NOTES FROM A WAITING-ROOM

ALAN REEVE

NOTES FROM A WAITING-ROOM

ANATOMY OF A POLITICAL PRISONER

heretic books

First published in Britain by Heretic Books,
   P O Box 247, London N15 6RW, England

World copyright © 1983 Alan Reeve

 British Library Cataloguing in Publication Data

Reeve, Alan
   Notes from a waiting room.
   1. Broadmoor Special Hospital
   I. Title
   362.2'1'0924   RC450.G72C7

   ISBN 0-946097-09-7

Designed by Aubrey Walter
Photoset by M C Typeset, 34 New Road, Chatham, Kent
Printed and bound by Book Plan (Billing & Sons) Ltd, Worcester

Introduction 9

★

Publisher's note

This autobiography was written after Alan Reeve escaped from Broadmoor in August 1981, and was originally to have been published by Penguin Books. But after his capture in Amsterdam, just one year later, Britain's leading paperback imprint had second thoughts about getting involved in a possible scandal, and the manuscript came into our hands.

No one who reads this book will accept that the tragic events in the Netherlands, where Alan is now serving a fifteen-year sentence for manslaughter, support the refusal of the Home Secretary to release him after seventeen years in Broadmoor. It is the British state that made Alan Reeve a political prisoner, then a desperate fugitive, leading to the death of a Dutch policeman. *Notes From a Waiting-Room* is written with an intelligence, honesty and compassion that immediately belie any charge of 'criminal insanity'. In truly heretical fashion, Alan turns the weapons of his jailers against themselves, and analyses the repressive system of the 'special hospitals' in the role of a political psychologist. The inhabitants of Britain's psychiatric prisons are usually denied any chance of making their story known. Alan Reeve has seized his chance: let his book speak for itself.

★

The strictness of the British libel laws has forced us to make a number of small cuts, totalling about 1 per cent of the text. This is where the author has made statements which could be construed as 'defamatory' by the persons referred to, and which we would not be in a position to justify. In no way, however, do these cuts detract from the main lines of Alan Reeve's story or his political analyses.

Caresses from sleep-filled thoughts,
gentle harmonies of long-awaited memories
structure flowing pieces of once fragmented desire:
freedom tastes of the future I sought.

Drunken illusions shatter on the rocks of hangover morning;
dawn brought raw-throated memories shrinking into the light
but they remained intact –
friendship and love forget everything and forgive nothing.

Happiness is reflected from a cracked mirror;
incomplete and shadowed by disaster:
in my pleasure the pain remains, tears
remember the tearing teeth ripping my family . . .

Did you think, writer,
omniscient scribbler of distant emotion,
that the mountain, the desert, the drought, the famine,
the artificial womb of official displeasure,
these would remove their taint,
their strictures,
their pain-full embrace of barbed-wire caress:
there is no rest in momentary pleasure,
for the anguished cry of oppression links
the future with the present.

The struggle continues . . .

Introduction

My Dear Allison:

This letter to you constitutes the Introduction to my attempts at sketching out an autobiography – as you were the first person to suggest that I write the thing, I think you deserve a preliminary comment! My doubts and reservations about the value of a work such as this are still very significant, but I am persuaded by the idea that my successful escape may, given fresh impetus through this volume, serve some useful political purpose in bringing attention to bear on what should only be referred to as the British Archipelago.

Dolores Price, an Irish political prisoner in one of Britain's prisons, wrote in a 1974 letter to Bernadette Devlin MP that she was sickened by the hypocrisy and double standards of representatives of the British state – they condemned the Soviet Union on the basis of a Russian dissident's hunger strike, issuing almost hourly bulletins, but totally ignored the identical action by the Price sisters. This hypocrisy, of course, should come as no surprise, for the bourgeoisie and their lackeys only take note of the actions of those people friendly to their own reactionary political practices: to be anti-communist is to wear the white mantle of purity, while to be anti-capitalist, anti-imperialist, pro-people is to be a "terrorist" or a "psycho-path", or just a "monster". Of course, the umbrella of the bourgeoisie is large, so they offer their support even to social-democrats and members of revisionist groups like the British Communist Party – I still remember with amusement the comment made to me about it being a pity that I wasn't a member of the CPGB, for that would make me respectable and therefore easier to release! Like the anti-colonialist freedom fighters in occupied Ireland, however, I am a committed revolutionary, so my actions are designated criminal, and, instead of being supported as a political prisoner legitimately escaping from persecution, I must remain a hunted fugitive.

In this volume I have attempted to show the way in which I moved from an anti-social position rooted in personal confusion, through a sense of social isolation and personal despair, to a burgeoning political consciousness and then a committed proletarian revolutionary stand. I have not hidden any of the nastiness of my own actions as I moved through my life, nor the hesitations and errors of my political and personal growth; my concern has been to show the myriad forces which have influenced me, locating my life in the context of a social web. The primary reason for this, and the factor which finally motivated me to write, was the fact that I felt this approach would be most useful in generalising any political benefits resulting from my actions: I remain convinced that the major significance of both my development and my confrontations with the state is the fact that I am merely the tip of an iceberg, one of the most public examples of a pervasive oppression.

The profound reality of oppression in penal institutions is a blunt instrument which conditions prisoners to accept an image of themselves as asocial and apolitical, exclusively individual agents engaged in a personal battle to survive: cooperative endeavour is actively discouraged, for this route leads to political consciousness. This ideological emphasis on individualism disguises the class bases of "deviance" as well as preventing the emergence of a solidarity rooted in class interest; prisoners, just as emphatically as their class brothers and sisters beyond the walls, must be prevented from breaking free of the false consciousness which hinders that unity which is the precondition for eradicating the bases of their oppression. Thus, any prisoner who becomes class conscious, and consequently politically active, immediately experiences a massive reaction from the institution, a reaction disproportionate to his or her personal competence as an activist; it is the ideological survival of the institution, and ultimately of the state, which is under attack, and this accounts for the savagery of the reaction – as it also partly explains the adverse reaction of many fellow-prisoners, for they are attempting to survive that institution and do not really want to find themselves forced to recognise the impossibility of their position.

When Udwin elaborated his "shift to the left" hypothesis, arguing that young "delinquents", experiencing the idealism of adolescence, would turn to class politics, to revolution, as a means of legitimising their personal inclinations to violence, he was merely formalising the ideological necessity of preventing prisoners from becoming politically conscious. The importance of psychiatric prisons for developing social theories sympathetic to the bourgeoisie must not be underestimated; the propaganda war launched against the anti-colonialist fighters in occupied Ireland, with its attempt to criminalise the struggle by the use of medical models of "psychopathic terrorists", was undoubtedly developed partly from models perfected by forensic psychiatrists. The bourgeois state does not waste its resources when it comes to isolating its enemies and controlling its population, and prisons are perfect laboratories for testing techniques of persuasion and control.

As you know, Allison, I didn't conjure these analyses out of thin air, they are the dialectical product of my experiences and my intellect: my twenty years in British penal institutions didn't succeed in completely numbing me, which is part of the reason why the Home Secretary considers me "dangerous". In this book, the analyses are largely mentioned tangentially, by implication, for a subjective account of one person's development doesn't lend itself to the cold rationality of analysis – but I think that on completing this volume the reader should be able to understand the bases on which my analyses rest. If this is the case, then I will have accomplished what I set out to do.

One thing remains, little one – the dedication of this book. It would be simple to merely state that it is for those I love, and thus say that I dedicate it to my class, but I want to mention some specific people and thus publicly recognise their influence on me. So . . . with love and gratitude in all cases, and solidarity in some, I dedicate this book to Walter, Audrey, David and Francesca Reeve, to Richard and Jenny Turner, Jane, Judith and Simon Grundy, John and Leslie Punter, to Ronald Greedy, Bob Windell, Alan Holland, Chris Reid, Alan Wilbourne, Ken Adamson, Nigel Price, Carol Rigby, Phil Batt and Bryan Knight, Don D'Eath and Veronica Pearson, and to the many others whose security I cannot jeopardise by naming them. And, with a gratitude, love, and solidarity beyond description, this work is dedicated to you, Allison

John Cook, and to my sister, lover and comrade, Patricia Ford.

That's it; I'm finished. For good, bad, or indifferent response, I cut this book free of me. I send you my love, Allison, along with a commitment that I shall continue to struggle – for my freedom, for the freedom of all victims of bourgeois mystification and domination, and for the liberation of my class.

Alan.

Childhood: confusion, despair, rebellion (1948–1962)

> "Consciousness is . . . from the very beginning a social product and remains so as long as men exist at all. Consciousness is at first, of course, merely consciousness concerning the immediate sensuous environment and consciousness of the limited connection with other persons and things outside the individual."
>
> Karl Marx, *The German Ideology*

My mother tells me that I was born on the couch in the front room of a small house in Northwood Hills, Middlesex, England. The date was October 24th, 1948. Although other people remember the event well, I have no recollection of it: such an important day for me, and I can't even remember!

Autobiographies, more than any other literary endeavour, show the material power of ideas: the attempt to resurrect the past, to deal adequately with forces and personalities which have had such a profound impact that they remain present in the consciousness with which we deal with the present, this is essentially a reconstruction of the model of reality which influences our every action. But . . . the past is not one coherent whole, easily contacted and made available to others, it is rather a patchwork of inadequately recollected events rounded out by reference to the collective memories of those involved in the period.

In my life the collective memories have been mediated through bureaucratic and psychiatric involvement: my contact with bureaucrats has resulted in their memories taking precedence over mine, and their interpretations possessing more validity than any simple memories I may possess. The fact that my late childhood, adolescence, and young adulthood has been examined, controlled and interpreted by psychiatrists has given me constructions rather than memories: I don't seriously believe that at the age of five I examined the shocked response of a German bus driver who ran over my leg in terms of the implicit and explicit racism of an army of occupation!

Although my preference is to record only that period I am fully conscious of, thus involving only the distortions of my memory and ideological position, the exigencies of an autobiography require at least an outline of early life. So, according to the memories of other people, themselves mediated by time and personal requirements, and the reconstructions of adulthood, my early life will be recorded. Essentially anecdotal, my own recollections could well be judged apocryphal from the perceptions of other persons involved with me in the period . . . but this is not really important, for it is the past I have experienced in terms of the model of reality I now possess.

When I was about eighteen months old my mother attempted suicide. The reasons behind this act are simply told – she had been attempting to live on inadequate funds, feeding my brother and me at the expense of her own health. Finally, she couldn't take any more and tried to kill herself. My father at this time was abroad on an army posting: he sent all his money home to England for my mother and the two children, but that money was not enough. Apparently, my brother and I were found walking along the street by some policeman; then my mother was found. My father returned immediately to England, and I understand my mother soon recovered enough to come home from the hospital. I remember none of this, but the psychiatrists found much interesting material in the process.

Soon after this the whole family moved to Germany – a lovely country, one I'd like to visit some day. We lived in several towns, but I have only sketchy memories. Vaguely,

14

images of childish squabbles, a kindergarten, parks, tears and laughter crowd into my mind as I seek to reconstruct that period; jumbles of peace, joy, security predominate. From my mother I learned that David, my brother, and I had indulged in a number of very dangerous games, including playing seesaw on the apex of our roof. The policeman who reported this first roof-top escapade of ours to our mother was met with a kindly "No, they're playing out in the garden", and I can well imagine the scene when she finally stepped out of the doorway, looked up, and saw us unconcernedly swinging up and down at such a height!

David, seventeen months older than me, looms large even this early: we squabbled endlessly, childish disagreements which rent the peace but did not estrange us. One thing I remember well was the occasional disagreement in our bedroom because of my habit of shaking my head from side to side on the pillow until I fell asleep – and humming, tunelessly, to myself all the while. The head shaking didn't disturb Dave, but the humming was sometimes too much for him! By the time I was seven or eight the humming had stopped, but the head shaking remained with me until I was nearly twenty-four.

When I was five my sister was born, completing our family. On the journey to the hospital to collect Francesca and my mother I fell asleep, awakening only when we arrived home, so I have no recollection of our first "meeting". I must have seen this new Reeve sometime during that day, but tiredness has swept the event away for ever. Fran is not really a memory for me until I was about eight or nine; she was there, but nothing happened of such magnitude that it stayed in my mind.

Sometime before we left Germany an event occurred which remains the most powerful memory I have of the period. It was an off-white winter, frozen pavements and grey snow. Like all the children in the neighbourhood my brother and I were frequently out of the house, building snowmen, having snowball fights, and sliding up and down the pavement on black ice. A Sunday morning, and several of us were out on the pavement frenetically attempting to outdo each other on the ice-slide; we were waiting for the Sunday School bus to arrive. My turn on the slide, and I'd wound myself up to really out-perform everyone – a five or six-year-old desperado putting his soul into a public performance. Just before I began to slide the bus came into the road; it drew alongside just as I went into a crouch, and I saw my chance to really shine. I jumped sideways, reaching out for the bar at the door – and missed. Hitting the side of the bus, I fell in a crumpled heap on the edge of the pavement, my body curling under the bus with my head and legs ready to be crushed. Reacting faster than he ever moved before or since, Dave rushed forward, grabbed a handful of my hair and sought to pull me clear . . . and my head missed being crushed, but my left foot was caught by the rear nearside tyre and pinned to the tarmac. The driver, having seen the accident in his mirror, was already braking hard; when he heard the screams of the other children he realised that he'd gone over me and desperately reversed in an obvious attempt to minimise the damage – and went over the foot again. Once more he reacted to the screams, slipping into forward drive and moving ten or twelve feet forward – going over my foot again in the process!

My memory tells me that I screamed, curling immediately toward the damage, my leg stretched out in front of me, and then turning and looking up toward the windows of our flat in a desperate search for my mother or father. Against this memory, my mother says that I was silent throughout the experience; she was convinced that my head had been caught under the wheel because I didn't scream. An interesting conflict of memory.

Within a couple of minutes adults outnumbered children on the slide; my parents, the parents of other children, and a couple of interested spectators. The ambulance arrived swiftly, and I was tenderly picked up and placed within it. Vividly, I recall the German bus driver standing over me, wringing his hands, tears pouring down his face, mumbling brokenly that he hadn't meant to do it, it was an accident. I recall, too, reaching out to pat his hand and saying earnestly that it wasn't his fault, not to worry, I'd be alright.

Memories of the hospital are vague, overshadowed by a clear recollection of the pain when the doctor ripped the scab off the ankle, swabbing the blood away and telling my mother that it hadn't hurt me a bit and that I'd be fine now. He was obviously a sensitive man, and I must record my admiration for the way he maintained his professional detachment in the face of my outraged scream; a superb example of humanity subordinated to expertise. Thanks, doc.

Each time I have remembered this incident, the most vivid period has been the wait for the ambulance; the behaviour of the bus driver continues to haunt me. It was clear that I alone was responsible for the "accident"; the driver had done everything in his power to protect me. But his behaviour was more than the response of shock, it was outright fear, a response which terrified me more than the damage done to my leg. Over the years, I have come to appreciate that the fear was a legacy of the war, an indication of the realities of occupation: I believe that this was my first experience of the insidious power of racism, with a member of a conquered people automatically accepting a position of responsibility regardless of the objective reality involved. I believe that the driver was fearful not for his life, but for his job: a child of the occupation forces had been damaged, and in the emotional aftermath of the incident any outrageous act of irrationality was possible. To this day, I don't know what happened to the driver, but even if he kept his job I believe that more damage was done to him than to me because of the incident.

My father was posted back to England, and we moved to Colchester, Essex. Our new home was in near-derelict army quarters. I remember that, along with the other children in quarters, I played a lot in the abandoned derelicts a street or so away from where I lived. Exciting memories, these, full of images of me up on roofs balancing while slates and roof-beams went crashing to the ground. Psychiatrists have told me that my disregard for my own safety during these climbs was an indication of some pathological development – but I put it down to the fact that children tend to be indifferent about the risk of serious injury or death because they don't understand either. I was most definitely reckless, but it was with a child's physical indifference to personal danger; the emotional warmth of excitement was far too rewarding for any sense of fear to intrude.

It must have been shortly after we moved to Colchester that I woke up one morning with all the symptoms of bad flu. I have a memory of some insensitive doctor trying to force my chin down onto my chest; I thought he was being really nasty. He wasn't. I was moved to the British Military Hospital, a friendly place where I was treated with care and compassion until, under the guise of "just another needle, Alan; it won't hurt a bit" I was subjected to a lumbar puncture which took three attempts to complete. Polio was diagnosed, and I was moved to Mile End Isolation Hospital.

The nurses at Mile End were undoubtedly caring and compassionate people; many of them must have wept as the polio epidemic devastated so many young – and old – lives. I remember only indignity and pain, though. A large, airy room, beds along the edges filled with very sick children; a large, plate-glassed window at the end through which we could see our visiting parents and friends. A soft-meat, high-protein diet with lots of rabbit – the little beasts are safe from me during my lifetime because of this experience – and bath-times leading to agony with physiotherapists rather than the sleep we so desperately sought.

I recovered quite quickly, being left only with tight tendons in my legs and a susceptibility to muscular damage. During my recuperation I was encouraged to walk around the corridors, visiting those children confined to bed. One day, going to visit a girl with whom I was friendly, I found her asleep and decided to explore the corridors further. Going to see each of the rooms in turn, I spent a few minutes in each of those which were occupied. Eventually, I came to the last room on the corridor; a closed door, which I opened and entered. My mother lay in the bed just inside the room.

I don't even have fragmentary memories from the meeting with my mother until a sunny day in Tripoli, possibly a couple of years later. A couple of psychiatrists have argued that the polio and the period of hospitalisation were so traumatic that, in consequence, I became fearful of other people, socially and emotionally withdrawn. One has argued that the disease left me with some brain trauma, some physiological distortion, while another told me during a consultation that the meeting with my mother caused a regression into infantile dependence on an emotional level. I find it interesting that they were able to conjecture in this manner about the past, but were totally unable to take into account the material conditions which prompted "aberrant" behaviour in their own, allegedly therapeutic, environments!

Anyway. . .

Tripoli holds fond memories for me, but they're at a gut level rather than constructively available in the present. Anecdotally, I remember things: an Arab family I used to visit who had lost a couple of children to diseases endemic in the area, and their dog, a mongrel, which I fell in love with. The dog died of another of those endemic diseases – rabies. A time when I faked drowning in an attempt to get some attention: I wasn't very successful, moving my tongue when the doctor told me to even though I was supposed to be unconscious! Lots of hypochondria, preferring day-dreams in an overly warm bed to the strains of being with other people. My attempts at attention-getting didn't seem to achieve much; I irritated and angered my parents rather than receiving the unconditional displays of affection which I sought.

We were frequently warned about contact with the "dirty wogs", but I preferred their company over that of Europeans. The music in the bazaars enthralled me, as did the food and the conversation. The people were universally kind to me, none taking advantage of the fair-haired child with the big eyes. I didn't like the soldiers much, they being loud and often brutal; their laughingly callous disregard of the Arabs pained me, making me cringe because I was one of "theirs".

School, large and pleasant in appearance, was a bore to me; I was several times in trouble because I would take the books out of the cabinet and read a volume or two ahead of the class. I rarely fought, preferring to be alone in the playground; I was an "odd" child, too withdrawn and susceptible to day-dreaming periods, but not yet condemned by adults or other children as "different".

In 1956, England, France and Israel conspired to attack the Arab peoples. The anti-colonialist attempt to reclaim the Suez Canal failed, defeated by a European-inspired anti-Nasser momentum, and signalled the confirmation of Israeli imperialism. In Tripoli, the families of servicemen were first confined to their quarters and then moved en masse to one of the army bases for "security". For the children it was one great holiday: all we knew was that we could run about and play, being given sweets rather than clips around the ear if we ventured into usually forbidden territory. The atmosphere of tension and the mood of adult concern did not seem to disturb us. Then we were airlifted out of the country, returning to England as "heroes". I spoiled things somewhat for my mother by appearing on the front page of a daily newspaper with my cap on – I was sitting at a table laden with food at the time. Tsk, tsk.

This period in England is another blank; I don't even remember if my father joined us at my grandparents' house, or if we didn't see him again until we flew out to Cyprus to join him. I do remember that my trust in adults was so low that I couldn't get as close to my grandmother as I would have liked: as I write this I feel sad again at her death, an event which cancelled out the walks and talks we had planned.

Although Tripoli was the place where my estrangement from my parents and my lack of closeness with everyone but my brother appears to have begun, Cyprus is the place where it became bureaucratically identified and confirmed. On this beautiful little island, amidst the violence of colonialist British soldiers and neo-fascist nationalist EOKA, I consolidated my "delinquency". Here in Cyprus I was first called a thief, and it was here that I first experienced the consequences of being known as a child who was "different".

We lived in a five-roomed flat in a two-storied building; I don't remember who lived on the ground floor, but it might have been Cypriots. The house was just outside Nicosia, in a predominantly Greek area. It was an interesting neighbourhood, and I used to enjoy running around the place. Dave and I were often together; he had more friends than I did, but he didn't mind too much me hanging around with him. Initially, I think, we went to the same school, but he soon moved out to the boarding school at Famagusta. This posed problems for me, because without him I felt lost and very much alone.

I remember running away from home once with Dave, but I think we got back again before we were missed! On a couple of other occasions we planned to leave, but we never got round to it. We did break into a post office just down the street from our home, looking for money, but we found only some stamps – which we took. This relatively simple exercise, resulting in a kind of success, made it far easier when we eventually turned more seriously to burglary several years later.

Our relations with the local children tended to be rather distant because of the immediacy of the national conflict. We got into several fights in the area, with Dave taking the leading part in the escapades and me willingly subordinating myself to his leadership; rarely, if ever, did the fights amount to anything significant. Usually, the exchanges consisted of verbal insults – grandiose and biological, full of vague sexual references to one's mother and specific Oedipal involvements! – followed by a mutually despatched volley of stones from our catapults. The only real danger consisted of inadvertantly looking up and catching a stone in the eye: I remember that Dave got hit on the side of the head a few times, while I got a couple of grazes on the cheek.

There were occasions when we actively helped to post EOKA leaflets on poles and buildings, but once David got his hand cut by a youngster we tried to hinder in leafletting. I remember chasing the boy, but failing to catch him – probably a good thing, because he was much bigger than me and armed with a knife which he wasn't too concerned about using! I was very frightened for Dave on this occasion, making more of the wound than was actually the case; by this time I was extremely dependent on him for emotional support and physical comfort.

Several times I contemplated running away from home to join up with EOKA and fight the British – really, I was seeking a way to fight back at my father. Family relations were deteriorating, with hypochondria, fantasy and the occasional theft on my part, and a dismissive attitude and a heavy fist on my father's. My mother was vaguely, even casually, protective of me when my father got angry, but I did not feel any real security in her actions. Brutality is too savage a word to use in relation to my father's infrequent beatings, but on several occasions I was so badly bruised that I could not take my shirt off at school because I was ashamed to show the extent of my injuries: too frequently do children collude in their own degradation.

When David won a scholarship to King Richard's boarding school by passing the 11-plus I was desolate; I didn't feel that I could manage to live at home without him. My behaviour became even more erratic, and even Dave sometimes got so irritated by me that he either hit me or ignored me, the latter reducing me more swiftly to tears and pleas for forgiveness. Increasingly I provoked my parents, seeking any demonstration that they cared for me, even if it involved my getting beaten. Unfortunately for me, my father's response was most often to shout at me, something which would leave me trembling and feeling sick; to be beaten was painful, but it was a gesture of concern as far as I was concerned, whereas shouting was a total repudiation which terrified me. I think my father felt he was demonstrating great forbearance by not beating me, but this was just the most dramatic example of the vast gulf in perception which separated us.

Soon after Dave went off to King Richard's I could take no more and decided to run away and join him. My behaviour was totally irrational, for there was no way that we could have successfully managed to be together without him leaving the school – and even for love of me, I doubt if he would have done that. But I was thinking with my fear and my need rather than any logical consistency – and I was only about eight years old!

With a friend who used to make a threesome with David and me, I made arrangements to go housebreaking and thus obtain the money needed to get to Famagusta. We chose a house occupied by an officer and, breaking in through the kitchen door, we ransacked the place. There was only a small amount of money in the house, about £15 I think, but it was enough for our purposes. We went straight from the house to a café just down the road and got the proprietor to telephone for a taxi for us. Although the taxi driver was doubtful about our request, the fact that we could pay in advance persuaded him to be compliant; we set off for Famagusta.

The trip took a couple of hours, and we arrived at the school just before nightfall. Hiding in the bushes near the entrance, we waited until it was dark and then crept into the grounds. Making contact with David was easy, we just called out at the windows until one of the boys went to get him – and a master!

We were placed in the school infirmary overnight, a telephone call to Nicosia having informed our parents that we were both fine. Early in the morning we were woken, given breakfast, and told that we would soon be collected; my father was driving down to pick us up. I asked to be allowed to speak with David, and the Headmaster, on the advice of the Matron, consented to our meeting for five minutes. It was a very fraught meeting; we both knew what was in store for me from my father. Also, my dramatic arrival had emphasised how much I was missing him, and Dave empathically responded to that.

Eventually, about nine o'clock, my father arrived and we were driven back to Nicosia: on the journey I listened to my father explaining what he was going to do to me once we arrived home. If I could have jumped from the car, even over a cliff, I would have done so. We dropped the other boy off at his home, and then drove the few miles to where we lived. Then my father beat me, up the stairs, in the living-room, and in my bedroom; there was no escape, it was like being in a cosmic boxing ring – only I wasn't fighting back! Once again, it was the accompanying shouting which terrified me the most. Even though this beating was, I believe, with one exception the most severe I ever received from my father, it caused me nothing more than pain – and that I didn't mind too much, because experience had taught me that it didn't last too long.

After the beating, dressed only in pyjamas, which I had worn on the journey back from the school, my father pushed me tumbling down the stairs and thrust me out of the front door, shouting that if I wanted to leave home I could do so. I remember gathering my clothes together from the heap where my father had thrown them and, walking about ten yards away from the front door, standing and just looking at him. I don't remember many tears, just trembling and an almost unbearable sense of loss: I loved that shouting giant at the door, and I had an overpowering desire to throw myself at his feet and beg his forgiveness for whatever sins I had committed or even thought of committing. But all I did was stand there and look at him. Several times he shouted "Well, don't just stand there, go!" I stood immobile, clutching in my pathetic grasp a little bundle of clothing. Then he told me to come back inside, and we went in together.

About an hour after my brief public appearance, a teacher arrived from my school to ask if I was coming to the football match I was supposed to be playing in as a school representative. My father said I couldn't go, and I had to return the football strip I had. I was not chosen to play for the school team again while I was in Cyprus.

Shortly after this escapade, and as a direct consequence of it, I received the most savage beating of my life from my father: I seriously believed he was going to kill me, and I resigned myself to dying. From my father's view, I believe this was one of the worst moments in his relationship with me as a child; after this he concluded that I was emotionally disturbed. It all came about as a consequence of my breaking into the officer's house.

Several days after the return from King Richard's, the

23

officer came to our house and asked what had I done with his telescope, a fine instrument which he desperately needed for his work guerrilla-chasing in the mountains. I didn't know what he was talking about, but my father believed I had taken it and, rather than face another demolition through shouting and beating, I constructed a story about taking it and hiding it in the sand-hills behind the British Military Hospital near the officer's home. My father immediately took me in his car to the spot I'd nominated and told me to recover the instrument – of course, I couldn't because it wasn't there! I scrabbled about in the sand for a couple of minutes and then announced that it was gone, probably stolen by some Cypriot. In a rage, my father punched me full force in the stomach and, when I collapsed on the ground, kicked me twice in the side. He was almost incoherent with rage, and through my pain I looked up at him quite calmly, accepting that he was going to kick me to death. Recovering his self-control, he walked away from me, told me to get up, and took me home.

For the next week I was constantly being asked to tell where I'd hidden the telescope; I kept saying that someone else must have stolen if from where I'd hidden it. My father didn't hit me again, although he shouted a lot. Then one evening the officer arrived soon after I'd gone to bed. I lay there terrified, thinking that I wouldn't be able to hold out much longer. After a few minutes, I heard the officer leave and, within seconds, my father came into my bedroom. He knelt down beside my bed, cuddled me, kissed me, and told me he was sorry that he had hit me; I saw that he was crying. After a short period of just cuddling me, he asked why I hadn't told the truth; the officer had found the telescope where it had fallen, behind the fridge. I answered that I had been too frightened to rely on the truth, and my father wept even more. We cuddled for a while, both of us slowly controlling our tears, then he kissed me good-night and left. The tragedy was that neither of us could break free from the trap of false perception into which my behaviour had led us: I loved him, was terrified of him and couldn't explain or reach out to him without fantasy and desperation intervening, and he believed that I was disturbed in some deep emotional sense. We merely tacitly agreed a brief and, ultimately, bitter truce.

During the week of uncertainty before the officer announced that he'd found his telescope, my memory tells me that I planned to shoot my father. Taking his service revolver from his bedroom cupboard where he kept it while at home, I pointed it out of the window and pulled the trigger. I planned to turn around and fire a second shot, straight at him, when my father responded to the sound. Either because of a heavy trigger pull or because I'd forgotten the safety catch, the gun didn't fire. I returned it to the cupboard.

My father assures me that this memory is apocryphal, the result of fantasy; he says the event could not possibly have occurred. As I am no longer sure, I relegate it to a brief comment, mentioning it only because for many years I believed it to be true – and I am convinced that this belief contributed to my self-image as capable of murder.

Vengeful fantasies are quite natural with children, and I wonder how many have been acted out with surrogate victims in later life. Memory or fantasy, if it influences self-image then it is important to recount it.

While at home my behaviour was deteriorating, I remember that I was performing rather well academically. At the school I attended, a rambling complex on a hill overlooking the Governor's official residence, I was in the top class; in addition, I was one of three boys following a special schedule in preparation for the 11-plus. Although I remember no particular conflicts with the teachers, they obviously felt there was something wrong because eventually they signed reports which hung like millstones around my neck for many years. With the other children I remember fairly amicable relations – no heavy problems at any time, although a boy I knew at the time told me years later that I seemed to him to be very withdrawn a lot of the time.

Because of the problems I was having at home, I was taken to see the army psychiatrist at the British Military Hospital. Reports given to him by the school suggested that I was a mass of contradictions: it seems that I was "hyperactive", constantly running around even when the heat was really oppressive, and simultaneously withdrawn and often sullen. It was said that my school work was sporadic, ranging from excellent to patchy; I sometimes failed to "apply" myself to the work in hand. The psychiatrist told me not to worry overmuch and recommended that I be given a drug – largactyl, AKA chloropromazine – to slow me down and make me more amenable. Obviously his motives were both honest and sincere, rooted in a real professional concern for my welfare, but I'm glad his advice was not followed! Many years later I was to see the personality disintegration resulting from this conjunction of "real professional concern" and largactyl – the popular, and grossly unfair, name given to people experiencing this conjunction is . . . zombies.

One day, while I was sitting in class, I was told to report to the Headmaster's office. I had no inkling of any "mischief" I might have ben accused of, but nonetheless for some reason I was fearful: it may well be that by this time I was in a constant state of suspicious trepidation whenever I had to contact "authority". The Headmaster's secretary gave me an envelope, sealed, to give to my father – and I began to cry, saying that I'd done nothing wrong! The secretary and one of the women teachers attempted to comfort me, saying over and over again that it was just a routine letter and there was nothing for me to be worried about: of course I'd done nothing wrong, they told me.

When I got home my father wasn't there, not yet having arrived back from work. Giving the letter to my mother, I went to wash myself. Returning, I found that my mother was weeping; I immediately joined in. She asked me what had I been doing at school, and I answered, truthfully as far as I was concerned, that I had done nothing. Then I heard that I'd been "temporarily suspended", allegedly for theft of a small knife used for cutting oranges at break-time – and also, something even more incomprehensible to me, bullying other children. Desperately, I rejected the allegations, maintaining my innocence of both charges . . . but what chance does a child have, especially one with a history of fantasy and lies, against the combined allegations of such respectable adults as teachers? I knew that I was now in real trouble.

My father arrived home and my mother gave him the letter. As I'd expected, his response was immediate, furious, and uncomplicated – he began to beat me! Falling to the floor, I attempted to hide under the chair in which my mother was sitting – a space about six inches high. My mother was telling my father to calm down, and after a couple of desultory kicks he did so. Yet again, it was the shouting which terrified me the most; I remember being almost incoherent as I tried to assert my innocence. The rest of the day is a blur, as is the rest of the time we spent in Cyprus, with the exception of one of the most horrifying memories remaining from my early childhood.

The army psychiatrist, whom I'd seen again after the suspension from school, recommended that I be placed under the "care" of a child guidance specialist, and to this end the army had posted my father back to England. My parents were distressed at this development, as I think was my brother; Fran was too young to voice an opinion. One of the problems we faced was what to do with our dog, a small white mongrel we called Lucky. There was no money available for a veterinary certificate of health because that would entail six months in a boarding kennel: Dave and I assumed that Lucky would be placed with someone else. However . . . one afternoon my father placed Dave, Lucky and myself in the car with him and we set off to pick up the vet. We went to an open space alongside the wall of Nicosia town, a quiet place near the army camp. Everyone got out of the car, and we stood and watched Lucky running around and enjoying himself. Then, my father called the dog to him and, holding him tightly, turned his head away from the vet – who shot him in the head.

The whole memory is jumbled in my head, with only an awful clarity when Lucky died. I remember that the vet alone was not weeping; we all loved that dog, and it was a terrible decision to kill him. I was very bitter, feeling in some way that I was responsible. To my bitterness at what I perceived as the injustice of my suspension from school, and my now confirmed rebellious certainty that adults were not to be trusted, was added a dimension of self-destructive rage which blamed the world for the death of a beloved pet. The specific target of this rage was the army, perceived as responsible, through the psychiatrist and his advice, for condemning Lucky. I was about nine years old and, although obviously irrational to an adult, this burden of bitterness and anguish was a heavy load to carry.

Back in England, we first stayed with my grandparents in Northwood Hills.★ Although I distrusted all adults, I achieved

★ Sometime after we returned to England from Cyprus the family, without my father, lived in Blackpool for a few months. I cannot remember when this was! I do remember, however, that this was where I held my one and only piece of paid employment other than a paper round. Dave and I worked as "washers-up" in one of Blackpool's leading hotels. We worked for about two hours one day a week, and we were paid five shillings each.

a certain closeness with my grandmother; she seemed more comforting to me than oppressive, but I couldn't get close enough to overcome the barriers I'd erected against the world.

In Northwood, I attended a local primary school while Dave went off to the Grammar. I didn't like the school very much; I didn't get on very well with the local boys, and the teachers were merely objects of suspicion to me. It didn't help much that I day-dreamed a lot, tending to answer any question asked of me in the broken language of whichever country I was remembering. The teachers' response to such anti-social behaviour was a thrown blackboard duster and the threat of more to come if I used such "dirty foreign languages" again. Perhaps they thought I was swearing at them, they being familiar with the fact that I was a "delinquent" receiving "therapy" from a child psychologist.

Once a week I'd leave the school and make my way to Ruislip to see the child psychologist. At the first interview I'd done a battery of tests, answered innumerable questions, and been assured that I could trust the person who would be "helping" me. The man I saw used to talk with me for a few minutes and then send me off to the local swimming baths, believing this was what I was keenly interested in doing with my time. We'd come to an arrangement that the meetings were to be used as excuses for me to get some time to myself; the psychologist thinking that was what I required in order to bring me back into the fold. When, years later, I read the official report of the time which stated that I was receiving assistance with reading at this weekly meeting, I realised that I had been perfectly correct to distrust psychologists – the person who had written the report had never met me, relying on the scribbled notes of my "therapist" and thus presenting a false picture of me to the Court which had called for the report. The trouble is, as the report was written by a professional, his "record" took precedence over my memory – and the image of delinquency I had was reinforced and expanded.

Both in and out of school I spent much of my time indulging in behaviour which, in the eyes of those adults who came into contact with me, merely confirmed my delinquent image. Disinterested in school work which was below the standard I'd attained, I retreated more and more into day-dreaming during "lessons": I fantasised myself as free from adult control, roaming the country and the world, weaving patterns of meeting people and being friendly with them. The conflict in my own life and my relations with those around me I resolved in fantasy; my inner world was populated with peace and love in direct proportion to the hostility and conflict in the "real" world. With my parents, my relations were cool and distant, the prime requirement being to minimise the shouting I had to endure.

Many years later I heard from my father that he found one of my exercise books, reading the fantasies contained therein with interest. One in particular caused him some concern; it contained fully developed plans to rob a sub-post office! I gather he took it to the police, and they were impressed with the planning! Nothing ever came of this fantasy.

From Northwood we moved to Mersey Island, just outside Colchester. We lived in a caravan for several months, my father spending most of his time at the army prison where he worked. It was a small caravan, so I doubt if the whole family could easily have lived in it. This period is something of a blur in my memory; the only thing I remember properly is an argument with my mother because Dave and I stole some eggs from a local chicken coop. There was nothing really dramatic about this period, and eventually we moved into army quarters on Montgomery Estate, Colchester.

10, Hitherwood Road, Montgomery Estate, Colchester – my last residence as a free person. It was from this address that I moved into the first of the waiting-rooms known as penal institutions. But when we first moved in that was three years in the future, and I had no inkling of what was to come.

David went straight into the local Grammar school, Fran into an infant's school on the neighbouring estate, and I went off to the army primary school I'd attended about five years previously. I enjoyed this school, settling down quickly and performing competently in academic terms. I remember being something of a rebel, establishing myself as an anti-authority figure and revelling in the occasional conflict with the teachers: my relations with other children were, on the whole, amicable. Years later, teachers from this school too were to accuse me of bullying, but schoolfriends from the period have told me that their memories do not include anything resembling my being other than a vociferous, quick-tempered and anti-authoritarian little trouble-maker. I remember on several occasions arriving at the Headmaster's study for some punishment or other and sending the other children back to their classrooms – telling them that as I had initiated the "conflict" with the teachers I would take the punishment due. In class, too, I tended to accept the teacher's wrath; canings did not disturb me in the least, for they would never match the pain I'd experienced from other beatings.

Eventually, it came time for me to take the 11-plus, and I was faced with a difficult decision. The Grammar school in Colchester required its pupils to wear a uniform, and the necessary clothes cost a considerable amount of money. My parents had already paid out for my brother, and I knew that fitting me out would bite deeply into their very meagre budget. I knew, too, that they would not begrudge the money spent: although I seriously doubted their love, I was always aware that they took good care of Dave, Fran and me.

I faced another difficulty too: although I wanted to go to the same school as David, I knew that the system would necessitate us competing with each other in terms of academic performance, and this was something I could not face. It was confidently expected by my teachers and my parents that I would easily pass the examination: whatever else I did at school, my ability was rarely called into question. (My school reports tended to be along the lines of: Performs well – when he chooses to do so!)

The examination was interesting: having read the paper through, I knew I would have few problems. I failed. I am still rather pleased with the way that I managed it – even in this I was rebellious. I answered each question in turn, and I believe I got most of them correct. The problem for the script-marker was that the answers were out of synchronisation with the questions – I shifted them about a bit.

When the results came through, it was assumed that my emotional imbalance had caused me to fail the examination. I did nothing to disabuse people of this impression. I'd succeeded in my aims, so I was unconcerned.

Somewhere around this time I was interviewed by a child psychiatrist with a view to placement in a Special School for maladjusted children. I found out years later that a place had been offered me, but my parents had decided to reject it and keep me at home – they still thought there was a chance that I would "grow out" of the problems I had, and felt that our home would be a better place for me than any school, no matter how good. Also, as my father told me later, they hadn't been too impressed by an earlier psychiatrist I'd visited because they felt he was out of touch with the "real" world; he had stated that what I needed was to be left to go my own way, and provided with everything I asked for. My parents felt that their resources were too limited to allow for this, and also that it took no account of the needs of David and Fran. One of the greatest ironies about all this was that the school, which might well have been of great benefit to me because of the freedom it gave to residents to explore their own needs, was rejected essentially because my parents wanted to surround me with their love and thus help me – but they did not explain this to me, so I went on believing that they did not love me. Too frequently, too, do parents collude in their own degradation.

A few months before my thirteenth birthday, Dave and I conspired together to break into the local NAAFI. It was on the estate where we lived, about a quarter of a mile from our home. We anticipated a relatively small haul of money, but a considerable amount of cigarettes and tobacco which we could sell. Because of the proximity of our home, and also because we were well known on the estate and possible suspects for such a crime, we planned to provide ourselves with alibis by doing the job during a break in a game with other children.

One evening, while we were playing something like rounders in the space in front of our house, I hit the ball over the houses and Dave and I set off to look for it. Actually, we raced off to the NAAFI. From the back, hidden by trees from the officers' estate, we broke in – and immediately set off a hidden alarm.

As we had anticipated some sneaky trick like an alarm system, we were not too dismayed – terrified, perhaps, but not too dismayed! Dave rushed through to the front of the NAAFI, heading for the cash desks where the tobacco was kept; he scooped several packets into a bag and then crawled back to where I was waiting. Through the plate-glass windows we could see people coming into the street in response to the blaring of the alarm siren. We ran off along the tree line, following the route we'd previously agreed.

This was the smallest haul either Dave or I ever received from a criminal act. As a first major excursion into crime it was a total fiasco. We got back to our home and joined the other children, thinking that our alibi was safe – but Dave had been seen by a young child as we ran along the trees, and the police were eventually informed. A few days later I found a policeman waiting to interview me when I arrived home from an Air Training Corps meeting.

The policeman had arrived a couple of hours earlier and had already spoken with David. With no prior warning, I found myself being questioned about the recent NAAFI break-in. I stonewalled all the questions, but it was obvious that more interviews were to follow. My father questioned us both further after the policeman had left, but we resolutely denied all involvement.

Dave and I discussed events with great care; from what had been said we knew that someone could identify one of us, probably David. I decided that I'd take the blame, but couldn't face the inevitable problems with my father so decided that the time had come for me to run away from home: I felt it would be better to be separated from David rather than face his being charged with breaking into the NAAFI. The next morning, or perhaps the day after that, I left home for school – but went instead to the railway station and headed for London.

My plans were to stow away on a boat, any boat, bound for anywhere in the world. I went to the Great Eastern Docks, planning to look around and speak with people about when the boats were leaving. I got kicked out of the docks as soon as I was seen! Walking around the wall, I came to a place where I thought I'd be able to climb over once night came; I crawled under a bridge, burrowing into a pile of rubble for warmth.

Just before nightfall a crowd of boys came under the bridge and began to torment me; I was an "outsider" on their turf, therefore I was fair game. Not wanting to fight in case the police came, I tried to pacify the group; they weren't having any of that. Eventually, the biggest among them decided the playing had gone on long enough – he came over to me and told me to fight. I didn't fancy the idea at all; he was bigger than me, and looked a damn sight harder! I picked up a brick and hit him with it. The others were rather surprised at my actions, and when I stepped over the fallen body of their "leader" towards them they broke and ran several yards away from me. I stepped back and knelt beside the boy I'd hit; he was groaning and holding the side of his head where the brick had hit him. Keeping an eye on the other boys, I took my handkerchief from my pocket and wiped a trickle of blood from the injured boy's forehead. He was surprised, and I think nervous that I was going to hit him again. I told him that I didn't want any trouble and, taking a risk, added that I was on the run and therefore couldn't afford to clash with the police. The risk paid off; the boy decided I was worth knowing, and told the others to go away. We talked for a while, me telling him, with suitable embellishments, of the circumstances which had led me to the bridge. He left me when it was completely dark, and I settled back to wait until ten o'clock – the time I'd chosen as most suitable for trying to stow away.

About half an hour after the boy had gone, a woman came under the bridge and called my name. The boy had told his mother about our meeting and she had brought a flask of soup for me! She told me to think about my parents, and that if I was convinced I was doing the right thing, to take care. I didn't cry while she was there, but I did when she left: such disinterested concern was not familiar to me.

Shortly after ten o'clock I climbed over the wall into the docks and cautiously made my way to the berths where the ships were tied. The first two had people standing at the top of the gangways, so I walked past them; but the third seemed deserted. Tentatively, always ready to run, I made my way aboard, crouching at the top of the gangway for about five minutes until I was sure I hadn't been spotted. I'd already decided that I wasn't going to hide in one of the boats on the deck, so I headed for the first open door I saw and climbed downwards. I found some cabins, but passed them looking for a storage cupboard. Just as I was going around a corner a man came out of one of the cabins and, seeing me, shouted in some foreign language. I ran! Back on deck, with the man running close behind, I ducked behind one of the boats – the man ran past, still shouting. Moving quickly behind him, I headed for the gangway and ran off the boat.

Because of the shouting, or possibly by coincidence, a group of people were coming off the other ships, so I headed back for the wall and climbed over. Dropping to the other side, I landed awkwardly and damaged my left knee. Hobbling away, I headed over the bridge and into town. Several minutes later a policeman came over and asked why I was limping. My answers were obviously unsatisfactory, because he "invited" me to accompany him to the police station!

At the police station I was told to sit down, given a cup of tea, and questioned by a policewoman and a desk sergeant. After ten minutes the sergeant asked me where I'd run away from – so I told him. They didn't hit me, nor even threaten me, so this was one of the few occasions when contact with the police didn't involve fighting. Remembering it now, I'm still rather surprised!

My father arrived a couple of hours later, accompanied by my brother who had been brought along, I think, to receive an object lesson from my father. The police willingly surrendered me to my father's custody; as far as they were concerned I'd committed no crime and was therefore of no interest to them.

The journey back to Colchester is memorable to me for the fact that this was the first occasion I remember my father using a tactic to control me that he'd learned as a prison officer. He made me take my shoes off in the car! I don't remember much of a beating on this occasion; I think it possible that my mother's distress inhibited my father, so he used a bit of emotional pressure – look what you've done to your mother, sort of thing. The next day I was taken down to the police station and, after being questioned, charged with breaking into the NAAFI – on my own – and bailed into my father's custody. At least Dave wasn't charged, I consoled myself.

The next couple of weeks were very difficult for me; my father had decided that I hadn't done the job on my own, and he kept on at me to admit that Dave had participated. Finally, I broke down and admitted that we'd done the job together. Then, to my anguished amazement, my father took the two of us down to the police station and had Dave charged as my accomplice! Nothing he had ever done before this affected me quite as much; I felt that I had been doubly betrayed, first because of the unremitting pressure which had got me to admit Dave's involvement, and, secondly, because of my father's decision to bring the police into the matter and thus get him charged along with me.

By the time we came to appear at the Juvenile Court I was in a complete mess: I was totally unable to relate to my father, unsure of my relations with my mother, at odds with David, and distanced from Fran because of her age. During the Court appearance, I informed the magistrates that I wished to be removed from home. They complied with my request and made a care order which placed me under the control of the local authority. I was taken to Evesbrook Children's Home just outside Chelmsford.

Evesbrook was a very pleasant place, and the staff went to great lengths to welcome me. But I was very unhappy: I didn't trust any adults, and the welcoming atmosphere of the Home seemed cold and sterile to me. I missed Dave and Fran – and, to my surprise, found that distance removed much of my hostility to my father. Home, my family, seemed much to be desired from the vantage point of a Children's Home. Thus does distance add blindness to youthful vision.

A week after I arrived at Evesbrook I ran away, was picked up, and ran away again. Every day I ran, and every day I was picked up and returned. There was never any problem in finding me – I always headed for Colchester! On the sixth day following this pattern, I arrived home and asked my father to take me back. He took me down to the Child Welfare Office in Colchester and we talked with an official. Somehow, and I still don't understand how, I was released into my father's custody, and a couple of weeks later the care order was rescinded. I was home again . . . but my relations with my parents, especially my father, soon deteriorated again.

I started at secondary modern school about a year before the NAAFI break-in. I'd been offered a choice of schools; either a modern, newly-built school on the estate next to where I lived, or an old school the other side of town. I'd chosen the latter – its reputation as the "learning place" of most of the recalcitrants in the Colchester area appealed to me.

Sheepen Road secondary modern gave me the chance to develop the fighting skills I'd been accused so often of possessing: on my first day there I was jumped in the cloakroom by a couple of boys who had heard that I was a bit of a handful at my last school. They made the mistake of fighting fair – I just wanted to end the fight, so I used my knees and my feet as well as my fists. It was all over in a couple of minutes; I had a bloody nose, they were on the floor. Strangely enough, this was one of the few fights I had before returning from Evesbrook; I was still unsure of my ability to survive without Dave, and I preferred to run rather than fight.

For a few weeks after returning home from Evesbrook I was on my best behaviour at home and at school. I was still in something of a state of shock at finding that I couldn't survive too well without my family – specifically, without my parents. However, as my relations with my father deteriorated again, my behaviour at school mirrored my anguish at home; I became sullen, withdrawn, bitter, and prone to react at any provocation.

Teachers found me difficult to deal with at this time: I'd lost almost all interest in the lessons, the exceptions being English and Drama, a combined class with a stimulating young teacher. On one occasion, my conflict with a teacher became physical: a new teacher, taking Religious Instruction, attempted to control the class by making us read from a collection of Bible stories, and I refused to read aloud when my time came. I stated that I didn't believe in the Christian mythology and would therefore prefer to remain silent. The teacher took this as a direct challenge to his authority, which of course it was – even though my statement was quite factual. He chose to order me to read – unfortunately shouting his instructions. I reacted against the shouting by slamming my book shut and restating that I wouldn't read. The teacher came down the line of desks until he reached mine; he opened the book and shouted in my ear that I must do as I was told. I slammed the book again; he hit me alongside the head. I stood up and, quite politely, told him that if he did that again I'd hit him back. He opened the book again, and once more I slammed it shut. He hit me again – and before he could move I'd picked up my chair and slammed it against his shoulders. He ran down to his desk, me pursuing him with the chair. Two other boys intervened, one of them a friend of mine, so I put the chair down and went out of the classroom. Five minutes later the teacher came out, looked at me, and then went along to the Headmaster's office.

When I was called by the Headmaster's secretary, I fully expected to be expelled. Still quietly raging from the provocation, I was unconcerned at any consequences. I was in for a surprise. The Headmaster called me into his office and asked me to explain my side of the issue, so I told him exactly what had happened. He sent me out of the room and called the teacher in again. I could hear raised voices, then the teacher came out looking very angry. He didn't even look at me as he stormed off down the corridor. Called in by the Headmaster again, I entered his office to find him standing by his desk. He told me that I should not have hit the teacher, no matter what the provocation. He asked me to apologise, and I refused, saying that I would only do so if the teacher apologised to me. I then heard the Headmaster apologise! He said that the teacher should not have struck me, and that his actions were as bad as mine! Finally, he told me that no further action would be taken against me, but that any repetition of the incident would result in my immediate expulsion regardless of the facts of the case – an example would be made of me to encourage the other boys. If the Headmaster had followed through on this interview, my distrustful barriers against adults might have been undermined. Unfortunately, he was overworked and could not spare the time.

This incident aside, I rarely had recourse to violence or even threats with the teachers; they tended to send me along to the Headmaster to be dealt with. After my appearance in Juvenile Court I was officially labelled a "delinquent", and at Sheepen Road that meant my reputation immediately became bigger than me: a punch became a full-blown assault, and anything resembling a real fight became incitement to riot! I remember very few actual conflicts which resulted in violence, but by this time the image was already far bigger than I was.

My estrangement from David took a couple of months to overcome after my return from Evesbrook; we were close, but there was something of a barrier between us for a while. I willingly placed myself under his tutelage again, subordinating myself to his counsel. In the few fights in which we combined against other people, I let him take the lead; I preferred to remain as passive as possible with Dave, and with many people we gave the impression that only he fought. I found out years later that I had three distinct reputations in the neighbourhood: with some people I was remembered as a quiet, polite young boy always friendly and willing to help; others thought of me as sullen, withdrawn, potentially vicious; and yet others remembered me as a "nasty piece of work, really vicious, obviously heading for a bad end". In Court reports, the latter two views predominated, and the favourable comments were dismissed as coming from myopic people or as indicating my competence as a manipulator. Personally, I think the first two most accurately portray the twin sides of my character at the time – the third comment is the type of thing which usually follows someone's incarceration.

When I wasn't with David I would prowl around on my

own, looking for places to break into or high buildings and objects which I could climb to practise my cat-burglary skills. Occasionally I would go looking for a fight, choosing always to scour other neighbourhoods at these times. Sometimes I would return to the army estate I'd lived on when I was younger, knowing that there would always be someone willing to fight in that area.

At this time, too, I'd started experimenting with the drugs which were available; purple hearts and benzedrine mostly. I used to go to a couple of places in Colchester where these drugs, and other users of them, were easily found: here, too, I made my first real contact with useful people like fences and other older "criminals". I was readily accepted, regardless of my age, but I didn't spend too much time at these places – I was still very much a beginner, a learner.

About four months after my return from Evesbrook, Dave was back in Court accused of theft and housebreaking. He was sent to Approved School, and I was left adrift, forced to fend for myself. I remember crying for a couple of days, then settling down to a life of sullen disinterest in anything other than trouble. At this time my father attempted to get closer to me, going out of his way to be both kind and gentle; my mother was her usual considerate self, probably the reason I don't remember too much about her at this time. I remember being convinced that my parents were having difficulties together, and that the reason for this was not just rooted in the problems David and I had been providing. I don't think I responded much to my father's advances, feeling we had gone too far along the path of mutual hostility to succeed in any rapprochement.

One day, a Friday, when I was out doing the collection for my paper round, David turned up. He told me he had run away from the school he'd been in, Kneesworth Hall, because of the torture of some of the school bullies and the indifference of most of the masters. He showed me cigarette burns on his arms, back and legs, and told me of some of the other practices: floggings, scalding water baths, and straightforward physical brutality. Appalled, I was walking along weeping, as much with rage as with anguish at his experiences. We discussed his need to get away, neither of us even considering approaching an adult for assistance, and also his obvious need for money. The conclusion was as obvious as the problem – he had to take the money I'd collected. One problem: how to do it without me being blamed?

We walked along discussing the problem, and eventually I suggested that he hit me over the head hard enough to draw blood and then run off with the money; I'd tell the police that I'd been jumped on by someone I didn't manage to see. He wasn't too keen on the idea, but I managed to persuade him that it was our only choice. (Strangely enough, I don't remember our discussing my running off with him; there must have been some good reason for it not being feasible.)

Putting the plan into action wasn't too easy; the first blow was too soft, not even stunning me. I suggested an improvement: I would walk along pushing my bicycle, and he would hit me, unexpectedly, thus making the wound look natural. We walked on, and suddenly I was on the ground, looking up at David's nervous face through stunned and tear-misted eyes. He already had most of the money, just having to reach into my jacket pocket, roughly, to pull out a couple of notes; this, too, was part of the plan to indicate assault. What happened next neither of us had anticipated!

Leaving me on the ground, Dave ran off along the lane. Concerned lest he had hit me too hard, he decided to notify the authorities that someone had collapsed and was lying injured needing an ambulance. Stopping at the end house, he knocked on the door and . . . said his brother was unconscious in the lane! Under stress, without thinking, he immediately referred to me as he knew me. He then ran off.

The ambulance soon arrived and I was taken off to the military hospital – the incident had happened on army property. In the hospital, the doctors decided to keep me overnight in case I was concussed. The police soon arrived to interview me, and immediately suggested that the assailant had been David. I strenuously denied this, pointing out that he was in Approved School and thus couldn't possibly be responsible. In addition, I'd seen a large man with black hair just before I was knocked out. The police assured me that they knew it was David, and that they would be charging him with GBH when they caught up with him. I complained of a headache, and they left.

When I returned home from hospital the next day, my parents weren't particularly happy with me! Once again my father kept on at me to admit that it was David who had hit me;

I knew better than to trust him again. Unfortunately, Dave was picked up a couple of weeks later and it became necessary to admit that we had conspired to commit the crime. In the Court, no attempt was made to examine the fact that David had been tortured, they were only interested in the fact that some poor shopkeeper had been deprived of about £18 or £19 by a couple of schoolboy desperados. David was recommitted to Approved School, and I was fined about £5 – which enraged my father as he had to pay it! Having already reimbursed the shopkeeper, this new loss was even more galling.

After this example of official indifference, there was no longer any possibility of my keeping out of trouble: at odds with my father and my teachers, I was now totally convinced that it was necessary to stay with David and fight the world with him.

Once again my behaviour deteriorated: my withdrawal from "ordinary" social life became more pronounced as I retreated into my bedroom or roamed the streets alone. I became more manipulative at school, seeking to gather around me a small group of like-minded "trouble-makers". I wasn't very successful; even the other boys began to realise that I was out for a bit more than simple "conflict" with the teachers. My infrequent carrying of a knife became more regular, eventually being a permanent feature. The fights I was involved in became more vicious. I extended my housebreaking activities, sometimes taking my anger out on the furnishings of the houses I broke into. I took more risks, climbing higher and taking more difficult routes. I was virtually disinterested in the money I gained from these expeditions; I usually gave it away, offering it to friends and giving generously whenever someone got married or needed money for a lawyer or a "coming out" party.

Around this time my mother caught me smuggling a pair of jeans out of the house one morning. She told me that if I wanted to leave home then I should say so, not move out surreptitiously. I answered that all I wanted the jeans for was so that I could change into them and play football during breaks at school; for once I told the truth! While the exchange was going on, I remembered a similar exchange my mother had had with David and me: she told us that she did not mind what we did with our lives as long as we were happy. I cried at the time, as did my mother; Dave was less overt with his feelings. I have never remembered the exchange itself, it always comes back to me as a memory of the jeans episode.

One day at school, I asked a boy I was vaguely friendly with if he wanted to join me in running away from home. Full of bravado, he answered that he did. We made a date to leave at the end of the week. He didn't know it, but he was going to be part of a deliberate campaign on my part to get myself sent to Approved School: I had decided that I didn't want to be separated from David any longer, so I was going to get myself sent down to join him.

On the Friday morning we met at school, and at lunch break we left the school and headed for the station. Half an hour later we were en route to London.

My plans for this expedition had been carefully laid over the preceding month: I was going to be a one-boy crime wave. The boy I'd invited along was one of three I'd picked out to accompany me; his function was simply to act as decoy and look-out. I had no compunction about using him, being determined to drive as many people as possible into outright rebellion. As far as I was concerned, I was doing him a favour by helping him in his first steps as a rebel; this way he would have some grounding before the adults could cripple him with their lies and deceit. I was reacting, with all the outraged passion of a thirteen-year-old boy, against the anguish and terror of my childhood.

From Liverpool Street station, the London terminus from Colchester, we headed for Uxbridge. I knew the place well because my uncle and aunt lived there, and I'd stayed there for a week shortly after the Court case. Behind my relatives' apartment there was the Lyons' Recreation Centre – at least, I think it was Lyons' – and my intention was to rob one of the pavilions. We were in luck; a bowls match was in progress, and there were quite a few jackets lying around. I spotted a likely-looking person taking his jacket off, and I noted where he put it. Walking over, I casually lifted the jacket, put it over my arm and went into the toilet. Extracting the wallet, I found that my "mark" was as affluent as I'd supposed: I got about £27.

We left the Recreation Centre and headed back into town; we caught the train back to Colchester. Overnight, we stayed in a greenhouse in the Castle part; it was too cold to sleep. In the morning, we slept out on the moat; no one noticed us, we were just two boys sleeping in the sun.

Later that day we went and bought an air-pistol so that I could pursue my plans. On the way to Sheepen Road school there was a sweet shop most of the children visited; it was run by a nice old lady who always gave full measure. I planned to rob it. I left the other boy outside as a look-out, going inside and waiting for the woman to arrive from her room at the back. As she came into the shop I pulled out the gun and said, quite casually: "Give me the money in the till and I'll leave." Equally casually, she answered: "No. Is there anything else you want?" I was so surprised at her response that I started laughing! Just at that moment the other boy stuck his head into the shop and announced that a policeman was walking up the hill. Still laughing, I asked the woman for a bar of chocolate – and paid for it! Then I left the shop.

We walked rapidly away, me laughing and the other boy looking shocked. He was very frightened by the action and decided to go home. I asked for an assurance that he wouldn't tell anyone I was still in Colchester, and he gave it. Like a fool, I believed him: he told the police almost as soon as he'd spoken to his mother. I found out almost immediately that I'd been informed on; there was a sudden influx of policemen at the Castle grounds.

I decided that I'd had enough; there was no chance, or shouldn't be, of my actions being misinterpreted now, so I knew that I'd soon be sentenced to a period of detention in an Approved School. With this in mind, I decided on a spectacular finale to my actions – I headed for the police station, determined to shoot one of the policemen as he came out. My principal concern was to be reunited with my brother, but my experience with representatives of authority had taught me to distrust them, so I thought that I'd better make my actions as extreme as possible and thus remove any possibility of their trying some sneaky trick like probation!

Outside the police station there was (is?) a carpet shop, and it was to the entrance of this that I headed. Somehow, I was recognised, and as I stood on the pavement I noticed a policeman I knew walking toward me. I turned to him, drawing the gun from my waistband as I did so . . . and another policeman hit my wrist with the edge of his hand. Thirty seconds later I was in custody, frogmarched across the road and straight into a cell. A few minutes, and a few back-handers across the face, and I was charged with "Attempted Robbery with Menaces or by Force". According to my calculations, I was on my way to a reunion with my brother.

My life to this point had been essentially reactive: I'd faced difficulties with my father, virtually ignored my mother and my sister, and been deferential and dependent with my brother. Outside the family, my relations with those representatives of authority I came into contact with, primarily teachers, were mediated by the problems I had relating to my father. In addition, because those problems had led to the involvement of child welfare agencies and officials, I had become labelled as "maladjusted" at a very early age, and this image, constructed so painstakingly by essentially well-meaning people, further intervened as a mediating factor in my relations with other adults.

I have been told by my mother that the first few years of my life were notable because of my sensitivity; I didn't become a "problem child" until I was six or seven. However, my quiet and amenable behaviour as a baby was marred by a tendency to express rage in a fairly common but peculiarly "passive" manner – I used to hold my breath until I went purple, sending my mother into near-hysteria until she was taught by a neighbour to pick me up and smack my bottom as a method of inducing normal breathing! Perhaps my "sensitivity" was rather an infantile caution. Whatever the reality of this period, it does seem that my other-directed interests gave way to a more introverted pattern around the time of our move to Tripoli.

The suggestion that a combination of physiological and emotional experience during my contact with polio resulted in a radical personality shift seems feasible to me. It seems to me that the material conditions of this episode were such that a traumatic response of this nature could quite well have occurred: the physiological problems of polio, combined with my fear and uncertainty at the time, could have made me susceptible to an extreme reaction when I came face to face with my mother. My infantile understanding could easily have resulted in a lot of guilt and terror in the meeting.

However . . . as a psychiatrist recently said to me: "We'll never really know what happened then. The period is lost in time, and those who were involved will lay too many layers on the memory." The beginnings may be lost, but the later developments are available.

The reconstructions of my earlier years are based primarily on the memories of other people; recent conversations with my parents are largely responsible. I have only fragmentary images coming to mind, and I am well aware of the distorting influences of my later experiences . . . this is why the period until I was thirteen is only sketchily recorded. I have far more vivid memories of my life as a "delinquent"–officially defined!

When around May 1962, aged thirteen and a half, I chose to invite a custodial sentence, I was seeking a peculiar form of security; I wanted to be with my brother, the one person I identified as both comforting and protective. This choice, merely the latest in a long series of essentially self-immolatory gestures of despair, gained me access to a route through the best education that democracy can offer. Rejecting adults, convinced that they were insensitive, deceitful, and brutal, I stepped away from my parents and straight into the welcoming arms of a determinedly adult-controlled world where I had no rights and no protections. I was very soon to learn that deception, manipulation and violence were the only required survival traits in my new world, and I gradually refined my skills at all three.

Still a child, my childhood was over. The real love of my parents, denied me because of misperception and miscalculation by the three of us, was no longer even a possibility of protection for me: the barriers between us were to be made even more difficult to break by virtue of the direct control now given over to the bureaucracies officially defined as my "protectors". I did not know what I was letting myself in for!

Custody and control (1): isolation, murder, despair (1962–1967)

> "A frog in a well says, 'The sky is no bigger than the mouth of the well'. That is untrue, for the sky is not just the size of the mouth of the well. If it said, 'A part of the sky is the size of the mouth of a well', that would be true, for it tallies with the facts."
>
> Mao Zedong, "On Tactics Against Japanese Imperialism"

While I was waiting to be taken off to the Remand Centre I was kept in a holding cell. My father arrived to speak with me, seeking some understanding of my actions. Predictably, I misinterpreted his anguish as rage; in my nervousness at his presence, the only time I smiled was when he told me, with an air of resignation, that I would definitely be sent down this time.

The next three months, covering my introduction to custodial life, run together and are blurred in my memory: Boyle's Court Remand Centre, located just outside Brentwood, memorable only for the vivid descriptions of the pleasures of homosexuality given by some of the boys who were introduced to the subject by a friendly master; the laughable date in Juvenile Court, sentence plus a homily from the chairperson about obedience to and cooperation with the people who would now control my life until I was eighteen;

45

Redhill Assessment Centre, where I experienced the first of my many periods in solitary confinement. The dominant theme in this period was investigation: tests, tests, and more tests!

At Redhill, comparisons were made between David and me; we both scored high on intelligence tests, and the psychiatrist and psychologist were intrigued at the way we both constantly referred to the other during interviews. The psychiatrist told me that he felt neither of us should be in Approved School; we should be located together in some "liberal" establishment and encouraged to express our obvious talents! The psychologist said something similar, but added that she felt it unlikely that we would be allowed to be together. I remained polite, obedient and cooperative . . . and told everyone who would listen that if I wasn't put with David I would run.

Eventually, I was offered a choice between going to Kneesworth Hall, the school Dave ran from, or St John's in Northampton. It was made clear to me that there was no way that I could be put with David because he was in a Senior Approved School (age 15 and above) while I was an "Intermediate" (age 12 to 15). Giving some thought to the matter I opted for St John's – there was more chance of running from there!

St John's, an old school, was in the process of being rebuilt when I arrived. The boys were used as unpaid manual labour. Immediately on arrival I was given the routine cautions about obedience by the Deputy Headmaster, and the equally routine threats by boys established as "leaders" (or "daddies", as they were more familiarly known) in the school hierarchy. Neither message made any impact, although the comments from the boys were forceful enough to make me think: six people hitting you with pieces of wood encourages careful listening to their argument!

My first night in the school began with an invitation to suck the prick of one of my tormentors from the afternoon: the invitation was extended not so much so that the boy could obtain sexual pleasure, more so that I would be totally subservient. My shy smile, coupled with my promptly getting out of bed, disarmed the boy – his initial scream was as much surprise as pain, I think, as I grabbed his balls and twisted. The next few minutes were very painful for me, but the boys hitting me didn't get off completely without pain themselves. As I was beginning to anxiously wonder just how badly hurt I was going to be, one of the "daddies" called the pack off. He told me that I could go to bed, and that the matter would be "resolved" in the morning. We all went to bed.

The next morning, during breakfast, the boy whose invitation had initiated the trouble the night before, came to me and said that he wanted to see me in the toilets when the meal was over. As this was the traditional place for settling quarrels, I thought that I was in for another fight; I was wrong. The boy told me that I could either join with the "daddies", although this would entail a few fights in order to find out how good I was, or I could stay alone and unmolested. I told him that I didn't expect to be around for long, so I would stay on my own.

For a few days, I remained polite and placid; I was looking for the best opportunities to run. Preoccupied as I was, I overestimated the "security" in the school. The masters had worked things out to a fine art; they didn't clamp down, they just used random and infrequent surveillance to cramp our style. Then, just as I was beginning to realise how easy it would be to walk off, I was assailed by a tremendous wave of loneliness and fear: I had been living on my nerves, placing my sights firmly on being with David, and the fact that I still hadn't managed it became too much for me. I broke down.

Sinking into a depression, I withdrew into my shell, breaking down into tears at odd moments. In the classroom I was so preoccupied with myself that the teacher had to walk to my desk and speak into my ear if he wanted an answer from me – and then I was just as likely to break into tears or ignore him! I wrote obsequious letters home, begging for help, and my mother wrote supportive and encouraging notes back – but she could do nothing for me, and I retreated from her.

Gradually I regained control of myself, the surface of my emotions gaining another layer of ice in the process. Superficially, I appeared self-contained again; conversations with friends from the period tell me that the other boys considered me a tough little bastard who used charm as a weapon of distortion while plotting anti-establishment actions! I went back to plotting a run, eventually choosing a day I thought was perfect – but which turned out to be one of my most embarrassing failures!

I stood on the sidelines, watching a game of football; it was an exciting match, with the spectators enthralled as much by

47

the action off the ball as the skilful manoeuvres toward goal. The masters, too, were watching closely, so they weren't likely to notice me going off. Unfortunately, another master chose to come onto the field just as I was disappearing into the tree line; I didn't see him, nor did I hear him give the alarm. I jogged complacently over fields for about an hour, heading for one of the main roads to the east of the school.

Reaching a main road at last, I lay down under a tree for a few minutes getting my breath back, then I went onto the side of the road and started thumbing for a lift into London. The first car to stop was a surprise; the driver told me that I was on the wrong side of the road! (I learned from this that it is never a good idea to state destination if in need of an urgent lift; always ask the driver where he/she is going!) A few minutes later, a van pulled up and the driver signalled me to get aboard. As he drew away from the kerb, the man turned to me with a smile and asked which route I wanted to take back to St John's – the long one or the short one! He was a young master I hadn't seen before, just returned from holiday; I was his first "job". I chose the long route.

The journey back, taking about twenty-five minutes, was quite friendly: we swopped holiday stories, the teacher telling me about his fortnight, and me telling him about my hour. Our reception was cordial, with a quick check-up by the Matron before I was taken off to see the Deputy Headmaster for the regulation caution–cum–threat. I wouldn't agree to stay in St John's, so I was told that next time I'd be "severely punished" – the Headmaster would soon be returning, and his reputation for canings had already impressed me. But the threats were a waste of breath; I maintained that I would run again. This was the start of a practice I was to maintain throughout my imprisonment – I was giving my opponents in the "game" fair warning of my intentions.

For the next week or so I alternated between bouts of sullen, depressed withdrawal, and superficially charming obedience. I had become friendly with a couple of the other boys, but, as they advised me to stay and "make the best of it", we didn't become too close. I was biding my time, preparing myself.

One morning, telling the teacher that I had a headache and an upset stomach, I got permission to go off to the Matron for help. I headed off into the rebuild section, making for the slip-road at the back. I expected at least an hour's start before I was missed – I found out later that I got forty-five minutes.

This time I knew which side of the road to be on, but no one seemed inclined to pick up a hitch-hiker that morning. I stayed on the kerb, always ready to jump the fence and take off across the field if it became necessary. For about an hour I walked, then a van slowed down as it approached me and I thought my luck had turned. Unfortunately, as I concentrated on the van, a police-car came from the other direction and, before I had a chance to run, a policeman came striding purposefully toward me. When he reached me, I smiled, pointed behind him and said, "That's a dirty trick, using one of those". He turned his head, and I ran straight past him and leapt over the fence into the field. The fence was about five feet high, and my trailing leg caught the top and sent me sprawling. As I hit the ground, my right knee went into a cow-pat – and I screamed as I felt something cut into me.

The policeman, recovering from his surprise, had jumped over the fence behind me; he grabbed my hair and pulled me to my feet. I was prepared to surrender, thinking that my knee was badly damaged, but as I came to my feet I got hit around the side of the head. My reaction was completely spontaneous – I brought my knee up into the policeman's groin and, as he fell backwards, ran off across the field again. The raw agony of my knee kept my pace slow, but the other policeman had gone to the assistance of his colleagues so I managed to get away.

I ran for about ten minutes, tears streaming down my face. Eventually, I fell down under a tree and examined the wound; I found a piece of glass embedded in the knee, rasping against the joint with every movement. For about an hour, I just lay there and tried to ignore the pain; I wasn't very successful. This was one of the few times I gave serious thought to giving up, even examining the branches of the tree with a view to hanging myself from one of them. I can remember feeling totally alone, a small and frightened boy having to act like a desperado. But I couldn't give up.

It took me half an hour to find a road again, walking over fields and skirting houses. I ran straight into the police at a crossroads; they were parked under the trees. One moment I was walking along quite peacefully, the next I was on the ground, my face pressed into the earth, a fifteen-stone policeman sitting on top of me. He was heavy! Pulled to my feet, I was spreadeagled over the bonnet of the car.

The police were quite gentle with me, just punching me in the kidneys a couple of times and grinding my face into the bonnet. I thought I was getting off lightly. Then another car drew up, and the policeman I had kneed got out and came over. He told his colleagues to turn me face up on the bonnet, and then he returned my blow. Fortunately, he must have been concerned about overdoing it, because after kneeing me he contented himself with one punch in the stomach – and I vomited over his trousers. There was one benefit in all this, however; I got to sit in the police car for about an hour before being taken back to St John's.

This time, the reception wasn't so cordial. I was sent off to get cleaned up, then ordered to report to the Headmaster's office. There I found myself asked to justify my actions, and thus remove the "necessity" for punishment – I didn't stand a chance, my inquisitors being satisfied with their predetermined conclusions. I found I was to be beaten, with a cane, on the backside. I pointed out that I had broken my back about a year before – which I had – and requested that I receive the blows on the hand rather than the backside; I offered to take twice as many blows if necessary. Not possible, I was told, because tradition called for a run-up by the Headmaster. I refused to be caned – so two masters grabbed me and forcibly bent me over a chair. I tried to resist, but the weakness in my back made it very difficult to stand up. The Headmaster left the room, walking off down the corridor. Then, turning, he called out "Ready or not, I'm coming!" and raced down to the office and lashed me across the backside with the cane. This was repeated several times; four or five, I think.

After the caning I stood up, tears streaming once again down my face, and listened to the cautionary tale of double strokes next time. Rather contemptuously, the Headmaster dismissed me; he obviously felt that my tears indicated a less than manly ability to handle pain. He was probably correct – but then again, I didn't particularly want to be a "man" if he was a model.

Following the second run, I was put under a new "security" regime: I had to report to the master on supervisory duty at regular intervals, and I was moved into the large upstairs dormitory which was locked each night. In this dormitory, the only window which opened properly was in the toilet, and it was confidently pointed out to me that no one could climb through that and successfully negotiate his way to the ground. A week or so later, I did so. I wasn't missed for a couple of hours, having chosen to go at four o'clock in the morning.

I walked into Northampton, sneaked into the station, and caught a train to London. At Watford station, I stole a bicycle and pedalled off to Northwood Hills; I had decided to visit my grandparents. When I arrived, my grandmother, who met me at the door, was surprised to see me; I told her that I was on leave. We spent a couple of hours talking, and then I went off to bed. The best night's sleep I had in months! Early the next morning I left.

I can't remember how I was caught on this occasion, nor the specifics of the treatment received from the police. What I do remember is that during this period there wasn't an occasion when they failed to beat me. Instead of being returned to St John's, I was taken back to Redhill: my campaign of disobedience, aimed at getting me with David, was still alive and going strong.

My first couple of days back in Redhill were spent in solitary confinement; I wasn't particlarly concerned. Then, on being let back into general circulation, I was told that I still wouldn't be put with Dave – so I ran. Going with another boy, I set off along the railway track; we were caught halfway across a bridge, the police coming at us from both ends. I was slapped around a bit, mainly, I think, because I insisted on trying to run for it, but it wasn't much.

To my surprise, the psychiatrist intervened to prevent me being caned; the other boy was let off too. Interviewed by the psychiatrist, he told me he felt that I must be moved out of the Approved School system, and that he was going to see to it. He did: I was packed off to the Adolescent Unit at St Augustine's Hospital, Canterbury. This was one occasion when the Home Secretary was prepared to move me out of a penal institution!

St Augustine's was a regular psychiatric hospital: grossly overcrowded, understaffed, not particularly clean – in short, a dumping ground. The nursing staff, overworked and harassed, functioned as custodians rather than therapeutic agents; the psychiatrists, with case-loads a minimum of four or five times the size they should have been, liberally prescribed drugs to prevent the "patients" being management problems: St Augustine's was "home" for a great many people, few of whom would ever again become "regular" citizens. The Adolescent Unit, a brave innovation by Dr Turl, was separate from the main units, occupying a house in the grounds. Quite a pleasant place, but I was determined not to stay too long.

My first interview with Dr Turl was a disaster: courtesy, one of my few consistent pieces of behaviour at the time, was transformed by nervousness into almost obsequious over-politeness. Turl went out of his way to be pleasant and put me at my ease, even telling me that I didn't have to call him "sir" – it seemed that artificial terms of respect were frowned on in the Adolescent Unit. But he was an adult, and no matter how friendly, that meant – enemy.

I was placed in a local school, a secondary modern a short bus journey from the Unit. Again, it was a pleasant place; the teachers were friendly, but the other children could smell the taint of "difference" on me and the other boys from the Unit. I couldn't settle there, feeling out of place and very lonely. A new dimension to my image had been formed: I was now "mad" as well as "bad".

Three weeks after I arrived, I left; instead of going into the school one morning, I went to the station and boarded a train for London. I was on the run again.

Several years later I read the report, submitted by Dr Turl, of my brief stay in St Augustine's. It had done me considerable damage, encouraging a foray into amateur psychiatry by a prison doctor eighteen months later. Interestingly enough, two incidents used to justify my designation as a conscience-less manipulator were completely false: it was alleged that I had manipulated the staff into buying me a new jacket shortly before I left, and also that I stole some money (3d – in the days before decimalisation!) from another boy. What I recall is that the jacket was pressed upon me, over strong objections, and the money never came anywhere near me! I think the boy used my run as a justification to get some compensation out of the hospital – although why 3d should be so important, I don't know. Once again, the main point is the power of official reports – and the fact that the "subject" has no right of comment or even review.

In London, I spent the first night sleeping rough, then set off the next morning to walk around the centre of the capital. During the afternoon I met a man who, for his sake, I shall call Paul. He noticed that I was rolling dog-ends to make a smoke, and offered me a cigarette. We talked for a while, an interesting discussion on how to live without money! He took me into a café and bought me a meal, still carrying on a humorous conversation which put me at ease. Then he asked why I didn't go home – and I told him that I was on the run. I don't know why I told him, nor why I felt that he wouldn't betray me: he offered to let me stay with him, telling me that it would be no trouble. Surprised, and a little unnerved, I accepted – for some reason I felt that I could trust him.

Paul was thirty years old at the time, a doctor, living on his own in one of the London suburbs. We travelled back to his place, him paying the fare so I didn't have to sneak onto the train. For a week I stayed with him, getting close to him – beginning to feel affection for an adult! He asked about my background, and I told him; he was intrigued, running some psychology tests on me, the only time I ever voluntarily submitted myself to such things without taking the precaution of fudging the results.

At the end of the week, Paul told me that he was going to the United States, and that he wanted to take me with him. He explained that he could get me a passport, and that he would be responsible for me in America. I came back to earth with a bang: I hadn't forgotten Dave, and much as I had grown to care for Paul, I was still determined to be with him. I stole £5 from the landlord's flat and left.

A couple of days later I was picked up. I'd been in Portsmouth, staying with a thief I knew, and I'd stolen a Post Office Savings Book which I used to get some money. Somehow, the police got on to me, and I only just managed to get to the station before being arrested. They telephoned along the line, and at the next station police came on board to get me. I ran off the train, dived under the legs of one policeman, ran through a luggage section – and straight into the arms of a police sergeant! I was picked up by my hair, my arms twisted behind me, lifted off the ground by my wrists (arms still twisted behind my back), and "carried" across the main road to the police station. When we reached it, my face was used to push open the swing door into the back of the station. For some reason unknown to me, the police were in a very bad mood; they beat me badly.

This was the first time I was crucified: my arms were hand-cuffed, spreadeagled, to the bars of a cell gate, and my ankles

53

were similarly locked. Then I was beaten, mainly on the body, with one policeman taking great care to run his truncheon up and down inside the front of my trousers. The beating only lasted a few minutes, then I was taken down and sat in the sergeant's area. I was finally asked who I was, and I laughed and told them that I couldn't remember! Someone hit me from behind with a truncheon, and asked me if I wanted to go back to the cell. I decided that there was no need for that: I told them who I was – then added where I came from. Within minutes I was lying down on a bed in the holding room, having my face bathed by a policewoman who solicitously asked if I wanted a hot meal!

The change in behaviour is simply explained: as an absconder from an Adolescent Unit in a hospital, I could easily be examined by a doctor less than totally sympathetic to the police. I couldn't be handed over with blood on me. The bruises stayed, but as it turned out that didn't cause any problem for the police – I didn't go back to St Augustine's. A couple of hours later one of the masters from Redhill came down in a van and picked me up – he used the same trick my father had used a year or so before, telling me to take my shoes off.

Back at Redhill, the master stood over me while I took the obligatory shower, resolutely ignoring the bruises, and then locked me into one of the solitary confinement cells. I was firmly back in custody.

For three days I sat in the solitary confinement cell, uninter-rogated, ignored: I asked questions when food was brought to me, but I received no answers. Then I saw the psychiatrist, and he told me that Dr Turl didn't want me back. It seems that no one knew what to do with me!

After about a week I was put back into general circulation. For a few days I was subjected to more psychology tests, with the addition of constant questions about my time on the run. Paul had been worried about me, and had made the mistake of enquiring at Redhill – the questions were designed to elicit from me a statement to the effect that I had been homosexually molested. The idea of disinterested concern was totally alien to my interrogators, and they didn't believe my consistent statement that Paul had just tried to help me. Fortunately, they didn't know what we had talked about, so there was no real chance of their bringing punitive action against him – or so I thought.

It was 1962, the year the Conservative dream came true; the heavily falling snow had turned England into a vision in white. In Redhill, we were cut off for a while, with deep snowdrifts making the roads impossible to traverse. In our thin corduroy uniforms, we froze; the nights were even worse, as we undressed after our showers and walked into the dormitories dressed only in thin cotton nightdresses. Instead of the usual pleasure at snow experienced by most youngsters, we cursed it for freezing us and for preventing any exercise.

With a couple of other boys, I decided to take advantage of the relaxed supervision – no one thought it possible that we would consider absconding in such terrible conditions. One night, about half past twelve, I crept out of the dormitory and, checking that the night supervisor was soundly asleep, went to the cupboard in which our clothes were kept. I removed my clothes and those of my two companions; it took two trips to get them all. We stayed huddled in our blankets until about five thirty, and then we climbed through a window and set off toward town through the snowdrifts.

A journey which should have taken no more than half an hour took us nearly two hours. In our thin clothing and plimsolls, we not only made heavy going through the snow but also had to stop every ten minutes or so and huddle together for warmth. Finally, we reached the station, sneaked past the ticket man at the counter, and went onto the platform; our train arrived very quickly.

We headed for Tunbridge Wells, planning to rob a house in order to get money to take us to the North-East where one of the other boys had a friendly family. Turning a house over was easy, once again someone had left the key under the mat and we just walked in. We made a meal for ourselves and ransacked the place, taking about £9 in cash and several pullovers! Then we went back to the station.

For some inexplicable reason, we caught the wrong train; it took us back the way we had come, straight into the waiting arms of the police at Redhill station! There was no real chance of making a break for it, so we surrendered quietly – and received only a few slaps as reward. Back to Redhill.

I spent that Christmas in solitary confinement, the only boy in the school to do so. It was rather flattering, but very lonely: I remember crying quietly to myself for some time. I was moved into the North Wing for the "festive season", then transferred back to my usual cell just before the New Year.

When we were returned from our winter run, I took the blame for organising everything; the staff didn't take much persuading. They considered caning me, but the consensus was that I wouldn't be overly impressed by such action: they were correct. Someone, one of the social workers, I think, asked me what it would take to stop me running again – I gave my stock answer: put me with my brother. This time, the staff decided to try and do just that – keeping me in solitary confinement as a precaution.

When, after Christmas, I moved back into my regular cell, the psychiatrist came and told me that a request had been made, on his authorisation, to the Home Office asking for a waiving of the rules – they were checking to see if they could put me with David. I took this as the usual bullshit, another tactic to slow me down: I was wrong.

At the beginning of January, 1963, a social worker came into my cell early one morning, and told me that I was being transferred. At first he wouldn't say where I was going, but just before he left the cell he told me – I was leaving for Ardale within the next few days. He hadn't meant to be nasty, refusing to tell me, it was just that he thought I knew! I didn't care: all the loneliness, all the fear, the beatings and the solitary confinement, all of them were worth it – I was going to David.

The significant thing about the journey to Ardale was that a social worker was my only escort: he acted as my chauffeur! It seemed that my protestation had finally been accepted – no one expected me to run because I was going to the place I had consistently asked for. I enjoyed the journey, looking with pleasure at the countryside as we passed through it: I didn't even bother to note the roads, or take note of bus numbers and stations – the one time I can remember failing to take such elementary precautions.

We arrived late in the afternoon, and our first task was the regulation meeting with the House Master and his wife. Mr Allen, known familiarly as the alley rat, was a small, round man with an almost perpetual laugh; his wife was taller and even rounder than the rat, with a less "sunny" disposition. After being formally handed over to him, the rat told me that he expected no trouble; he had had long discussions (and arguments!) with David about me, so didn't think I was going to run again. I was then told that some tea had been kept for me, and that there was someone in the dining-room to keep me company. David was sitting at the table, waiting.

The reunion was heavily charged: we embraced, cuddling for about a minute, then sat down to talk. I found that the House we were in, Nelson, had about sixteen boys in it; one boy had a room, the rest of us in dormitories. I was to be in the same dorm as David. As in St John's, and all other Approved Schools that I know of, the system was that each House was effectively run by "daddies", and they set the ground rules for the rest. Nelson was relatively settled, the key "daddy" being unchallenged in his position: beneath him were two other boys, only one of whom, an ex-champion of schoolboy boxing, was unsure of himself and therefore likely to cause trouble. Dave's position was secure in the hierarchy; no one gave him trouble because he had proved his prowess. Overall, he was well entrenched in the school.

After about half an hour Dave took me into the day-room and introduced me to the other boys. It was an interesting meeting: the usual first contact was brittle, with waves of aggression rolling out to meet the newcomer, but with me everyone was more circumspect. My arrival had been heralded by the rat; he told everyone of the fight I'd put up to get to Ardale, and had cautioned them about pressuring me too soon! Dave, too, had prepared the ground by telling of our lives. One benefit of all this was that the boys who had no reputation to protect were more friendly right from the start; they didn't have to watch for any power struggle. My difficulties in getting to Ardale had the effect of making my arrival much easier.

My first week was spent settling in. The system in Ardale gave two options permitting a choice of emphasis to the boys: we chose between three days education and two on a trade, or two days education and three on a trade. The trades were plumbing, mechanics, electrician, or bricklaying. I chose three days education and two days bricklaying: David was learning plumbing and I was tempted to join him, but we decided that it would be best if I went into something else. The deciding factor was that the alley rat was also the bricklaying instructor, and we felt he would be more amenable if I wanted to take time off for more education. The choice was correct.

The schoolrooms in Ardale were in a new building, a single-storey structure with a quadrangle. The teachers were excellent, among the best in the country – they needed to be, for one of the peculiarities of the school was that all of the boys had recorded high IQs, and for all their tearaway style tended to be questioning and critical. My educational competence was below par at the time because of my lack of interest in schoolwork and my conflict with the authorities; it improved during my stay at Ardale, and my greatest benefit from the school was the opportunity to read widely and participate in critical debate. Several years later I was to draw on my memories of this period of learning in order to survive and grow as a human being.

I had quickly become very friendly with a couple of the boys in Nelson, and I discussed with them the dilemma I found myself in concerning the inevitable conflict I would face when someone tested me to find my place in the hierarchy. My position was complicated by the fact that now I was with David I didn't want to fight; my preference was to use the facilities of Ardale to develop my academic interests. They sympathised, but their experience, too, was that I would have to find a way to assert my right to live unmolested.

At the end of the week, the expected test arrived: the ex-boxer taunted me, seeking to provoke a fight – and I refused to fight him. He hit me, twice, but I just took it; I was setting the pattern for the next few months, but it was difficult to stand still and let someone hit me. My passive response relegated me to a lowly place in the hierarchy, but luckily enough the fact that I didn't seem particularly dismayed by the blows added to the image of "difference" the alley rat's warnings had given me: I wasn't to be one of the "daddies", but nor was I subjected to much harassment. I think Dave might have been a bit disappointed in my passivity, but he understood my dependence on him, so we remained close.

About ten days after I arrived I participated in an escapade which confirmed my right to be unmolested, indicating some strengths beyond simple aggression. With David and two other boys, I climbed to the top of the school chimney (about 65 feet, perhaps 70) and tied a dustbin over the opening. I can't remember why we did it, although it was probably in response to an escapade by boys in another House – there was a lot of competitiveness in the school. The climb was made more difficult by the fact that we made it at about one o'clock in the morning! We almost got away with it, but unfortunately the night supervisor came around just as we returned to the House and caught us sneaking in.

The next morning there was much excitement in the school; the teachers had to find a way to get the dustbin down. Eventually, one of the boys who had put it up there had to climb up and cut the rope – the falling dustbin just missed a teacher. The escapade over, the punishment followed: we all lost a month's remission. We didn't particularly care – it was fun.

Apart from this moonlight climb with a dustbin, I was not in any trouble in Ardale. Very quickly, I managed to recover the lost month's remission; the alley rat was very pleased with my "progress".

Three months after my arrival I became eligible for a one-day leave of absence. Initially these were granted once a month, becoming more frequent as the time passed and culminating in one pass a week for the final month or two of detention. David, eligible for more leave than I was, had his days changed so that we could go out together. The first leave came, and we set off for Colchester.

This first Sunday back at home was very strange; we were all rather distant from each other, reserved, over-polite, courtesy overdone. But it worked out, and I returned to Ardale emotionally drained but happier about our relationships than at any time previously. I still didn't trust my parents very much, especially my father, but I was no longer so nervous.

Slowly, over a number of visits home, we all became more relaxed:. tolerance began to give way to a cautious liking. On one occasion, thanks to a special dispensation, Dave and I left Ardale early in the morning to attend a Gala Day at the military prison – this was one of the two days in the year that military families were allowed into the camp, the other day being Remembrance Sunday. (I remember several of those: long, boring hours seated in the church, the only good part being when the Last Post was played – it's one of my favourite pieces of music.) By getting a taxi from the station – the money provided by my father – we managed to get to the camp at ten-thirty. It was a good day, given special meaning because my father finally had to recognise that I was "growing up" – I bought him a pint of beer! Dave and I returned to the school pleasantly light-headed.

By mid-summer it seemed that I had turned the corner; I was well on my way to becoming a "normal" adolescent. My school-work was adequate, relations with masters were amicable if not particularly friendly, and I was getting on well with the other boys. I had a few fights, and I passively accepted blows several times when I didn't feel like fighting, but there was no real heavy pressure any more. Dave and I had grown closer, and I had begun to experiment with something resembling independence. It was an Indian summer.

In June or July, Dave and I set off for Colchester to enjoy our two weeks annual leave. The family was working well together, and we all anticipated a pleasant fortnight.

For a few days, things went well; Dave and I settled in and everyone relaxed. Then, one afternoon, when the rest of the family had gone out somewhere, I went for a walk – and ended up smashing my left foot. I'd gone into the children's play-ground near our home, and one of the older children had asked me to demonstrate the principles of long-jumping. After showing them the basic things about measuring run-up and taking off properly, I put in a very good jump to round off what I had been speaking of – and crashed into the far wall of the sand-pit! When my family returned, they found me, moaning quietly to myself, sitting in front of the fire with my left foot propped up on a chair.

The next morning, after a night of agony during which I hadn't managed any sleep, my father took me off to the military hospital. He was very annoyed with me, and suspicious of my story; he told me that if the doctor found nothing wrong with the foot, he'd beat me. At the hospital, a doctor came out to make a casual examination – and sent me straight into the X-ray department. I had broken three toes and badly sprained the other two: I now knew why I was in agony instead of simple pain. My father apologised for doubting me.

Over the years, I had broken my right wrist three times, on the last occasion being warned that another break could cost me the use of the hand, been run over, fractured my spine, and gashed quarter-inch holes in my leg by running through barbed wire – none of these things hurt anywhere as badly as this damaged foot. For a few days it was raw agony, and the rest of the holiday was characterised by a slow-moving Reeve family and a limping Alan. It didn't put too much of a damper on us, though; we managed to get out and visit quite a few places.

The holiday over, Dave and I returned to Ardale refreshed and confident for the future; the family seemed to be growing closer. We thought that everything was going to work out well, and we applied ourselves conscientiously to our work. Almost as if the authorities were doing their best to confirm that things were going well, the alley rat called me into an interview – they were held each month, with every boy called in and questioned about his attitude and expectations – and told me that if I continued as I had been doing, then I would be given an accelerated discharge. Then they dropped their bombshell.

Even though he had been re-convicted and sentenced anew after absconding from Kneesworth Hall, and though he had lost some remission because of various escapades, David was further advanced than I was in the discharge process. One day he came to me and said that Morris, the Deputy Headmaster, had told him he was to be moved into another House for his last month or so in the school. It seemed that the staff wanted to split him from me in preparation for his leaving. Together, we argued that it would be better not to split us, but the authorities were adamant. I was desolate.

During the next month, my behaviour fell back into its old erratic patterns. I was cautioned that I was heading for trouble, but I didn't care – the authorities had ripped the bottom out of my world, and now they were accusing me of being a problem! David, concerned that I was becoming increasingly and visibly depressed, took to visiting me "illegally" after lights out. He would sneak out of his House after the night supervisor had done his rounds and come back to Nelson to visit with me. Perched on the side of my bed, he argued that everything would be fine, they wouldn't split us up completely. He was wrong.

Dave was due for release somewhere around the end of August, and as the day drew nearer I became ever more nervous. Unknown to me, he had approached Morris and begged him to be allowed to stay for the extra three months which would see me released – Morris refused. Finally, he was sent off on terminal leave; arrangements had been made to place him in the Merchant Navy. I didn't know what to do with myself; I retreated into a shell, coming out of it only to fight with a ferocity which left my opponents wondering what I'd been doing over the past few months. I felt betrayed, totally betrayed; the staff had built me up, encouraged me, and then hammered me on the one point at which I was mercilessly vulnerable. All the work that they, and I, had put in over the preceding eight months was shown to be worthless.

About two weeks after David left I was due for a day pass. The alley rat called me in and told me that I was definitely going to get my accelerated discharge; I would be released in three months. I wouldn't be joining the Merchant Navy, of course, so I would still be separated from David, but I was going to be released. It didn't mean a thing to me. I went on the day out and didn't bother going back.

My behaviour had, once again, become totally irrational. Separated from David, I felt so terribly alone that I couldn't work on any basis other than retreat: after the build-up in my hopes and expectations, the feeling of vulnerability was beyond my capacity to handle – I was completely estranged from any source of comfort and/or protection. In seeking to make a "man" of me, the authorities had succeeded only in driving me into an anti-social isolation.

An absconder again, I found that my short period of conformity had ruined my skills. I lasted for only a couple of days. One of the problems was that I was running scared; I no longer had the goal of being with Dave as a life-line. I spent the first night sleeping rough, and then set off to Paul: I felt that he would welcome me, and I had a vague notion of taking him up on his offer to go to the United States. I found that even this refuge was denied me: when he had contacted Redhill they had notified the police of his interest, and the consequence had been a vicious interrogation during which they accused him of homosexual assault. His position as a doctor made him extremely susceptible to this type of reactionary pressure, and he buckled under it. All this was unknown to me as I went, desperately, in search of some sort of assistance from him.

I arrived at Paul's place early in the evening; he wasn't at home. As it was getting dark, I felt safe enough to wait in the bushes outside his front door – I was dozing when he arrived back from work. He let me in without question, and then told me what had been said to him the year before. I was stunned.

He told me I should give myself up, and that he would go with me to the police station: I rejected the suggestion and left the house.

I remember feeling numb, walking the streets and not knowing what to do with myself. About half an hour after leaving Paul, I was standing at a bus stop when a police motorcyclist drew up and asked me what my name was – I ran, blindly. Down one street, over a fence, running through gardens and trampling on the flowers. Eventually, I stopped running, climbing up onto a ten-foot wall and just lying there. I could hear police dogs and knew that for some reason they were out to get me; the energy expended was in excess of my worth. Fifteen minutes later, with blood running down over my hands from where I had ineffectually attempted to cut my wrists, I walked through a couple of gardens and came to the road. A police car was standing there, two constables lounging against the bonnet. They saw me and ran over.

My intention was just to surrender, give up, but once again I wasn't to be let off so easily. The first policeman punched me in the face and, as I fell backwards, the second man kicked me in the leg. On the ground next to me was a broom, and I jumped to my feet with it in my hands – they backed off hurriedly as I swung at them. With torn clothes, dishevelled hair, tears running down my dirty face, and blood flicking out with each swing of the broom, I doubt if I looked very inviting! Two more cars drew up, and the occupants came to assist their colleagues. I looked at the half circle of big strong policemen – and decided that it just wasn't worth going on. Dropping the broom, I walked over to the window of the house, broke the glass with a blow from my head, and then rammed my neck down on the shards. It didn't work, my collar stopped the glass from cutting me – then the police were all over me, throwing me to the ground and handcuffing me.

There was no beating on the way to the police station, and only a few blows to my kidneys when we arrived. I was sat in a chair in the corner of the charge room, and a steady procession came to view the "wild animal" – the sergeant's ready-witted designation. The worst thing was the way they gloatingly told me that it had been Paul who had alerted them: he was leaving for America in a few weeks, and he didn't want to be delayed by police harassment. I felt dead.

For the next couple of hours I sat in the police station; then someone came down from Ardale, I think, to take me back. Attempts to question me broke against a wall of indifferent silence. Morris interviewed me, cautioned me about having to go to Court because of a couple of counts of housebreaking, then sent me back to Nelson. The alley rat spoke with me, letting me know that he was "really disappointed" with me. I ignored them all, not really caring a damn what they thought, or what they did with me.

I lost remission for absconding, so I was confined to the school again. For a month or more I wandered around, getting in everyone's way, sullenly complying with orders. One day, Morris told us at roll-call that a psychiatrist would be visiting the school and anyone wanting to speak with him should give advance notice. I decided that it would be a good idea if I had an interview – even in my withdrawal, I was aware that I was going further and further away from other people. The interview was a farce: I was asked what the problem was, and I spelled it out quite clearly – I was missing Dave, felt lonely and isolated, and experienced so much bitterness at the adult world that I feared I would lose control and kill someone. The psychiatrist told me to pull myself together, and told Morris that I was faking it. That was my last attempt to seek assistance from anyone in authority; from now on it was to be straightforward manipulation.

Although my cooperation with the staff was sullen, marked by "dumb insolence", I did not get into any official trouble during this period; I was biding my time. It would have been easy to just walk out of the school and disappear, but I wanted to see David again and tell him just how badly I was feeling. Perhaps, in my dependence on him, I felt that he would be able to work some magic for me: there was no one else I could think of to talk with. Eventually, the waiting paid off – I was given a Sunday pass.

David was at home, on leave from the coastal vessel he was currently serving on. My parents, disappointed at my "relapse", were very tentative with me, so I managed to spend more time with my brother. We talked about the problems I was facing, and Dave told me that he was unhappy too at our separation. He suggested that I serve out my time, doing my best to stay out of trouble; I told him it was out of the question. Before I left, I told him to keep his eyes open – he might be getting a new shipmate soon. I didn't go back to Ardale.

For two weeks I was on the run, establishing a base in Plymouth and commuting up to London for talks with some thieves I knew. I was taking pills most of the time, and drinking a lot as well. Several fights, some of them very bad, knives as well as fists, boots, bottles, and assorted blunt instruments; a number of crimes, most of them when I used my climbing skills to assist friends in opening places. It was wild and rowdy.

In Plymouth I experienced the one really bad "trip" that I can remember. Coming back from London on the last train, stoned out of my head on purple hearts, benzedrine and whisky, I walked down the brightly lit exit tunnel – only to find myself being pursued by a woman dressed in red and waving an axe! I was terrified, forgetting that I carried a knife and knew how to use it. I ran. Confusion covers how I got back to the hostel I was staying in, and I don't even remember locking and barricading the door. The next morning, sober, I went back to the station to work out what had happened – and found, after looking around for a while, a red fire-extinguisher with a flared nozzle. That was my woman in red!

Although I was vicious, getting a street reputation as someone uncaring about the number of opponents, berserk and indifferent to blood, I had a few friends in Plymouth. Two homosexuals, a man and a woman, married, who ran a pub; they took care of me a few times when I'd been fighting, on one occasion putting me in bed between them so that I'd be kept warm. A young woman, daughter of a family of thieves but herself honest; she too took care of me sometimes – on one occasion I staggered to her door and collapsed unconscious at her feet. The next morning she told me we had slept together, and that we had even made love: my memories of this incident, after the collapse, are non-existent. In addition, several thieves – and a Merchant Navy petty officer who was trying to get me a job.

Apart from some routine housebreaking, bread and butter stuff essentially, this period introduced me to some very heavy law-breaking. On six occasions I was called upon to help some people by climbing some rather interesting buildings; my role was a simple one, merely having responsibility for short-circuiting alarm systems by coming in from above. Security was very primitive in the early 1960s! I was paid a flat rate for these jobs. On another occasion I did a difficult climb for myself, making several thousand pounds out of the feat. The last job was the most interesting, at least in terms of learning the "trade" – I participated in a hold-up. I shall not make any further comments on these episodes; there is no Statute of Limitations in England, and although I am not particularly worried about myself (I can't receive any heavier sentence!), the other people involved were not apprehended and would therefore be at risk.

Whatever money I made during the fortnight was quickly gone; I continued to be indifferent to cash, letting it flow through my fingers like water. Whenever I heard of someone needing assistance with lawyer's fees, or getting married, or having a party, I gave without reservation: I loaned just under four thousand to two friends, both in their early thirties, because they were getting out of "crime" and wanted to set up a business as market gardeners. I didn't call in the loan, although both men gave me some help a few years later by watching over someone for me.

I was eventually picked up by the police as the result of an act of gross stupidity. I had spent all night at a party, joining in the celebrations welcoming someone home from prison, and I had all but emptied my wallet during the collection. I had a cheque book in my pocket, the spoils of a housebreaking expedition the week before, and I decided to cash one of the cheques! I should have been alerted when the clerk went out of his cage and into the manager's office, but I wasn't thinking very straight. When I realised that a lot of time had gone by, I turned and made to walk out – and the doorman decided to be a hero. I was armed with several knives and a couple of sleeve-guns (small pistols) which I had no ammunition for. I pulled one of the guns out of my pocket and invited the man to step aside; he lunged at me, but I pushed him off and ran out of the door. Three policemen tackled me as I reached the street – they had just arrived in response to the clerk's warning. It was a very brief struggle, a truncheon blow to the nape of my neck making me unresisting. I was back in custody.

At the police station I was taken into one of the detective's rooms and questioned. The police thought at this time that I was just a silly youngster trying to cash a stolen cheque, and for a few minutes I thought I might actually manage to make a dash for it. Then a policeman came dashing in and told the detective about the gun. I stood up, thinking to make a fight of it – then saw the crowd of policemen standing just outside the door and sat down again! The questioning had been heavy but verbal up to now, but everything changed with news of the gun. I was finally searched, and then beaten around the room when the men realised their mistake in not checking me out beforehand. Why I should be beaten up because they had made a mistake I don't know, but it's a familiar occurrence. This time a boot knocked me out – I decided that the kicking was getting too bad, so I led with my chin. I woke up in the cells.

After cleaning myself up, I was taken out and finger-printed. About an hour later a detective sergeant came into the cell and asked if I would tell him who I was; I did so, knowing that was the only way I was going to get out of the place. The sergeant went away, telephoned through to Colchester police station for confirmation of my identity, and made arrange-ments for someone to come down and pick me up. Early the next morning two detectives arrived and, after making sure I was firmly handcuffed, took me off to the station. It was rather pleasant travelling in a reserved carriage!

Back in Colchester, I was met with a barrage of verbal abuse. It wasn't that they hated me, just that they were tired of me turning up and posing problems for them. I only got punched a couple of times, so I wasn't complaining much. Over the next few hours I engaged in the time-honoured practice of examining the books to see which crimes I would have TIC'd – Taken Into Consideration, a process whereby the police get to keep the charges down to a minimum, but improve their figures by hooking a multitude of offences onto one person. I had been playing the TIC game ever since I got sent down the first time. Discussing the matter with a detective sergeant, I agreed to clear up a few housebreakings in return for any charges concerning the weapons being left off. He made on the deal, while I didn't really lose because it was obvious to everyone that I was heading for a Borstal sentence this time unless a miracle occurred – and they were in short supply! In addition, even given a miracle, the fact remained that I was already in custody; my Approved School sentence had been re-applied the last time I was in Court.

When all the dealing had been concluded, I was formally charged and then returned to the cells to await transfer to a Remand Centre. The police found themselves in difficulty: a check was made with all the Remand Centres in the area, but none of them would take me because they believed they couldn't successfully hold me. Finally, Ashford Remand Centre – a minimum security prison – agreed to take me. The police sent me off quite happily, contenting themselves with descriptions of what they would do to me if they found that I'd broken out of Ashford. My escort were even kinder – the three of them asked if I'd let them have my autograph when I made it to the death cell. The driver remained silent, being interested only in confirmation that my handcuffs were secure.

In December 1963 I was only just over fifteen years old; officially, I was still a child. Prison Regulations quite specifically maintained that a child could be kept in an adult or young person's cell only under exceptional circumstances: Ashford catered for children by having a special wing, H Landing, set aside for them. For a few days I was kept on H Landing, then, with no warning, I was moved to another cell – and away from the children's wing. I found out later that one of the prison officers had seen me looking out of a window on the way to the showers, and my reputation was such that this was enough to panic the administration into relocating me in a more secure cell.

I spent Christmas in my new cell on E Landing. We got no exercise over the "holiday", being confined twenty-four hours a day. On Christmas Day I was taken down to the main mess, but I didn't stay long because, ordered to sit on my own – I was too young to sit at the main tables, and too much of a risk to sit with the children – I refused. I had several friends in the mess at the time, and they set up a howl of derision when the screws began to try the heavy image. I was removed to my cell, sent on my way with a chorus of good wishes from the other prisoners.

It was a lonely time, made worse because I hadn't heard from home; everyone was unusually silent. Fifteen years later I found out why I'd heard nothing. My mother had sent me a package of food for Christmas, and included a card with the box. The prison staff refused to deliver it to me, sending it back to Colchester. No one told me. My sense of isolation was increasing, and my ability to deal with anyone other than fellow "outcasts" was rapidly decreasing; I felt that I had nothing in common with the outside world, and that the people who inhabited it were insensitive dullards. Prison de-sensitises to such an extent that ordinary citizens become identified with the oppressive authorities who represent them behind the walls: the world was my enemy.

At the beginning of January, 1964, either the 1st or the 2nd, I went to the Quarter Sessions. The trial was rapid: I pleaded guilty to the charges brought, the judge said that he was accepting the negative reports and rejecting the positive ones because the people who wrote them obviously didn't know me, and then I heard the sentence I had expected. I was sent to Borstal Training for a period of six months to two years. I understand that I was the second fifteen-year-old to get the benefit of the recent law which lowered the age for Borstal Training from sixteen to fifteen – I had a feeling that 1964 was not going to be my lucky year.

I was taken straight from the Court to Wormwood Scrubs prison, along with several other boys who had received Borstal sentences. We were booked in, bathed, issued with prison uniforms, and then escorted to our cells. It was about eight or nine o'clock, and we hadn't eaten since midday, but all we were given was a cup of cocoa. A good beginning, just the thing to welcome us into our first full prison.

For two or three weeks I stayed on A Wing, the allocation centre, going through yet another battery of tests. Bored, I complied with everything they threw at me, coming out of my shell only on one occasion: a young psychologist interviewed me after I had completed another set of IQ tests, intrigued, once again, by my high scores. I can't remember the bullshit I came out with, but it ended with a comment that my intelligence should help me destroy the bastards who had damaged me. The psychologist was upset at my bitterness.

I was informed that my age and intelligence warranted an Open Borstal, but that my record indicated a need for security – I had no hand in the decision-making, having given my opinions through my actions over the past couple of years. My destination was Rochester Borstal, the prototype of the system, located in Kent. I was then moved to B Wing to await transport – i.e. a place being available.

My stay in B Wing was quite pleasant really; I had a couple of fights, met some old friends, and took part in a mini-riot. The screws consistently attempted to act heavy with us, but few of us felt anything other than contempt for them.

Sometime in February I was moved to Rochester, having my last look at the countryside through the windows of the bus which took us down. The only interesting part was when we stopped off at another allocation centre, an ex-prisoner of war camp, I believe, to pick up some more boys. I found that a friend of mine from Plymouth was coming down with me.

My induction at Rochester was interesting: I was wearing my own clothes, a black leather jacket and black trousers, with a black shirt and black shoes, and the first screw to see me called out: "Hey, a nazi!" I was used to the comment, having heard it several times before, and I had given up explaining that it wasn't very good going housebreaking in light-coloured clothing. I decided that this was as good a mask to wear as any, so I answered by raising my right arm in a nazi salute and snapping out "Sieg heil!" The screw wasn't very pleased with me; I'd spoiled his fun.

Once again I found myself going through a settling-in period; there weren't quite as many tests this time. As one senior screw put it: "We don't need to run too many tests because we've got all the reports on you. We know everything there is to know." One person, though, did seem very interested in me for a while; the Borstal doctor spent several hours quizzing me about David. I found out a couple of years later, when I finally got the chance to read the reports written about me during this period, that he had strayed into amateur psychiatry, noting that "the possibility of this boy being an early psychopath must be considered". I was very impressed, until I noted that the date on the report was September, and by that time everyone was trying to get into the act.

My behaviour was initially circumspect; I was determined to learn the manipulative skills of my opponents, and to this end I wanted to remain out of trouble for as long as possible. Unfortunately, as a direct consequence of the taunt on my first day I found myself involved with several other boys in the formation of a nazi "cell". We were playing games, choosing one of the few things we all knew to be abhorrent in an attempt to irritate the screws. Eventually we were punished, but I was singled out as the ring-leader and as a result got my first taste of the punishment block.

Two things remain in my memory of that first encounter: my meeting with the Governor in the Adjudication Room, when it seemed to me that I was being punished more for not knowing anything about nazi-ism, especially failing to spell "führer" properly, than for any act of commission; and, secondly, the fact that the screws boasted their punishment exercises were worse than the Foreign Legion punishment camps! I didn't like the experience, but it gave me the incentive to give up my infantile posturing.

I was kept in the Induction Block for an extra month because of my time in punishment, then I was moved to Hawk House. This had a young warden in charge – I can't remember his official title. He was pleasant but "firm" on discipline; I was charming and polite with him, but I kept my distance. I didn't get on with any of the screws at all. During my first two weeks I had two fights, neither of my making: the first, in public, I lost, being effectively battered by another boy with a thick piece of wood; the second, a re-match, in private, I won – I had to sit with the boy for ten minutes while he came back to consciousness. We cordially hated each other for the duration of my stay, and he took every opportunity to cause trouble for me. I remained outside the "daddy" system, not joining any of the cliques and getting involved only when there was trouble involving the whole House.

I was put to work in the laundry, a boring job which I did well; it required no thought, so I just learned the actions and then performed them automatically. It left me free to examine the gate and check for opportunities to run; none presented themselves.

For the first few weeks I was in Rochester I was on full-time education, forced to spend two hours a day, on my own, with a teacher. I didn't like it much, but the teacher was sufficiently impressed to get the warden of Hawk to "persuade" me to take up evening classes when I moved. I made the mistake of writing a decent essay, and I found myself submitting to an "O" level examination in English. I failed it – pleasurably. The evening classes at least got me out of the House for a couple of hours every few nights, and because of the English teacher's interest I managed to get greater access to books in the library. I continued to read as widely as possible, but took no great care in choosing the material.

One day, when I had been in Hawk House for about two and a half months, I was picked up in the laundry by three screws and taken to the punishment block. I had no idea at all what was going on. I was put in a cell and left for several hours; no one said anything to me. Then, early in the evening, the Governor and the vicar came to the cell to speak with me. I thought, automatically, that someone in my family had died; I assumed it was David, and I nearly fainted. The Governor told me that I was in the cell for my own protection – David was being hunted by the police for stealing some shotguns, and it was thought that he was coming to Rochester to attempt my release! When the deputation had left, I sat in the corner and cried: it was very much an experience of "no greater love hath . . ."

I was in the cell for about three days, and then Dave was picked up. I found out later that he had been in a car chase, and the police had forced him off the road and straight into a tree at about eighty miles an hour. He was unhurt, but the car was a total wreck. I moved back to Hawk House.

David received a Borstal sentence for his plan to free me, a fact my father told me when he and my mother next visited me. They came fairly frequently, beginning a visiting process which was to last for many years. We discussed the matter, but there was no real communication; my father couldn't understand at that time just how close my brother and I were. I told him that I would do the same for David if I got the chance. It came, disastrously, in August.

In July, 1964, I heard that my father, still a serving soldier, had been posted to Malta – or, perhaps, Gibraltar; my memory is hazy on this point. On the strength of this news, I applied for a compassionate day leave; I didn't expect to get it. Called in by the warden, I heard that the staff thought my behaviour warranted my getting this day out. It seemed that miracles were beginning to occur for me. The date was fixed for Wednesday, 16th August.

The day before I was due to go out, I heard that the long-expected and anticipated clash between the two major opposing cliques in the House was due to come off that night, straight after tea. I was rather annoyed by this coincidence, but resigned myself to losing my pass. The fight didn't occur; someone informed the staff, and immediately after tea the House was swamped with screws – we were individually escorted to our cells and locked in. Searches of the cells immediately began, and I was one of the first to be done. I had nothing untoward in my cell, so I was unconcerned – then, to my surprise, I was ordered to report to the kitchen to do the washing-up. The screw who let me out of my cell told me that everyone thought I would be unlikely to be involved in the fighting because of my day pass! With another boy, I did the washing-up, carefully hiding the blades, filed-down rings, and razor-edged coins I took out of the teapots. Then I went back to my cell.

Wednesday morning dawned cold, but clear. After drawing some clothes from the stores, trousers and a sports jacket, I dressed, picked up a railway warrant from the office, and was escorted to the station by a screw. We had a fifteen-minute wait for the train, and then I set off for London in order to catch the connection to Colchester.

I arrived home somewhere around eleven o'clock, and I had only five hours before I had to leave again. It was an enjoyable visit, but rather sad; I remember that Fran was very upset when it came time for me to leave, and I cried as I left. My father came up to London with me, and several times asked if I wanted him to accompany me all the way. I turned his offer down, knowing that the decision I had to make would not be possible if I had company. We parted at the terminal, and I caught the train for Rochester. At Gravesend, I left the train. My decision was made, I was going to break David out of Borstal by whatever means were necessary.

The first thing I did was to call on a friend in the East End of London. I found that much had changed: Freddy had been in a fight and had his face badly slashed with a bottle, and the incident had ruined his taste for illegal activity. He wouldn't help me get the guns and dynamite I wanted – but he did give me a hundred pounds, so we parted amicably. I headed back for Plymouth.

On arrival, I went to see a thief I knew, seeking information about two friends of mine. They were both in town, so I went pub-crawling until I found them. I explained the situation, outlining the material I wanted and asking them to get it for me. They agreed – both owed me favours, both were ex-Borstal boys, and neither one had any affection for the police or prison authorities. I had to pay seven hundred pounds within two days, but the material wouldn't be available until the following Tuesday.

I went housebreaking that night, making just over three hundred pounds. My next stop was a café I knew, looking for someone to sell me some dope; I wanted some purple hearts and bennies to keep me going for a while. I rounded off the night at a party, drinking heavily and dropping pills regularly. Not having had any sleep, I headed back to London early next morning; I was on the money run.

Getting the seven hundred was easy; people cooperated with burglars in 1964, leaving cash lying around in cabinets and under their beds. I was back in Plymouth by Friday afternoon, getting about half an hour's sleep on the train, the only rest I'd had since Tuesday night, and even that was confined to a couple of hours sleep. I delivered the money and made arrangements to pick everything up on Tuesday morning. Then I headed back to London again.

That evening I went to see the last half of the Beatles film *A Hard Day's Night*. I went to the cinema because, arriving in London, I had been overwhelmed by a sense of desolation; everything seemed so damned futile. I wanted somewhere warm to crawl into. When the film was over, I came out of the cinema and broke into a car; I just sat there, staring at the dashboard. Some time later, I decided that I'd had enough; I felt lost, alone, and very, very small in a vast hostile world. I settled on the idea of driving the car to Colchester and crashing it into the police station, planning to take a couple of the bastards with me. The idea fell through – I couldn't get the car started, finding that my hands just couldn't cope with hot-wiring that night. So I dropped some more pills, and left the car.

I wandered around for about six hours, the benzedrine keeping me awake, and the purple hearts preventing me from throwing myself under the wheels of any car which happened along. Continuing to toy with the idea of suicide, I found myself getting angrier and more bitter as the hours passed. Finally, I passed through the anger and reached a cold resolve: I'd go to Colchester and kill one, or perhaps two, of the people I knew had betrayed David, turning him into the police at some time.

I caught an early morning bus into Colchester, arriving just after six a.m. Going straight to Montgomery Estate, I hid in the coal house of one of the betrayers' homes. At seven-thirty I knocked on the door – and came face to face with someone I'd never seen before! The woman I was after had found herself a new lover, and I could see a couple of children at the table behind him. I made some excuse and left. I didn't think I could follow through on this one.

The other person I had thought of lived on the edge of town, and I thought that there might be too many police around for me to go in so early. Instead, I headed off to the fields behind the officers' estate, planning on staying there until mid-morning.

I was feeling very tired, but too charged with emotion and benzedrine to sleep. Lying in the field, I watched the clouds, trying to rest. At ten o'clock, on my way out of the field, I saw that one of the houses looked empty; I decided to break in and get some food. After having a small snack out of the kitchen, I looked around for anything worth taking – and found a shot-gun, shells, and a cartridge belt in the bedroom. There was also a carry-case for the gun, so I left the house well-armed but not too obtrusive.

Once again the person I wanted wasn't available; no one answered my knocking. I headed into the town centre, meaning to rest up in the Castle Park. Going down the High Street, I suddenly remembered that I had obtained a Youth Hostel card first thing on Friday morning – I could stay at the Hostel off East Hill. A perfect scheme, I thought, because the Hostel was so close to the police station that it provided absolute cover – no one would expect me to be there.

The Youth Hostel was similar to the ones I had stayed in before; self-catering, and a bed in a dormitory. I had stayed in the Park most of the day, and by the time I arrived in the Hostel it was getting dark. I made myself a meal of beans on toast, sharing it with a boy who threw in some extra bread and butter; he introduced himself as Barry Richards. We talked during the meal, Barry telling me that he was on a bicycle tour of the area, me saying that I was just walking around. He wanted to go touring the town with me afterwards, but I excused myself: I had checked the gun, in its case, into the bus depot luggage store, and as this was right next to the police station I was feeling a little rattled. I wanted to go to a pub and have a few drinks – my pill store was getting low.

I had four or five whiskies in the pub, but vomited most of it into the road on my way back to the Hostel. As I went in, I swallowed more pills for the night – even if no one would expect me to be staying this close to the police, I intended to be alert.

There were only three people in my dormitory; Barry, another boy – the oldest among us, who came from the

North-East – and myself. We had several bunks to choose from, and ended up scattered around the room. The others slept well, I heard them, but I only managed to doze for a couple of hours. It was a long night.

Early the next morning I breakfasted on pills, leaving me just enough for lunch, and then joined Barry while he cooked and ate a meal. We carried on our discussions from the evening before, and I suggested that he spend the day with me; I said I could borrow a bicycle from a friend and, when I had done so, we could go touring together. He thought the scheme a good one, so we made arrangements to meet in the Castle Park at ten o'clock. I left to pick up my bags from the bus depot – and to look around, checking for untoward police activity. Sleeplessness, pills, anguish, and a terrible sense of isolation had by this time made me into a raw-nerved mass of suspicion; I felt that the whole police force were looking for me, and I conjured up visions of desperate shoot-outs as they came for me.

Just after ten o'clock I arrived in the Park to find Barry waiting for me. He asked about my bicycle, and I told him that I was to pick it up at about two o'clock – I intended to steal one. We walked down to the river Colne, running along the bottom boundary of the Park, talking about our itinerary. I sought to ingratiate myself, determined to use Barry as my cover for the next two days – then I could collect my stuff from Plymouth and get on with the job.

Leaving the Colne, we walked back up to the Roman Wall and left the Park by going into St Peter's Street, heading for the Cattle Market. As it was a Sunday morning the Market was deserted, but we stayed there for a few minutes as I explained the usual scenes occuring during its operation. My vivid, almost frenetic description seemed to make Barry nervous, so I hurried him along Sheepen Road and then into the fields next to the Technical College. We were to wait there until two o'clock.

We had a radio with us, although I can't remember whose it was, and we switched it on to listen to some music while we waited. I excused myself, went into the bushes, and swallowed the last of my pills; I had been getting fuzzy-headed, but they soon cleared the cobwebs away. For about an hour we talked, sporadic and desultory conversation. I took the shot-gun out of the case and showed it to Barry, loading it and pointing it out across the field; for some reason I couldn't get it to fire, so I stripped it down again. Somehow, the conversation turned to juvenile crime, and Barry indicated a very conservative outlook – I started to get annoyed, but he maintained a stubborn anti-crime attitude.

Just before one o'clock we started to talk about Borstals, and Barry made some derogatory comment about people who were sent there. I jumped to my feet, holding the butt of the shot-gun in my hand, and told him to apologise – I said that my brother was in Borstal, and I wouldn't allow anyone to make snide comments about him. Barry started to get up, kneeling on one leg, and I smashed the gun butt down onto his head, sending him full-length in a sprawl on the ground. He wasn't unconscious, much to my surprise, and I told him to turn around so that I would see the damage I'd done. At this stage, hitting him had been enough; I didn't intend to take it any further. Not surprisingly, he refused my request, and this enraged me: he jumped to his feet, pushed me, and ran off down a track with me in pursuit. I had dropped the butt, which had shattered when I'd used it as a club, and picked up the barrel of the gun – when I caught up with Barry, I knocked him to the ground with it.

Standing over Barry, I told him to get to his feet; he just curled into a ball and whimpered. I decided to kill him, thinking that he would be a useful warning to the police that I meant business – I didn't see him as a person any more, just as an enemy, one of the many objects of my hatred. I clubbed him several times with the barrel, stopping only when he whimpered: "Mummy, please don't let him hit me any more." He was unconscious at this time, he had to be, but the fact that he could talk was too much for me; I dropped the barrel, pulled out my knife, and started to stab him. Several times I hit him with my knife, finally stopping only because I'd stabbed him in the neck and it took considerable pulling to retrieve the weapon. He was still breathing, stentorously, but I knew that he was dead. I dragged him into the long grass and walked back up the hill to where we'd left everything.

After I had dragged Barry's body into the long grass I had gone through his pockets and removed all his papers – and his wallet. When I got back to where we had left our belongings, I examined everything in his pack, removed what I wanted, and threw the rest, along with the gun and its case, into the bushes. It wasn't that I wanted to prevent the police knowing I had murdered Barry, merely that I saw no reason why I should make it easy for them.

I took Barry's bike and rode off down the hill. On my way out of the fields, I met a man walking his dog; we exchanged comments about the weather, it was very mild, and I left. I cycled back to the Castle Park, and walked the bicycle up to the High Street. Going to the bus depot, I parked the bike against a wall and caught a bus for Southend. Somewhere along the route I threw Barry's Youth Hostel card out of the window – I decided that I didn't want it.

Arriving at Southend, I posted a couple of postcards I'd taken from Barry's wallet – they were addressed to his parents, and I wrote on them "D.O.A.", meaning "David or Alan". (A month or so later I listened to Barry's father explain to a judge that he thought the letters stood for "Dead On Arrival" – I didn't think of that, and thus caused even more pain.) I caught the train to London, intending to go to Plymouth on the late night express.

I felt incredibly relaxed, free of all pressure, very loose. On the train to London, I carried on a casual conversation with two adults and their little boy; it was all so easy, as if I hadn't a care in the world. I thought about Barry, but his death was so distant from me, as if it had occurred somewhere else and in another time.

When I got to London, I decided that I was too tired to travel down to Plymouth that night, so I caught a train for Lydd, in Kent. I was going to an address I had been given by another Borstal boy – he had told me that he used to live there, and that his father kept a gun in the house. I had to get a taxi into Lydd from the station because the train didn't go all the way; it cost me almost all the money I had, but I wasn't worried because I thought I could steal some more the next day. I found that the boy had lied to me; the address he had given didn't exist, so I had to break into an empty house to stay for the night.

I was so tired that I fell into a deep and dreamless sleep within seconds of my head hitting the pillow. The next morning, I awoke to find two policemen and a civilian looking down at me. I didn't even have the chance to pull my knife out from under the pillow as my arms were grabbed and I was pulled from the bed. I was under arrest yet again.

The policemen were the only two in the area; they ran a small sub-station from Lydd. I found that I had been arrested by chance: the house I had broken into belonged to the army, and the man who had notified the police had decided to make an early morning check before handing it back to the authorities. He had walked around the building and noticed that one of the windows was broken, but had thought no more of it until he entered and found me asleep. I had actually been roused when he came into the room, but in my dozy condition had dismissed the incident and gone back to sleep!

When I was questioned, I realised that the policemen didn't know who I was, so I attempted to bluff my way through; I claimed that I had only broken into the house because I was drunk and tired. For a while, I thought I might get away with it – then the younger of the two policemen looked into the Incident Book and, on seeing my description in it, rushed back into the room and told his colleague that maybe I was the wanted Borstal escaper and murderer, Alan Reeve. It really was all over.

After a couple of hours in the cells I was taken off to the central police station in handcuffs. On the journey I listened to the two policemen discussing how they were going to report my capture: the younger policeman was to receive the credit, he needing it more than his colleague. It was an interesting discussion.

At the central police station I received a couple of slaps around the face, maintaining the police record for their relations with me. I was surprised it was so little; I had expected a full-blown fight! A detective inspector told me that a car was coming down from Colchester to pick me up; the matter would be dealt with down there.

The policemen who collected me and took me back to Colchester were ones I had known for some time. We talked during the journey, but I said nothing about the murder.

Back in Colchester I freely gave a statement, secure in the knowledge that it couldn't be used against me because, as a minor, I was supposed to be protected from such immediate questioning. That was a mistake. I was asked to show where I had put the gun and the other material I had taken from Barry, and I gladly cooperated – I hoped to get the chance to run. In handcuffs, I was taken back to the field where the murder had occurred – I couldn't run, being held all the time I was out of the car. Then, back to the police station and into the charge room: I was formally charged with murder, taken before a magistrate, and remanded into custody for a week. That evening I was in Brixton prison, all the Remand Centres, including Ashford, having refused to hold me because I was too great a security risk.

While I was on remand, my father arrived back in England and came to visit me. Although he was still reticent with me, I realised that he really did care for me; he came to see me frequently, spending other periods giving information to the police and welfare authorities about me. My mother and sister remained abroad, and David wasn't available because he was located in another prison.

I was kept in a cell in the hospital wing, kept separate from the other prisoners because of my age; even exercise was a solitary event. Interviewed by the prison doctor, I heard him expound the theory that my experience with polio had resulted in brain damage; I was not responsible for my actions, he said. My response was simple and to the point: I told him that he was a stupid bastard.

Dr Peter Scott, the psychiatrist called in to interview me, spent several sessions discussing my life. On the last occasion I spoke with him, I asked: "Well, doc, am I mad?" He answered: "No, you're not mad; you just need lots of love." As I walked out of the room and back to my cell, I laughed and said: "Yeah, well, I'll get a lot of that in the nick!" He didn't answer.

Finally, I got my day in Court – October 15th, 1964. The "trial" was soon over: I was asked how I pleaded and, on the instruction of my barrister, I answered "Not Guilty to Murder". There was a short silence while all the officials looked at me, then, as my barrister waved his hands in a gesture indicating I should speak again, I said ". . . but Guilty to Manslaughter by reason of Diminished Responsibility." (The capital letters are straight out of the law books.) Barry's father was called to the bar to state that he had received postcards posted after his son was dead, and then a young boy testified that he had found Barry's Youth Hostel card on the roadside. Then the police were on the stand, and I listened to them "verballing" me – I didn't recognise any of my alleged comments. The last thing was the reading of my confession – so much for protection of minors!

The judge didn't waste any time: in a very avuncular voice he called for the psychiatric evidence. I heard myself called a psychopath, dangerous and in need of special security. A short silence, then the judge looked over at me and explained that what he was about to do was in my best interests. Then he sentenced me to be detained in Broadmoor Special Hospital under Sections 60 and 65 of the 1959 Mental Health Act. I shrugged, smiled, and said softly: "Thanks, your honour." Then I was taken down to the cells.

Twenty minutes later I was taken out of my cell and led down the passage to a closed door with a glass panel. My father was on the other side. We spoke for a couple of minutes, but our words didn't make much sense: my father was weeping, and within a minute I joined him. It suddenly dawned on me that he didn't just care for me, he loved me, he really did. With that realisation, my defences crumpled and the full import of what I had done hit me: my tears were no longer sympathetic ones for my father, now they were for Barry, his family, my family, myself, and all the wasted years. I was taken back to my cell, still weeping.

Back in Brixton for the night, a screw came and gave me a sleeping draught. He was an old man, a regular hospital screw, and he told me that it was no good feeling sorry for myself: that did me good, because it brought my defences back up. I told him to fuck off.

The next morning, handcuffed and escorted by several very large screws, I was taken by car to Broadmoor. On the journey, the screws echoed what the police had said to me – I should have been hanged, but at least they could be confident that I'd never see the outside world again. I ignored them, securely back inside my shell.

October 15th, 1964: Harold Wilson led the new Labour government into office, Nikita Khrushchev went off in disgrace to manage a power station, and I received what amounted to a life sentence for the crime of murder. I entered Broadmoor on the 16th, a fifteen–year–old virgin: I was physically, emotionally and intellectually immature.

Barry had died as a surrogate victim, the sudden focus of all my rage and anguish: he was the scapegoat for the years of betrayal and terror. The few minutes of concentrated hatred which took his life paradoxically brought me back from the abyss; his death gave me a form of emotional release. Superficially, it seemed that I was indifferent to the murder I had committed, and to the pain I had caused so many people, but the reality was that I was distanced from the event because it had left me drained, once more just a child: at a critical moment in my life, Barry's death took just enough pressure off me to enable me to survive. The doctors, classifying me as a psychopath, argued that I had a "personality disorder" characterised by extreme immaturity; they maintained that a hospital was the best environment for me as it would permit a pressure-free period in which I could mature. Barry's death was to be the key to my life.

When the escort took me into the gatehouse at Broadmoor, we were met by the Principal Nursing Officer who surprised me by angrily demanding that the handcuffs be taken off me – he said that I was in a hospital now, and that as a patient I should be treated with respect. I was overjoyed: my imagination had conjured up a place similar to St Augustine's, just having high walls to keep the "loonies" securely in place. Dr Scott had told me I was not mentally ill, so I thought I would shine out among the less fortunate in Broadmoor; I had visions of getting leave within a few months. Doctors, nurses, treated with respect and consideration – I really thought that I now had a chance to make something of my life. I was correct about the walls.

Escorted by two white-coated "nurses" to Block One, the Admission Ward, I was still locked in my day-dream of a brave new future. The booking-in procedure didn't disabuse me, although I was slightly unsettled by the surly attitude of the people I came into contact with. Then I was told to strip naked on a gallery, watched over by about eight people, and locked into a cell. Doubts started to creep in. After about half an hour I was taken out of the cell and along to the bathroom by four "nurses".

Four inches of luke-warm water was the ration for my bath; I wasn't particularly concerned, having had to bathe in cold water on occasion in other prisons. Then I had to listen to the "nurses" making homosexual references to my future; they were laughingly talking about how, as a fifteen-year-old, I'd soon find a queue of people after me to give me the fucking I obviously wanted. The comments irritated me, but I put them down to introductory provocation; I'd heard worse. Then my tottering illusions were shattered – I was told, bluntly, that the first step out of line would earn me a kicking.

I had made a conscious decision that I would no longer use

violence; Barry's death had been enough for me. Also, I had decided that no matter what the provocation, I wouldn't start fighting the staff in Broadmoor – no matter what they were called. This threat, however, dismayed me; I knew that I had to answer it, otherwise I would be used as a doormat. I laughed softly, leaned back in the bath, and answered the threat with a promise: as long as I wasn't touched, I wouldn't fight, but if any screw attacked me I would kill the first one I could get my hands on – regardless of whether he had taken part in the attack or not. I thought that my non-violence was going to end right there, but they just snarled at me and, when I had finished bathing, took me back and slammed the cell door shut behind me. I now knew that I was dealing with screws – and I wondered how wrong I had been in my imaginings of other matters. The next morning I found out.

My first night was relatively quiet: I lay in bed thinking about my situation, knowing now that I had merely exchanged one prison for another, but still hopeful that I would be able to make headway because I would be surrounded by people who swung from chandeliers, ran naked down high streets, and frightened children and small dogs with their grimacing faces, gibberish, and hideous habits. When the screws got everyone else up the next morning, I waited impatiently for them to get to me; I was left locked up. When breakfast was brought, I asked what was going on; the screw told me that I would be getting up at ten o'clock – or when they felt like unlocking me. They didn't feel like it until just after eleven o'clock.

I strolled into the day-room, casually, with my hands in my pockets and a carefully arranged look of boredom on my face – I was determined not to show any fear about the forthcoming encounters. In the event, my hardest job was stopping my jaw from hitting the ground.

The day-room held about twenty people, with three screws sitting just inside the door. Only a couple of people looked up at me as I walked in, one of them being a man I knew from Brixton prison. He called me over, gave me a cigarette, and asked me how I felt; I told him I was shocked. He misunderstood me, saying that I would soon get over it and settle in. I told him, no, it wasn't shock about the sentence or being in Broadmoor, it was the scene of normal people in the day-room which had got to me. He laughed and told me that I would probably see more "strange" behaviour from the screws than any of the other prisoners. He was correct.

During the rest of that first day I sat and talked with Paddy, my friend from Brixton. He was about forty years old, an expert safe-breaker, who had been sent down this time because he'd cracked up, thought he'd killed his baby son, and fought savagely with the police when they prevented him returning home to check the body. It was all a figment of his imagination; the baby was unharmed. Pat took being in Broadmoor quite lightly, waiting for the opportunity to kill himself – he tried three times in Broadmoor, succeeding only when, six years later, he got access to a rope and beam in a real psychiatric hospital.

For several days Pat kept me in tobacco and provided me with company as I adjusted myself to the new environment; he also introduced me to some of the other cons. I was the youngest person in the prison at the time, and there were only about four other people under twenty; a sixteen-year-old, two seventeen-year-olds, and a nineteen-year-old. Graham Young was the next youngest after me: initially, Graham and I stayed clear of each other, neither of us finding the other of much interest. I spoke with the other adolescents, but the person I got closest to was a young man in his early twenties. As Pat spent more and more time turning in upon himself, so I got closer to Tony, the young man I just mentioned.

As I settled in, not quite becoming part of the furniture, I became more adolescent in my behaviour. I was no longer constantly on the alert for violence – which was remarkably absent in Broadmoor, coming most frequently from a handful of screws who used their position of authority to pick on the weaker cons – and, newly connected with my childhood, my behaviour began to resemble that of a young fifteen-year-old. A pattern I vividly recall from this early period came about because Tony claimed, quite seriously, that he could hypnotise people. I allowed him to try his "talents" out on me – he failed to influence me, but I pretended to be susceptible – with hilarious, though childish, results. For about a week we maintained this game, getting on everyone's nerves as I performed ridiculous acrobatic feats or pretended to be re-living a life from a century past. Eventually, the screws decided that my behaviour was getting too disruptive, so they locked me up for forty-eight hours. The period of detention seemed a bit excessive, but this was probably one of the few occasions when there was some justification for the screws to intervene. The things that most interested me about their response was the fact that it was straightforward punishment, no question about "therapeutic" value – and, as no doctor was involved in decisions such as this, there was no check or hindrance to their arbitrary use of detention cells for any purpose.

After a couple of months, Tony and I fell out over some trivial incident which I can't remember; I was back on my own again. I spent a month sitting around and reading, waiting to get my "privileges" which would enable me to go to the sports field on Wednesday and Saturday afternoons, weather – and screws – permitting. (During the summer months, the hours we could spend out of the Block rose from four to seven; subject to the same provisions, we were able to go to the sports field on Monday and Thursday evenings as well as the two afternoons.) I also began putting together my thoughts about escape, a subject which came back to the forefront of my mind as I sat in the bath being threatened by the screws on my first day. I still had visions of being with David, my first impulse to "reform" having been wiped out by my realisation that Broadmoor was just another prison.

One day, about six months into the sentence, I was called along to the Departmental "Nurse's" office and quizzed about a mass escape attempt I was supposed to be leading. It seemed that another con, whose name is unimportant, had hidden himself in the toilet down the sports field, a can of beans in his pocket, planning to escape when everyone went back to their respective Blocks. Of course, as soon as the toilet was checked prior to everyone leaving, he was found – and immediately attempted to prevent himself from being sent to Block Six (the Refractory Block, more familiarly known as the Punishment Block) by informing the authorities that I was master-minding a mass escape. The Departmental "Nurse" threatened me with the Punishment Block; I was unimpressed, said nothing, and was told that my Responsible Medical Officer, Dr Udwin, would be coming in to see me shortly.

Dr Udwin had become my RMO shortly after I arrived in Broadmoor, but I had only spoken with him on a couple of occasions prior to this meeting. He hadn't made any great impression on me. When he came in on this day, he too threatened me with Block Six unless I made a "full confession" – and also told me that he wanted all sixteen names! I had, as it happens, been discussing with a couple of people the idea of an escape, but not by any stretch of the imagination could it be said that there were sixteen people involved. I continued denying all knowledge of the charges, wondering just how far Udwin would be prepared to go with the charade – then the Departmental "Nurse" came back into the room and produced a handful of three-inch pieces of string, allegedly found under my bed, from which he said I was going to make an escape rope. I pointed out that the string wouldn't hold a baby's weight, let alone mine, even if it was enough to make a twenty-foot escape rope – but they were seriously accusing me, so I knew that I was in real trouble. Udwin sent me back to the day-room for five minutes to think things over: it was a straightforward choice, names or Block Six. When I was called back to the office, I categorically denied the allegations, so I was sent to the Punishment Block.

I was taken to Block Six by only two screws, which I thought was adding insult to injury. Rumours abounded about this place, some of them as horrific as stories I'd heard about the nazi concentration camps; I was to find that some of them were true. Stripped naked, I was pushed into a double-door cell: I had a mattress on the stone floor, two blankets, one sheet, an open chamber pot and no paper. Later I was given a pair of pyjamas. In this cell, twelve feet by six and a half, the walls covered with shit and the floor with piss, I spent the next sixteen days – one for each year of my life. There was a window, high up on the far wall, but it was kept permanently shuttered. I was finally given exercise on the day I was moved to Ward Two.

Block Six, in 1965, had a medieval regime in a Victorian building. On the ground floor the prisoners were locked up for a minimum of twenty-three hours a day, with most of them doing the full twenty-four. The cells were unhygienic; apart from the daubs on the walls and the pools on the floor, they were consistently damp. Periods of detention ranged from several days to several months – with some people spending several years behind the door. One prisoner was kept in solitary, I believe, for a period longer than my lifespan at the time; he was in solitary when I first went there, and was still behind the door when I went back on each occasion over the next few years. He was completely unable to face coming out from his cell by this time; if forced into the day-room he would smash a window in order to go back into solitary.

Conditions on the other two floors – or Wards – were slightly better. The day began at seven-fifteen a.m. and ended at seven-thirty p.m., but the intervening period was spent in the day-room. At this time, the rules were harsh: prisoners were allocated a seat on one of the benches around the wall, and there they sat unless given special permission to move. In the centre of the room was a table, at which two prioners could sit and play chess or some other game; permission wasn't always given. Going to the toilet depended on the duty screws; again, they didn't always give permission. Pens could only be borrowed from the screws' desk – permission was sometimes difficult to obtain. Exercise was at the discretion of the screws – we sometimes got it, usually for half an hour.

This was the routine I moved into when I was sent to Block Six – but I missed out on the welcoming committee. In fact, during my seventeen years in Broadmoor I was not physically assaulted once.

On Ward Two when I got there I found Graham already firmly ensconced. We quickly became friendly, being the only two youngsters on the ward. Although separated by several chairs, and forbidden to talk to each other because the rules were that talking was only between immediate neighbours, we managed to carry on quite a few conversations by getting permission to meet at the table in the middle of the room. We played numerous games of chess, with Graham winning by a ratio of thirty or forty to one – he was much better than me. When, eventually, the rules were relaxed somewhat and we were able to play bridge with two other people at a table in a bay-window area, we always partnered each other; we were unbeatable for many months. I heard Graham's life story as we swapped information about each other, and I became angry at the way he too had been the victim of prejudicial official reports which reflected their authors' bias rather than factual commentary.

Several months into my stay in Block Six I got talking with another prisoner about the possibility of making an escape. The man, whose name I cannot unfortunately remember, was an engineer by profession – and our first plan entailed making copies of the screws' keys by memorising them. We made rough wooden copies, but they weren't good enough. We then examined our environment, looking for weaknesses in security – and we found several. The one we chose involved our going to the canteen together on Monday morning, a difficult feat because the screws tended to randomise each group of six. It took us several weeks to get the conditions we needed, but they finally arrived.

Two screws escorted a group of six prisoners from the Punishment Block to the canteen each Monday morning, the schedule starting at about nine-fifteen. We had planned the escape carefully, seeking to take advantage of the fact that the escape siren was tested at ten o'clock the same morning as our escape – our reasoning was that the siren was a familiar Monday morning sound, so few people would suspect that this one was for real. We set off for the canteen at about nine forty-five, walking casually with the others. As we went around the corner onto the Terrace, we speeded up our walking, and the others followed suit. Reaching the Chapel, where we were to turn into the canteen, we started running – along the Terrace, around by Block One, and up to a shack which leaned against a connecting wall to the outside wall. From this wall no one could reach the main wall; it was about nine feet higher. The other man knelt down, I got onto his shoulders, he stood up – and I pulled myself onto the outside wall, looking down into the coal house. I spent about three minutes trying to pull my friend up, but he had an acid stomach which chose that moment to burn him badly; he couldn't straighten up properly, and I couldn't reach him. He kept urging me to go, and, finally, I shouted goodbye and jumped down into the coal stack.

The coal house had an open gateway onto the road and I headed for it. Before I could get through, one of the senior screws stepped in and blocked my path. "Give up, Alan", he said – and I dived at him, rugby-tackled him around the waist, shoved him to one side, and ran through. Unfortunately, the few minutes I had spent trying to pull my friend onto the outside wall had given the screws time to sound the alarm – and I found three screws, plus the Physician Superintendent, Dr McGrath, waiting for me as I turned right, heading for the trees. I dodged two of the screws, but the third one, Barry Goswell, dived full-length and managed to ankle-trip me – on the wet grass I didn't stand a chance. With McGrath jumping up and down in the gutter and screaming in what suspiciously resembled a hysterical voice, "Get him inside! Get him inside!", I was hauled to my feet and, arms twisted behind my back, frogmarched back into Broadmoor. As we went through the gate, the siren sounded – I had got over the wall, thirty yards, thirty seconds, and the timing had been perfect . . . but we didn't make it. Barry and I laughed at the irony of the siren sounding as I came back inside.

As I had spent sixteen days in solitary for planning an escape, I would ordinarily have expected at least three months for making one. On this one occasion, however, luck was with us: the Punishment Block was being redecorated, and my friend (Cliff?) and I spent only one day locked up. We didn't get to go to the canteen for a long time, though, and never again together! Udwin, who interviewed us when we got back to the Block, seemed amused by our temerity – I was beginning to like the man, a phenomenon which had started a couple of months earlier.

Shortly after I moved onto Ward Two, Udwin came to see me. We spent about thirty minutes talking, and he assured me that he would be back. To my surprise, he came. Several times he came in and we talked, backtracking over my life; him listening, me talking. He is a South African Jew – or so legend has it – and when he questioned me about my nazi "past" I played the game with him for a while. It had an interesting consequence – one day, early, he came and asked me if I was willing to be interviewed by him for a BBC radio programme on violence. I agreed, and the interview took place: Udwin asked me loaded questions, and I answered – and made a garbled anti-semitic statement. It was so childish, so obvious what I was doing, that I am surprised Udwin didn't stop the interview – but, on the other hand, I should imagine that it served his purpose, indicating the irrational nature of violence in terms of a Broadmoor detainee. After getting this infantile attack out of my system, I began to like the man; over the next eighteen months I was to grow increasingly dependent on him.

In mid-summer 1966 Udwin moved Graham and me to Block Three, one of the "front" Blocks. For the past few months he had been treating us similarly, encouraging us to be together and give each other support. We were moved onto

Ward Two, located in the same dormitory, and placed together for meals.

At tea on that first day in Block Three we met the other two men who shared our table. I can't remember the name of one of them, but the other was Allison John Cook – who I thought was the most beautiful human being I had ever seen, and whom I immediately loved with a passion greater than anything I had ever known.

I was seventeen years old, only tentatively beginning to reach out toward some form of maturity, unsure of myself, bitter and with a tendency toward self-destructive reactions against the futility of my existence. I had never before felt the emotional turbulence which Allison caused me: this was no childish reaching out for security, a need for dependence, but, rather, a desperate desire to reach out and crush him to me, envelop him, protect and cherish him. The surging sexuality of my desire stunned me – until this time I had been sexually neuter, disinterested even in masturbation. I had had homosexual advances made to me, but on the whole I had rejected them with good-humoured tolerance; only with insistent and unpleasant pressure did I react angrily and, on occasion, with violence. I thought that desire, sex, passion, love, all these were games that other people played; I loved David, and Fran, and I was beginning to love my parents, but this was a totally different dimension.

Immediately after tea I asked Allison if I could talk with him, privately. He agreed, and we went off into the gallery together. In my bemused state I lost whatever delicacy I had, and my first comment was: "Are you a homosexual?" I think he was amused by my gaucherie – but he answered: "Yes. Why?" I could hardly keep my hands off him as I said, simply: "I think I'm in love with you." He didn't laugh, nor did he walk away in anger or contempt; the smile left his face, replaced by a rather sad expression, and he said, softly: "Oh." We spent the rest of the evening talking, covering many things, none of which I can remember. We parted at lock-up, him to his dormitory, I to mine.

For the next five weeks Allison and I spent as much time as possible in each other's company. Our talks, at first intensely intimate and self-directed, began to range more widely. Allison encouraged me to fly, to reach out and use the intellect I had left dormant for so long. He also encouraged me to talk about myself, not that I needed much prompting! I wanted him to know everything about me, all the weaknesses I had and my few strengths. Toward the end of this period he began to criticise me for wasting so much of my time, telling me that I should not waste my life in futile rebellion; he was also the first person to tell me to write my autobiography, but I argued that there wasn't enough life to justify it at the time.

Then we found that we were being pressured by the screws to split up – our feelings were too open, we were told. We contemplated escape, and I turned my attention to spotting a flaw in the security. I found it – or thought I did. I noticed that one portion of the wall was still fairly low, and worked out that we could get over it quickly if I could find a hook. The only thing I could find was the handle of a mop, a metal pipe. We smuggled the handle and a length of flex out of the Block and into the exercise yard – and then I ruined the bending of the pipe and we had to leave the stuff outside overnight. That was our undoing.

The Block next to ours – number Four – had evening exercise and someone found the bent pipe and the flex. Instead of keeping his mouth shut and his hands to himself, he reported the find. There was an immediate search around the Blocks, and it was found that the flex came out of Block Three. I was suspected, but left alone for the evening. That night, after lock-up, I developed intense stomach pains and the screws were called. McGrath came in and examined me, saying that it might be appendicitis. I should have been moved down to the infirmary downstairs, but one of the screws pointed out that I could smash my way out of the Block through the back so I was moved to Block Four infirmary. I was violently sick during the night, but next morning I was told to get out of bed and then made to walk, still in pyjamas, to Block Six.

McGrath came to interview me, and said that he was convinced I was guilty of attempting to break out; he told me that Allison was implicated, too. I denied the whole thing, saying that we were being framed – there was no evidence against us, it was all prejudice. My complaints were ignored, and I was put back in solitary. Later that day, McGrath moved Allison back to Block Three, saying that he had been led astray by me. I was locked up, alone again.

I cannot remember how long I was in solitary on this

occasion; within a day or two I had sunk into a massive depression so deep that I lost track of time, had no interest in eating, couldn't sleep, and would have killed myself if the chance had arisen. When I finally left the cell, I sat in the day-room of Ward One, a recent innovation of Udwin's, and wrote pathetic, love-lorn poetry to Allison. I was sinking deeper and deeper.

Unable to handle my anguish, I turned to David; I asked for an inter-prison visit on compassionate grounds. One morning, Udwin called me into the office and told me that the visit had been arranged – I thought he was lying, attempting to humour me. I went out onto the exercise yard and, when the screws walked five yards away from me, quickly climbed up the bars to the second storey and then made my way up the drainpipe to the roof. I'd started a method of protest which became identified with me over the next few years.

It was a bitterly cold day, but I kept myself relatively warm by ripping up slates and hurling them to the ground. I took great care not to hit anyone, although several of the screws were badly frightened. Even when Udwin came out and maintained that the visit was arranged, which enraged me as I still thought he was trying to trick me, I didn't try to hit him; I had no desire to hurt anyone, my protest was self-destructive.

At about eight o'clock I decided that I might as well give up; I was going nowhere, and maybe they actually would allow Dave to visit me. I called for Udwin and made a bargain that if he stood alone in the exercise yard, keeping the screws completely out of the way, I would come down. He agreed, and told everyone to stay away. I found out a few minutes later that he expected me to climb down the ladder they had called for, but by this time I was in the process of climbing. My feet were badly cut, dripping blood, from where I had kicked in some windows, and this made the climbing dangerous because I kept slipping. When I reached the ground, Udwin, visibly shaking, gave me a cigarette and said: "Please, Alan, whatever else you do, don't do that to me again." I told him I wouldn't – and never did.

My feet needed several stitches, so Udwin took me into the medical room and got to work with a needle. I lay on the examination trolley, smoking and eating a meal that had been provided on my descent – and carrying on a conversation with Udwin. As a local anaesthetic was not possible because of the siting of the injuries, and a general was out of the question, I had to endure a rather painful few minutes; Udwin was very good with the needle. Then I was locked up.

I had a very peaceful night; a deep and dreamless sleep. The next morning I woke up in agony as an assortment of sprains and torn muscles revealed themselves. Part of the deal I'd made with Udwin about coming off the roof involved my not being locked up, so I waited with considerable interest for the screws to arrive. The other cons were unlocked and taken down to the day-room – but I was left in solitary. When my breakfast was brought round, the screws told me that Udwin's orders were that I should be unlocked at ten o'clock; he wanted me to have an early morning rest! Much to my surprise, I was allowed up later that morning.

For a week after coming down off the roof I hobbled around the Ward; my feet were heavily bandaged, and most identifiable muscles ached badly. Udwin spoke to me only in passing, but I didn't want anything more from him – I was waiting to see if David was going to turn up. As I wasn't allowed out on exercise, the screws locked me up when the other cons went out – and took great care to inform me, gloatingly, that I wouldn't be receiving a visit. They were wrong.

At the end of the week David was escorted down to visit me, and we spent two hours talking about how our lives were going. He warned me about overdoing things, saying that it was time for me to settle down and make some constructive arrangements with the authorities. I listened carefully to what he had to say, but couldn't really see any way of doing as he asked. When he left, I went into the day-room, sat in a corner with a newspaper over my face, and cried – I felt so incredibly lonely, separated from David and denied access to Allison. While the visit was good for me, it didn't break the depression – I was still locked in a self-defeating, self-destroying spiral of despair.

In the ensuing weeks, a period which remains very blurred in my memory, I sank ever deeper into depression: I was exhausted, feeling a bone-deep weariness, an emotional and intellectual lethargy. Udwin came in frequently to speak with me, urging me to write or speak or do anything which might break the pattern – but he couldn't reach me. Finally, in a departure from normal Broadmoor practice, and setting the pattern for such things with me in the future, he asked if I wanted any drugs. I wouldn't accept any of the regular anti-depressants, but said that I would take sodium amytal, a sleeper. I started taking six grains four times a day – and this kept me in a constantly soporific state, exactly what I wanted.

During this time I developed really savage headaches, and no matter what analgesics I was given the pain remained. Eventually Udwin brought a specialist in to see me – and even though I was unconscious when he examined me, my head was so sensitive that I tried to punch him! (One of the screws told me this some time later.) A disease of the jawbone was diagnosed, and I was put on a course of antibiotics which gradually reduced the pain – but a later X-ray showed that a residue of the disease remains, so I may suffer from it again at some time.

Gradually, Udwin managed to get me to talk; he offered me a course of psychotherapy, with him as the therapist, and I accepted. Although a qualified psychiatrist, Udwin was not a psychoanalyst, so we were involved in a mutual learning process! Over the next few months I spent several hours a week – more than many cons had in a year – speaking with Udwin: we discussed anything which I wanted, ranging from politics through an extensive review of my life. David and Allison figured largely in these talks, as did the problems I had experienced coming to terms with my father. I had unre-stricted access to Udwin when he was in Broadmoor, being able to go into the office and ask to see him – and he would come in. The screws didn't like this development, and they went out of their way to be unpleasant to me: of greater interest, though, is the way they slandered Udwin, calling him a homosexual – and a communist! I ignored them, only com-plaining to Udwin when they became particularly insistent in their attempts to turn me away from him.

The interviews became intensely emotional over the months, and I became increasingly dependent on Udwin. As we explored my past and my visions of the future, I began to place more and more trust in him, accepting his argument that he was only concerned with helping me. It was like a drug – I needed my daily fix of Udwin. I pushed him hard, and he accepted it; he encouraged me to talk out my fantasies of revenge, and all the pain and loneliness and fear came spilling out for him to see and feel. I stripped myself raw, leaving my nerves exposed, making myself vulnerable because I had come to accept that he would not betray me. I had stopped taking the sodium amytal, choosing to face the reality of my life and work through the pain as I related it during our talks.

While all this was going on, Allison was sent to the Punishment Block for attempting to escape – he and another con climbed through the roof, or tried to, but they were caught. For a short time he was on Ward One with me, but at this time he wasn't too keen on staying with me: he had become emotionally involved with another con (the one he had tried to escape with) and preferred to be with him. We talked about his problem of being moved, and he went into a depression, asking me to kill him. We went into the toilet and I put my hands around his neck, squeezing, but I couldn't do it – I loved him, and I wanted to ease his pain, but I couldn't kill him. The next day I went to Udwin and requested that he move Allison off the Ward because he was causing me too much distress – thus he was moved upstairs, to Ward Three, and reunited with his friend. Udwin congratulated me on making a wise choice, and I became ever more dependent on him, even starting to refer to him as "Uncle Edgar".

Eventually, Udwin moved me upstairs to Ward Two, but our talks continued in both frequency and intensity. The screws continued to get at me, provocatively telling me that I was behaving like a child or asking if Udwin was fucking me during our private interviews – they didn't like the fact that Udwin was spending so much time on me, or that he had agreed to my condition that the screws be excluded while we talked. I didn't react to the provocation, secure in my relationship with Udwin.

By mid-summer I had reached crisis point in re-living my life during the interviews, and I sank into a depression again. Udwin slowed down the tempo, relaxing in his questions, and meeting with me only about three times a week. I didn't like the cut-back, but it was about all I could stand. Then it came time for Udwin to go off on two or three weeks' leave – and I became desperate. He told me that we would continue when he returned, but while this reduced my anxiety somewhat I didn't have a very pleasant time while he was gone.

During Udwin's leave the screws became even more obnoxious, no longer letting me sit quietly in the day-room, reading, writing, or just thinking; they harassed me, constantly calling me down to the office and then sending me back without comment, ordering me to do more Ward cleaning, continuing with their provocative comments about my relationship with Udwin. I tried retreating back inside my shell, but I couldn't do it successfully, and by the time Udwin returned from his leave I was in a state of complete panic.

For several days after his return, Udwin stayed away from the Ward; the screws gloated. When he came in, he saw me for only a few minutes – I couldn't believe it, thinking he would come back and see me later that day. He didn't. The next time he came in, I managed to catch him on the gallery and walk down to the office with him, demanding that he speak with me. I was trying to test him, so I reminded him of his promise to move me to a "front" Block the moment I thought I could handle it; I asked for a move – and he refused. I was shattered, feeling an overwhelming sense of betrayal: I had let down my defences, come to trust him and even to love him, going through the classic psychoanalytic process of identifying with him – I felt that I had nothing left, nowhere to hide. I didn't know what to do.

I retreated as far as I could from everyone; most of my time was spent sitting in a corner, ignoring everything going on around me. I often went off to the toilet and wept. My sleep pattern was erratic, I spent hours just lying in bed staring at the ceiling; I ate very little. Some of the other cons became disturbed at my slide and reached out to me, but I couldn't connect with them.

One day I went into the dining-room and, standing at the window with my back to the room, I burnt Allison's name into the flesh of my left forearm, using the cigarettes which I was chain-smoking. It was a childishly self-destructive act, but there was no other form of expression open to me. The same day, on exercise, another con came up to me and asked me to kill him. The coincidence of events was later to become very interesting.

Billy Doyle, the man who asked me to kill him, knew that I was feeling desolate; he was in the same state. He had been released from Broadmoor some time before, but had been returned after killing someone. He felt that his life was over, suspecting that he wouldn't be released again – not just a question of several years, or even many, but a total life sentence was how he put it. We walked around the yard, talking, and his sorrow managed to get through even my self-centred anguish – but I told him that I couldn't kill him, partly because the burn on my arm made it difficult for me to use, and partly because I had vivid memories of Barry, and I didn't want yet another nightmare on my life. I thought, too, that Billy was just severely depressed, and while I could sympathise with that condition I knew that suicidal ambition was a passing phase if something else intervened. None of this was conscious logic, more an emotional response to the problems as I saw them, but Billy seemed to understand and agree with what I said. He went off to speak with another con, leaving me to wander around the yard.

The next day, after lunch, Billy and another con came up to me and asked if I would stand watch while they played the knock-out game in the toilet. The game consisted of someone having a neck-lock put on until they became unconscious, then released so they could experience a "buzz" as they came round: it was similar to the game played in school playgrounds, only the children used chest-squeezing combined with breath-holding after deep exhalations to induce unconsciousness. I agreed to stand in the dining-room and keep watch, turning any other con back into the day-room until the game was over and intercepting any screw with loud questions. They went off to the toilet.

About ten minutes later, during which time my interceptions weren't needed, the other con came back alone, walked past me, and went into the day-room. I went along to the toilet to see Billy – and found him dead on the floor of the end cubicle.

Standing over Billy's body, feeling the absence which is the reality of death, I experienced the full force of what I had done to Barry Richards. I could hear again his whimper: "Mummy, please don't let him hit me any more." I was shaking uncontrollably and had to lean against the wall of the cubicle. I straightened the body, then, knowing in advance that it was pointless, checked for a pulse; there wasn't one. I left the toilet and went back to the day-room.

The body wasn't discovered for several minutes, and I spent the time attempting to play snooker. I wasn't very successful, my hands shaking so much that I couldn't hold the cue properly: I rolled the worst cigarette I ever made, spilling tobacco on the table and the floor. Someone spoke to me, but I was stuttering so badly that he went off before I could answer him.

After a while, two more screws came into the day-room to join the three already there. They told us all to sit down; McGrath was coming into the Block, and he would then be told what was going on. Noticing that I was shaking, one of them went off to the office to report the matter, then came back and told me that McGrath wanted to see me in the office on Ward One. I went downstairs.

McGrath asked me what I knew about Billy's death, and I immediately said that I knew nothing and, what was more, didn't want to know anything. He told me that he would stake his professional reputation that I hadn't done anything to Billy, but that he felt I probably knew something about what had happened. I continued to deny all knowledge of the incident. I was sent back to Ward Two, but McGrath ordered that I be kept in solitary until Udwin arrived to speak with me because I was so obviously distresed. Half an hour later Udwin came onto the Ward and, after asking me if I felt able to go back into circulation, let me out of solitary.

A week went by, during which I spoke to the con who had killed Billy, learning that assisted suicide had been the plan all along and also hearing the details of the act. The screws kept asking me what had happened, telling me that I would gain considerable advantage if I gave the details. I ignored them, locked away in my anguish over Udwin's betrayal and my shock over Billy's death and the flash-back insights I had gained about my murder of Barry. The screws kept up the pressure, convinced that I knew all about the incident and determined to make me talk.

At the end of the week, I had had enough – I decided to tell Udwin what I knew. I went into the office, having come in from exercise to see the man: I sat down and, as Udwin prompted me, told what I knew of the details of the killing. The only thing I wouldn't give was the name of the man who had done it. Udwin was very gentle with me, but kept asking for a name – in my depressed and devastated condition, I could take no more, opened my mouth and said . . . I killed Billy Doyle. I don't know to this day what I intended to say originally, but in the few seconds before I gave myself up into complete destruction I remember thinking to myself that I had a chance to get out of Broadmoor, to go to a regular prison, to remove myself from Udwin, Allison, and all the other pressures of betrayal, rejection and loneliness. I had arranged myself on the crucifix – the nails weren't long in coming.

For three or four weeks I sat in solitary confinement, coming out only to be interviewed by the police and to speak with Udwin and McGrath. I wasn't surprised to find that my story was accepted, but then several screws told me that they didn't believe I had done the killing, each of them nominating the same person as the "guilty" party and asking why I was protecting him. I saw the police for a second time to withdraw my "confession", but I wouldn't name anyone else. By this time I had realised how irrational my action was, and I attempted to protect myself – but I wouldn't do it at the expense of sending someone else into the dock. In some unbelievably innocent part of myself, I suppose I believed that I would not be convicted because I wasn't guilty – and I knew that if my statement was accepted as accurate, and used as the basis of the prosecution, I had to be acquitted because the suppurating burn tissue on my left forearm would not be found by forensic examination of the body. If I had killed Billy in the manner the prosecution would specify, then the forensic report would have to refer to the burn tissue – and it couldn't, because I hadn't done it.

I was taken to a Magistrates' Court and sent for trial after committal proceedings. Instead of being taken back to Broadmoor, I was remanded to Winchester Prison. During my time on remand I was kept in a cell in the hospital Wing – locked into a canvas miniskirt the whole time. When I went on exercise, I realised that they thought of me as particularly dangerous; six screws, all of them larger than me, accompanied me at all times. The prison doctor, another man with pretensions to amateur psychiatry, asked me if I wanted to go home – I told him that I did, but not if he meant Broadmoor! A well-known psychiatrist came to interview me – a Dr Neustatter, I believe – and spent approximately six and a half minutes interviewing me before deciding that I was as close to being a homicidal maniac as it was possible to come: yet another report from a "professional" which was to cause me problems. I was in Winchester for about five weeks.

Billy died on September 9th (?), 1967: a couple of months later I was convicted of the same thing as last time – only this time a jury said it, I didn't. My innocent expectation of being protected by the truth was blown away by a legal charade: I would have received a better defence if I had been given trial by combat with a pack of lions. I don't blame the jury, they were faced with a young man in prison clothing, possessing a pallor which related him to Dracula, and heard nothing but well-presented circumstantial evidence – and a "confession" which I repudiated in anger during an ill-matched confrontation with the prosecutor. The decision took only a few minutes to arrive from the Jury Room, and about an hour later I was en route to Broadmoor after listening to the judge describe me as a merciless killer.

When I arrived back in Broadmoor, I was just nineteen years old, a convicted double killer, condemned as a savage maniac. There was nowhere else for me to go; I had reached a nadir, even for my bitter life.

There are episodes of violence, mine or other people's, which I have chosen to leave unrecorded from this period. Repetitive accounts of my fights, or my experiences of police and prison-officer brutality, or recollected verbal confrontations with the authorities, these could easily have filled another twenty or thirty pages – but the only real purpose they would serve would be to titillate the bored palates of sensation-seeking readers.

People and places, too, have been recorded only in terms of their significance for me: I am writing an autobiographical sketch, not a travelogue, so I have left out long descriptions of the institutions in which I spent my time. Also, I experienced them as waiting-rooms, places from where I would run as soon as the occasion presented itself.

As in Part One, where my father was portrayed in terms of the anguish which I experienced as an enervating reality, Part Two recalls my relationships in terms of my responsiveness to them. I have sought to show the significant occurrences, the key events, but each time it has been in terms of my life: autobiographies can be very unkind to other people, dealing as they do in interactions from the perspective of only one participant.

What is recorded here represents the world as I saw it, as I experienced it; it reflects the style of perception I had at the time, and, as much as possible, I have left out benefits of hindsight. I was still essentially reactive; my view of the world was narrow, self-centred, and I judged all issues in terms of my direct experience. Like Mao's frog, I could not see beyond the lip of my own well, and I thought the whole world was an oppressive place.

I started the period innocently enough, seeking the protection and support of the one person I perceived as willing and able to provide this, and I ended it in a solitary confinement cell, effectively buried. The intervening period saw my behaviour become increasingly erratic; my sense of isolation, of suspicion, of bitterness and despair, all these combined to create an irrationality almost psychotic in its intensity.

Udwin, during an interview in 1965, told me that I was not a psychopath, nor had I ever been; the classification had been used, as so often, as a catch-all to justify my detention in Broadmoor. Further, he said that the closest I had come to being psychotic was when I stood over Barry's body, but that I had not succumbed because I retreated into an emotional shell. I think he was wrong: my behaviour was consistent with the clinical descriptions of both psychopathy and paranoia – I perceived the world as infinitely hostile, a source of irredeemable anguish; my response was to retreat into a schizoid shell from which I emerged only as a suspicious, and erratically aggressive, reactive being. However, while maintaining that I exhibited all the symptoms of a psychopath edging toward psychosis, I locate the source of this irrationality in the relational net within which I was embedded – unlike bourgeois psychiatry, I do not think that a reference to intra-psychic conflicts is an adequate explanation of my development.

By the age of thirteen, the model of the world which served to guide my actions was sufficiently distorted to make me perceive myself as an "outsider", the target of official disapprobation. That the model was inadequate, I do not dispute – but it was the only one I had, the one I worked with, and I lacked both the personal and the social competence to either recognise its inadequacy or to take any step to alter it. During the ensuing years, my contact with the authorities increased my isolation as an individual and as a social being: this wasn't their plan, of course, but it was the consequence of their actions. As I pursued the tactics which I thought would get me to David, so the authorities pursued the tactics which they thought would result in my control – the dialectic took me progressively into higher and higher levels of conflict, resulting in the death of Barry at one peak, and the wrongful conviction I experienced in 1967 at another.

None of these arguments is designed to minimise my personal responsibility for the pain and anguish I caused other people during this period of my life: I seek to show the social responsibility which envelops the personal, the network of social distortion which results in personal irrationality. The intervention of psychiatric authorities disguises the dialectic between personal and social responsibility – it locates the source of conflict within the individual, thereby making him or her responsible, and then produces the miracle of absolution on the basis of a personal distortion, sometimes influenced (but never caused) by social factors. I believe this reasoning to be false: the individual is responsible, but that responsibility is embedded in a context of wider social responsibility – the burden is shared. Comprehension of any "aberrant" act requires an understanding of the individual's view of the world, and that view is shaped by a dialectic involving personal and social factors.

In 1967, during the intensive psychotherapy sessions I went through with Udwin, these ideas of individual and social responsibility were beginning to emerge in my reasoning; I was coming to grips not only with my own life, but with the social relationships within which that life was embedded. By September, my ability to grasp the complex problems with which I was faced was tentative, I was hovering on the threshold of maturity – and then, as I experienced the crisis of moving from a dependent and childish existence into some-thing resembling an adult, mature independence, the whole thing collapsed. Uncertain, insecure, grappling with the tottering edifice of my own distorted life, I reached the abyss – and dived straight into it.

Barry's death had, paradoxically, saved my life, giving me the emotional release which prevented my total collapse: now, Billy's death was the instrument of that delayed collapse taking place. If I was to survive, I had to find a route out of my sense of bitter and despairing isolation.

Custody and control (2): despair, growth, dissidence, revolution (1967–1981)

> "... the essence of man is no abstraction inherent in each separate individual. In its reality, it is the ensemble of social relations."
>
> Karl Marx, "VIth Thesis on Feuerbach"

The woman doctor who gave me a routine medical examination on my return to Broadmoor treated me as coldly as if I were a cadaver on the mortuary table – then the screws, as they left the cell, casually told me that I had seen the sun for the last time. I was left in no doubt that my life was effectively over; I had become the ultimate in pariahs, a convicted double killer.

For about a week I wallowed in the morass of a self-centred despair, hating myself and the world in equal measure. Before returning to Broadmoor I had spent about ten weeks in solitary confinement, four waiting for the DPP's decision to prosecute me, and then another six on remand in Winchester Prison, but that was a throwaway period compared with what was before me: pacing my cell, four steps up and four steps back, I measured out my future. The cell hadn't changed since I had first experienced it in 1965; it stank, and I was constantly damp. When, at the end of the first week, a screw decided that keeping my light on during the day was a waste of electricity, a decision his colleagues gladly agreed with and supported, my isolation was completed and compounded by almost perpetual darkness. Fittingly, the only light entering my cell came from the Judas slit – a narrow eighteen-inch high by one-and-a-half inch wide glass-covered opening which the screws could unlock if they wished.

Losing the light didn't really bother me; the glare had given me a constant headache, and I felt much better lying in the darkness. When the light was flicked on so that screws from other Blocks could come and stare at the "animal", the contrast did begin to disturb me: I would lie there immobile and let them stare at me, but when the light was switched off again the darkness would make my despair press even heavier. I let myself drift down into a reverie of suicide, examining the few articles in my cell with a view to using them as self-destructive weapons – I thought of some really strange methods, but the only things I achieved were a sore throat and a savage headache. There was nothing to do, and nowhere to go.

About three weeks into my new sentence I decided that I had to fight back: I couldn't kill myself, and I wasn't prepared to become a vegetable, a natural target for the screws. My reverie on suicide had at least forced me to get my brain working again, and I turned my thoughts toward creating some sort of schedule of activity, something to keep me intact. I worked out a physical exercise programme based on yoga and kata, and started each day off with a mile walk – four-hundred-and-forty times four paces, touching the wall at the end of each reach of my cell and stating the number softly to myself in a chant which kept the rhythm going. This wasn't enough, though, for I still had to have something to pass the time away; it gets very monotonous just listening to your own heartbeat, and all too easily you can sink into a twilight world, lulled by its gently insistent murmur. I thought about where I was, the obvious thing for me to concentrate on; I wanted to find out how and why I had arrived at this terminus. Over a couple of weeks, as I looked back into the past few years of my life, I realised that there was something worth looking at, examining, and thinking about in depth – who was I, what was I, why was I? . . . not in some vast metaphysical sense, but in terms of the concrete developments which had led me to this cold, damp, stinking, dark and silent cell. I was going nowhere, and I had nothing to prove or to hide any more – also, as I was constantly alone, locked in darkness, there would be no one to hear me laugh or see me weep. It seemed that the conditions were perfect!

Going deep within myself, I found a chaos which my interviews with Udwin had only hinted at. I had no barriers left and soon touched the raw emotions which had driven me so despairingly to this cell: face down on the mattress, chewing the pillow and soaking the blankets with tears, or pacing the cell and adding blood to the walls as I smashed my fists against them, I was engulfed in waves of almost primal terror, hatred, anguish, pain. It was fortunate that the screws never took any notice of screams emanating from the cells, but intermittently, during brief periods when I collapsed, drained, into a numb silence, I could hear other cons shouting encouragement to me, telling me to "just hang on in there, Alan", and "don't let the bastards break you". Finally, after several days, I reached a point at which the intensity broke: using the yoga technique of passively observing the flow of consciousness, I settled into a routine of just drifting through my memory, replaying scenes whose repetitiveness indicated their salience.

Timescales are difficult to remember during this period, but it must have been a couple of weeks or more before I realised that I was experiencing contradictions between what had been at the forefront of my mind for years – suspicion, bitterness, self-pity, self-centred concern – and the more extensive reality of the relationships I'd had. Through the barrier of bitter memories which had crowded my consciousness, recollections of happier times made their way: I felt again the humour, the gentleness, the compassion and protectiveness of my father; remembered the unfailing love of my mother, her warmth and acceptance even when my behaviour was causing her so much pain – the caresses from both of them outweighed the punishments, and the happiness was more extensive than the pain. Now, without the childish distortions of immediate terror or the rose-coloured spectacles of self-pitying need, I looked back on my life and saw the misperceptions, misjudgements and misinterpretations which had flawed my reasoning – and I began to understand that I had to examine and grasp the social context of my life if I was to answer the questions I had posed. If I simply accepted that my behaviour had been selfish, conceited, brutal and uncaring of other people, then I would have only one part of the riddle in hand: I had to look further if I was to understand myself and other people, but understanding wasn't enough – I had to change myself, and, in the light of the insights I was tentatively gaining, that would involve my seeking to change the world in which I was located. Concentrating on myself, I had reached the threshold of a social consciousness of the world.

During this period I have a vague memory of speaking with Udwin at least once, but no details survive. Having reached the point where I needed to "go out into the world" to obtain more information, I applied for an interview with him in order to get permission to buy some books with the few pounds I had in savings. The interview was coldly formal, with my tentative attempt to discuss what I was thinking being rebuffed – but I did get permission to buy some books. I wrote off to Penguin, the only publisher I could remember who provided low-priced books and a large catalogue.

During the week or so it took the catalogue to arrive, I spent my time attempting to systematically examine the ideas which had emerged over the past few weeks. Casting my mind back to the wide and uncritical reading I had done in Ardale, I remembered some texts by Marx, Engels, and some of their disciples: there was an echo from those works in my current thinking. Vaguely, I recalled things like "the past constrains the perceptions of the present", and "social awareness is determined by social experience" – I knew that these weren't direct quotes, but I was reasonably confident that the substance was correct. I chose from the catalogue a book called *Selected Readings from Karl Marx* by Bottomore and Rubel – the other titles I can't even guess at, but I remember that they covered philosophy, psychoanalysis, contemporary history and economics.

As the screws still weren't prepared to waste electricity on me, I read the books in brief passages by the light from the Judas slit. Actually this helped me, because I spent half an hour or more thinking about each passage before going on to the next. I walked up and down the cell, no longer smashing my fists against the walls, but still talking with myself – or, more properly, carrying on debate and argument with the authors whose works I was reading. When, about a month later and three months after they had turned it off, the screws permitted me to have my light on during the day, I read each book through again in one sitting – with a day of critical re-examination of my thinking between each book. It was an exciting process, and not even my recurrent, but brief, bouts of personal doubt and anguish at my situation could seriously interfere with the stimulation I was getting.

From the Marx extracts I gained a firmer understanding of the social basis of individual existence; I found the class analysis very impressive, but filed much of it away for future reference because I didn't fully understand it. The other books gave me a wider perspective on the world – what, and to a certain extent why, things had been happening. Reading through the history of the twentieth century, and also through the individual case-histories in the psychoanalysis text I had, I examined again the destructive aggressiveness of my own past: I found here a position on which I had some disagreement with Marx, feeling that perhaps evolution was preferable to revolution. In repudiating the terror from whence I came, I rejected the whole notion of violence. To my rather naïve Marxism was married an even more naïve pacifism.

I had now spent about six months in solitary confinement, and I had reached a position where I felt a deep and thorough-going change had occurred in my life: from a level somewhere near the bottom, if not actually on it, I had reached out and inserted myself into society. I was still incarcerated in a cell, cut off from human contact and denied an even rudimentary human dignity, but I felt more aware of myself and my surroundings than at any time in my past. Emotionally, I still suffered from swings of depression, but during my self-examination I had been quite ruthless in bringing to the surface the contradictions I had found – I didn't like what I had been, and I wasn't satisfied with what I was, but at last (and at least) I felt that I wasn't totally worthless. Intellectually I had found my feet, tentative and sometimes rather fearful, to be sure, but nonetheless at last in contact with the world as it was rather than how, in my fear and isolation, I imagined it to be.

The screws told me, sometime around this period, that Udwin had thought of getting me out of the cell, but that McGrath had categorically refused to even consider it. They were quite pleased with this decision, and had great pleasure in "confirming" that I would be locked away for life. I wasn't so sure that they were correct: having recognised that there really wasn't a conspiracy against me, that I was just another con, I had worked out that I was just undergoing a fairly routine punishment in the solitary confinement cell rather than a total repudiation by humanity. The people dealing with me had their own problems, and their actions were in contradiction with any notion of humanitarian concern, but they wouldn't bury me away forever – of this I was sure. It was unpleasant to be locked up so long, but I settled back to continue thinking and feeling about the world, laying the foundations for the future.

May, 1968 . . . around the world momentous events were occurring, with the ordinary people feeling their own strength and frightening their masters. Just over fifty years after the Bolshevik revolution, Europe trembled on the brink of a Red future – and then the fearful bureaucrats of revisionism, waving the red flag to hide their lack of any real communist analysis or understanding, cooperated with the bourgeoisie to re-establish "order". As this period of popular revulsion and exciting innovation was getting under way, I came out of solitary confinement: I had been back in Broadmoor just over five months, and in isolation for nearly eight months.

Udwin had interviewed me one morning, telling me that I would be moving upstairs to Ward Two the next day; he also told me to expect some harassment from the screws, but no assistance from him. So, whey-faced, my hair hacked short by an enthusiastic screw, clutching my few books in my hands, I re-entered the "community".

My reception was hostile: the screws called me into the office and told me that the first step out of line and I would be returned to solitary – adding that the other cons had been warned about getting too close to me lest they suffer the same fate. Only three cons would talk with me at first, the screws' threats having been forcefully delivered, but this only lasted for a couple of weeks. It was a bitter time for me; I had ripped out of myself much of the emotional core which had supported me over the years, and I wasn't yet secure in the strength of my new ideas and feelings. I still had much work to do.

The harassment I experienced from the screws consisted mainly of interruptions to my reading, being assigned to the dirtiest and most time-consuming cleaning jobs, and being isolated from the other cons because of the threat of punishment for associating with me. There was also an attempt at physical intimidation on occasion, but I maintained a policy of not "biting" – no screw actually assaulted me, though several threatened to give me a "taste of the boot" to remind me what it was like. Gradually the harassment died down, becoming less and less frequent over a period of a couple of months: unlike later efforts to intimidate me, this period was merely a case of the screws not wanting to seem soft on a "domestic" killer.

Throughout 1968 I concentrated my attention on reading: I used most of my meagre wages to buy books, and regularly took the maximum permitted from the Mobile Library which visited us every fortnight. I read widely, though critically, seeking all the time to build on the basis of my development in solitary. Philosophy, politics, history, economics, psychology and sociology, these were the subjects I consumed: I didn't concentrate exclusively on Marxist material, choosing to compare and contrast ideas and styles rather than be dominated by one structure. One author I came across during this period, a man whose writings were to exert a tremendous influence on my develoment, particularly excited me because of the purity and commitment of his work – he was Mao Zedong.

I had emerged from solitary confinement a rather naïve pacifist–communist, although this was more a social–worker mentality than anything resembling political activism. In my reaction against the terror, violence, and bitterness of my past, I sought to be a "servant" of society. As a firt step away from the reactionary nature of my childhood and adolescence this romantic commitment to "society" was fairly standard – but it could not be maintained in the face of the information I was obtaining from my readings, and from my application of the analytical tools I was learning to the concrete reality of the social relationships in which my life was embedded. My development in solitary, and the further development during that first year back in Broadmoor, made it impossible for me to retreat from the conclusions my studies were forcing me to reach – I moved increasingly toward a firm and committed Marxist position, with my consciousness being rooted in a class perspective. Objectively I was lumpenproletarian, a reject, an outcast, but my family history was working class, proletarian, and this was where my identity and my loyalties ultimately lay.

My political consciousness developed unevenly, being generated by an emotional reaction against the futility of my existence and then fed by an intellectual grasp of social theories. From out of the degradation of a solitary confinement cell I found, through examination of myself and my history, a social consciousness which linked me with all other people; and from this basis, through reading, applying what I learned in analysis of my immediate social environment and the wider community in which it functioned, as well as conversation/debate with other cons, I moved on to achieve a political consciousness and a class commitment. My initial pacifism, rooted in an emotional repugnance at the violence I had experienced and perpetrated, remained part of my dream of the future, an aspect of communism which is rarely understood, but it could not remain as a viable tactic in the face of the oppression and exploitation which even a rudimentary social analysis demonstrated as endemic in class society. By the end of 1969, I had accepted the need for revolution – my development wouldn't permit me to maintain a social evolutionary stand.

During this period of personal, social and political growth, my relations with other people had been tentative, strained. I had gradually become just another con to the screws, and their harassment dribbled away to intermittent pressure. With the other cons, I started to rebuild contact, but their fear of retaliation from the screws, and their doubt about what had really happened with Billy Doyle, made this a difficult process – one which was further complicated by the process of growth I was undergoing.

I had been in regular correspondence with my parents; they were still in Malta (or Gibraltar?), where my father had been posted in 1967. We didn't really cover anything hard in our letters, but the contact was being maintained. Corresponding with David was more difficult; our letters were doubly censored, first at my (his) end, and then at his (mine). He had finally been released from Borstal, but had now graduated to an adult prison. Within Broadmoor, too, I corresponded – with Allison. We had regained contact when I returned, and we remained in touch over the months that followed: it was in these letters that I first outlined the major changes in my thinking, and Allison was the first person to know that my development was taking a specifically political line.

Udwin remained distant, unapproachable, but this just meant that I was being treated like any other con – something which made my relations with the screws a bit easier! Like everyone else, I only saw McGrath when he came round on ceremonial occasions like Christmas or when some visiting dignitary graced us with his/her presence.

All told, this was a quiet period for me. Engrossed in my books and thoughts, maintaining contact at a distance, I just passed the time away. Superficially, it looked as if I were settling into a routine of slightly eccentric conformity; I was becoming a model long-term prisoner. One incident in 1969, however, gave an indication of what was going on beneath the surface: in October, on my twenty-first birthday, I received a card from David which had a large key on the cover. The screws confiscated the key, telling me that it was a "security risk" – and I spent ten minutes in the office giving an analysis of the key as the true mediator of relations between prisoners and their custodians. One of the screws mentioned that I seemed to be getting rather political!

Early in 1970 Udwin came into the Block and called about six of us into the office. We were told that a new scheme was to be started in order to get us into "front" Blocks – we were the cons who no one wanted! Udwin had made arrangements for us to work in the Occupational Therapy Unit – the fancy name given to a work-place in Broadmoor. To facilitate this scheme the dining-room on Ward One was to be turned into a changing-room for us; we would have to change our clothes each time we left or re-entered the Block for "security reasons". We accepted the constraints gladly, feeling that we would lose little and gain much – several hours each day outside the Block.

It took a couple of months to get the scheme under way; many of the screws opposed it, thinking that Udwin was being too "liberal" with us. When we finally got into the workshop, we found that we had a choice of occupations; I chose printing, a unit which was always busy. My reasons for the choice were simple: printing interested me, offering a means of information–dissemination which I could utilise for the plans which were beginning to take shape in my mind; in addition, I knew several of the people who worked on the unit – one of them being Allison.

Being with Allison again was painful, making me realise just how much I still loved him. Like the other dimensions of my emotional life, the specifics of that love had changed, being I think more mature and less ruled by blind passion; but the love

111

was still strong. Fortunately, I had the printing to interest me, so any initial temptation to concentrate exclusively on my love was quickly tempered by my need to learn about the presses and their processes. I also got friendly with the other cons and, with their assistance, quickly learned what I needed to know.

During the first month, I found that printing didn't just interest me – I was fascinated by it, becoming excited by the seemingly endless possibilities the machines offered. I borrowed books on printing from the library, and then added the theory of the craft to my list of subjects to study in depth. After about six weeks I produced a small booklet demonstrating the type faces available in the unit – and thereby published my first political tract: each type face was shown through the device of a political poem or statement. I didn't get "rave" reviews; primarily, I hope, because I only produced a limited edition of about twenty-four copies, but the cons who read it were interested and this encouraged me in the thoughts of political organisation which I had been nurturing.

Of the six or seven people who worked in the unit, four of us openly avowed homosexual experience; we didn't make a big thing of the way we felt, but we didn't hide it, either. My reading had included a few papers on the Gay Liberation Movement in America, and I decided that it would be a good thing to start a GLF section in Broadmoor: I spent several hours discussing the possibility with the other cons, and their response was cautiously enthusiastic – with the emphasis on caution. It seemed that I had to wait until I was out of Block Six before I could get anything under way.

Throughout the spring and summer of 1970 I continued with my efforts at self-education, spending all the hours I wasn't at work in the print unit concentrating with my books. On several occasions I attempted to get some of the other cons interested in forming a self-help group, aiming to establish links between us and also prompt debate about those subjects most important to us. But at this time it was too early, and Block Six was too threatening for most people to enable them to take such a step into cooperative life – especially as the screws resolutely opposed any efforts at organisation by the cons. I was forced to work alone.

In 1968 and early 1969 I had written a couple of short pieces for the *Broadmoor Chronicle*, the prison magazine: they were essentially liberal-humanitarian essays calling for peace on earth and racial harmony. Now, I concentrated on writing for myself; positional statements which helped me clarify my thinking on a range of issues that seemed to be of paramount importance for prisoners in Broadmoor. I made a list of all the incidents of brutality which I had heard about on the "grapevine", had reported to me, or witnessed myself; then I broke them down into those in which an assault on a screw had prefaced the brutality, and those which had occurred without even that spurious justification. I found that there were few assaults on screws, but many incidents of brutality – and this formed the basis of my first positional statement: the significance of brutality in closed institutions was not directly related to any level of overt physical aggression manifested by the inmates. Next, I looked at the relationships between the staff and the inmates, dividing the staff into four groups – screws, office screws, doctors, and auxilary medical staff such as psychologists and social workers. This brought some interesting thoughts.

The bulk of the screws on the Wards were simply doing a job; they did not physically assault cons, nor did they go out of their way to do anything for them. A small number, only a few in each Block, regularly participated in assaults on cons; these were the "boot merchants", the "heavy mob". The other two groups, the office screws and the auxiliary personnel, did little to involve themselves in the lives of the cons: the office screws remained aloof, and the auxiliary personnel ran tests or were involved only at the end of the sentence.

This truncated schema of relations I found to be agreed with by most of the cons, but few of them would say it out loud, in public, for fear of the screws. Also, many of them would agree and later seek me out to repudiate their agreement – it is difficult to accept this view of an institution's relationships and still cooperate with that institution and regard oneself as a "patient" in a "hospital". Without this cooperation and this self-image, the majority of cons knew that they had small chance of being released some day. But this was a positional statement for myself, reflecting my perceptions, and at this stage I wasn't too worried about the problems of communicating my position to other people.

These preliminary positions made me think hard about the relationship between Broadmoor and the outside world – but I lacked the analytical skill, and the experience of manipulating it, to pursue the matter further. I had to simply file the whole thing away for future reference, and then carry on trying to educate myself.

In autumn 1970 Udwin told me he was moving me to Kent House – the Blocks had been given names by McGrath, who felt that it made the prison more "humane". Kent House (Block Three) was where I had been with Allison, and I asked if the screws were objecting; I was told that they had been, but they were now prepared to accept me. In November I moved out of Block Six (Monmouth House): I was going back into general circulation, sent on my way by screws who said that I had changed beyond recognition. They didn't know the half of it.

Changing the name hadn't changed the regime; Block Three or Kent House, it was still a prison wing. Somewhat to my surprise my reception was relatively cordial – all the threats were implied! Like everyone else, I was initially located in a dormitory on Ward Three, although I resided on Ward Two: there were only enough cells (officially known as "side-rooms") for about a quarter of the population. During the day I continued going out to the printing shop; evenings were spent reading or watching television, at least in the beginning while I got to know the other cons.

Sometime near to Christmas, I was given a cell on Ward Three; I could only use it for sleeping, the Ward being locked off during the day. I'd made a couple of friends among the other cons, and I now spent quite a lot of my "free" time discussing politics with them; I had decided to try and get a group going for self-help and self-education, and I was determined that it would be a consciously political thing for everyone. I had also spread the word that a Broadmoor section of the GLF was now in existence, its function being to give whatever help was possible to any gay who needed it – and many did, for the screws used gay people as tools to pacify certain cons, while the rest of the time they treated us with contempt. Several people asked me how I could call myself "gay", seeing as how I'd never had the opportunity to find out if women interested me as emotional/sexual partners; my response was to say: "If I died today, and it was necessary to specify my sexuality on the death certificate, then I would be nominated as gay – I can't comment on the future." In addition, I felt that I could get more response from the other cons if

I showed that there were options other than the ones approved by the screws – and some of us weren't afraid of taking them.

Initially, four other cons met with me for discussions: Bryan Knight, Phil Batt, and two other Brians whose surnames I have, unfortunately, forgotten. We were all on the same Ward, which made it easy for us to get together. Another con, in Cornwall House, began to speak with me at this time; we worked together in the print shop for a while, but most of our meetings were on the sports field – his name was Ronald Greedy, someone who was to become probably my closest friend and comrade in Broadmoor.

In April, 1971, almost six months to the day after I had left Monmouth House, I was granted internal parole – there is no external parole in Broadmoor. When McGrath interviewed me, he told me that Udwin was putting himself on the line by recommending I have parole, and if I used the "privilege" as an escape-route, then he would suffer. I said that I wouldn't try to escape while I held that parole card, but that was the only assurance I gave. I moved out of the cell on Ward Three, and into one on Ward Two – this one I could use during the day, one of the benefits of parole.

Immediately after I was given parole, Udwin gave me a job which involved my going outside the walls. With two other cons and one screw, I had to load and unload lorries carrying wooden pallets which were used in the OT. The job was part-time, with a couple of days a week outside and the rest of the time sitting around in the House doing nothing. In January, I had taken two "O" levels, and intended taking another five that June – my plan being to take five "A" levels in 1973, preparatory to seeking an external Degree in Economics from London University. I asked Udwin for permission to spend my "spare" time on education; he agreed, and permitted me to open an unused room on Ward Two as a classroom. Phil, Bryan, and one of the other Brians decided to join me – the last Brian was due to be released shortly, and he wasn't interested.

We quickly turned the classroom into a centre for political study, with me taking responsibility for giving lectures on Marxism, economics, and broad sociological issues. We encouraged other cons to come into the room, and several took advantage – with one or two screws sitting in on occasion! The lectures were based on the principle of "he who learns, teaches; he who teaches, learns", and some of the time we had really exciting discussions with everyone learning the additional principle of non-personal criticism.

The Education Officer in Broadmoor, Ieuan Williams, was one of the few officials in the prison who was prepared to assist the cons; we called on him for books, writing materials, and the occasional tutorial. I had known Ieuan since I arrived in the prison, and we had quickly established a working relationship – I now offered my services as a teacher in the school, and he accepted. The school-rooms were in the Admission Block (Norfolk House), and I went there on two mornings a week to take classes in English language and basic mathematics; I employed the same principle of mutual learning in these classes, and the cons seemd to appreciate it.

During the couple of months between my getting parole and the exams in June, I spent less and less time going outside unloading pallets; I felt that it was unfair that I should get the opportunity to touch the outside world while the cons I was working with were stuck inside. It seemed to me that Bryan, Phil and Brian were getting increasingly keen on the political arguments I was advancing, and the logic of those arguments demanded that I make greater demands on their time, energy, and understanding. I thought it was time to expand, forge more links with cons in other Houses, and perhaps lay the foundations for a prisoners' political organisation.

At this time, McGrath, in his attempts at liberal cosmetic surgery, was still permitting formal debates to be held on one evening a month in the Central Hall. Ian Dunlop, the con who organised and acted as chairperson at these events, asked me to nominate some of the subjects to be debated; I took the opportunity to open up political arguments. Some of the subjects I put forward were: the role of the police in bourgeois society; the function of parliament; the oppression and exploitation of women; gay liberation and its relationship to revolutionary politics; and several issues dealing with prisoners' rights. These evenings were well-attended, and the arguments often became heated as people fought out their personal views from the floor. On two separate occasions Ian asked me to tone down the strength of my arguments, telling me that McGrath would end the debates if I continued ramming politics down everyone's throat – I refused, answering that the response I was getting from the other cons indicated not only their interest in politics but also their thirst for polemic.

One evening, when we were debating something to do with the functions of parliament, we had a couple of guest speakers, people from outside who had been asked by Ian to come in and give us the benefit of their "knowledge" – the excitement generated led to the banning of these political fronts! One of the guests, a young man who kept drinking from a bottle of cough mixture, gave a fiery defence of extra-parliamentary opposition, sprinkling his arguments with extremely "earthy" language. From our position directly in front of the table, several of us gave vocal support to the anti-state arguments, taking the opportunity to make categoric statements of support for direct political intervention by the people. The debate was finally halted by the screws, the guests removed (the young man being interviewed by the police, I believe), and all the cons taken back to their Houses. The next day we heard that there would be no more debates – McGrath's liberalism didn't extend to political discussion which showed that the cons, far from exhibiting some anti-social illness, were mirroring the political arguments being used outside the walls.

A major value of the debates, while they lasted, was that we got the opportunity to sound out many other cons; we pursued those who indicated a real interest with further conversation down the sports field. Gradually we forged a network of supporters, linking the Houses and attempting to lay the foundations for the organisation we now knew we would be starting in the near future.

After the June examinations, I approached Udwin and told him that I wanted to take five "A" levels: Economics, Sociology, British Constitution, History, and English Literature. (I had intended to take French rather than English Literature, but I had failed the "O" level and decided that I needed more work with the language.) I asked if the Education Committee would fund me with two-thirds of the cost, and he agreed – adding that he would attempt to get one of the lecturers from Reading University to come in and assist me with the Sociology. It seemed that education was viewed as possessing pacific qualities for cons!

Early in the autumn, two significant events occurred: firstly, Bryan, Phil, Brian and myself formed ourselves into a committee to organise the Broadmoor prisoners on a political basis, and, secondly, a lecturer and several students from Reading University started coming in to visit me once a week and help me with my studies. These two events were quickly combined, with my comrades joining me in the classroom for discussion and debate with our visitors. The lecturer didn't stay long, and most of the students quickly gave up when we started pushing – but several remained, joining us in criticism and self-criticism sessions, and giving us support and encouragement. From this interaction came the first avowedly political public document from Broadmoor prisoners – the Provisional Manifesto of the Revolutionary Action Committee for Broadmoor – RAC(B).

For the first eighteen months or so after coming out of solitary I had concentrated on developing the ideas and insights I had gained for myself; I did little in terms of generalising this development. Following this period I turned outward more, seeking not only to apply what I had "learned", but also attempting to reach through the barriers and made contact with the other cons. When I got to Kent House I quickly stepped up my activities – and people began to look upon me as a new political spokesperson generated by the prison environment. I found myself often regarded as a "leader", and this caused me immense problems because I wasn't yet ready to assume such heavy responsibility: I was wrapped up in thinking, and the social pressure to be a direct activist, a "leader", was rather frightening.

As the "group" began to develop, this problem of mine became increasingly acute – so I turned to my brothers for assistance, offering myself for self-criticism and group criticism. We discussed the issue in depth, but the pressure didn't abate; my brothers, too, demanded that I give political leadership. When our friends from Reading University started to engage in political debate with us, we threw the question over to them – and they pointed out that I would be shirking my responsibility if I didn't work without reservation, even if I wasn't too confident. The key question, it was pointed out, was how the brothers perceived me: no one wanted to develop a "leader" as a cult figure, but it was necessary that some figure be identified completely with the arguments we advanced because this represented the level of consciousness reached by the majority. Thus I found myself not only the most argumentative of the brothers, but also the one considered to be the single most dynamic representative of the political position we espoused – colloquially: Marxism, Leninism, Mao Zedong Thought. We agreed among ourselves that this unfortunate state of affairs would have to be resolved as quickly as possible, and this meant an increase in our workload as we took the question of leadership out into the prison.

When, in January 1972, we determined to call ourselves the RAC(B) rather than simply an organising committee, the four initial cadres, joined now by Ronald Greedy for discussion, decided that one of the first tasks we faced was the publication of an internal study document which would, eventually, form the basis of a Manifesto from the prisoners. We put out feelers into the other Houses, calling for comments, and were encouraged by the response. By the end of February we were ready to begin.

Contrary to the comments of McGrath and his allies, the writing of the Provisional Manifesto was completely the work of prisoners; our friends and comrades from Reading and elsewhere merely commented on the finished product. Three drafts were written, with two separate versions each time: Phil Batt produced one version, I wrote the other. About seven people were involved in the direct discussion of each draft, although some twenty or so people had prepared initial papers on which the discussions and drafts were based. After the first two drafts, it was decided that we had achieved the basic structure of what we wanted to say, and Bryan, Phil, Brian, Ronald and I had a three-hour meeting to hammer out the points for the third draft: this was to be the document upon which the Manifesto would be based.

It was the unanimous argument of my comrades that I was preparing drafts which, while excellent as polemic, presented too convoluted political arguments for a document purporting to represent the political consciousness of the mass of prisoners in Broadmoor. I was instructed to make my writing more comprehensible to the majority. Phil's drafts, on the other hand, were thought to be too anarchic – but his writing was at least understandable! We spent a week-end writing out our final versions – and once again I was criticised for using too convoluted a style. During the discussion of this version I took notes of the arguments we used, and then I went away to write the final paper: it had been decided that I should do the final writing on the basis that I had more experience of précis writing.

119

We discussed the completed text with our friends from outside, listening to their criticisms – primarily, a disagreement with us about the frequency of the word "pig" – and then had fifty copies run off on a duplicating machine. (I cannot be more specific about the reproduction because even now there is a need for security – "subversive" techniques and facilities available to prisoners must be protected, as must those people who remain unknown to the authorities.) We distributed six copies to each House, excluding only Monmouth; we had friends in the Punishment Block, but we didn't yet have access to it. Then we waited for responses.

For about a week we heard nothing, then comments began to dribble in: on the whole, the reaction from the other cons was favourable, although several people informed us that they couldn't go along with our total repudiation of the system. The reaction of the screws was mixed: some found us "amusing", others made it clear that we were a threat to "good order and discipline", while yet others came to us and made serious enquiries about how we saw relations with them developing. We kept a relatively low profile, speaking with anyone who sought us out, but preferring to listen and absorb responses before we went any futher.

Eventually, the new editor of the *Chronicle* went to McGrath with one of the copies of the Manifesto – McGrath decided that it would be a good idea to publish it in the magazine, thinking that the cons would unanimously reject it. He was wrong: from a fairly small distribution, publication in the *Chronicle* made the document available to everyone – and it became a leading topic of conversation. Several people wrote to the magazine and subjected us to a barrage of personal abuse, claiming that we didn't represent the views of the majority, but in the Houses the comments were very favourable to us. We found that we were still a minority in the prison, but those cons who really did oppose us were an even smaller minority; the majority still hadn't been reached in terms of making a significant response. Finally, a con named Bob Shaw wrote an attack on us in the *Chronicle*, and we decided that it was time to respond – but the editor wouldn't publish our document, telling us that the subject was now closed.

McGrath's gamble failed miserably; the cons began to discuss the issues we had raised, and even when they were not in favour of our political statements they made it clear that they supported our demands for radical alterations in the administration of Broadmoor. The screws began to get heavy with us, attempting to intimidate those people who hovered on the fringes of the group; we were threatened with violence by a couple of the heavy mob, but they quickly retreated when we told them that we would fight together against any attack on one of us.

While the controversy simmered around us – it never reached the stage of "raging' – the RAC(B) continued to discuss tactics. I had been pressing for greater contact with our sisters in the Female Wing, something the whole group agreed with, and we now delegated Phil to make as many contacts as he could. Bryan Knight took on responsibility for improving the organisation of cons in Kent House, and was also responsible for maintaining our personal security, while the other Brian started to look into the possibilities of our establishing some sort of quartermaster's store. I was to continue with my work of analysing Broadmoor and its relations with the state, collating the information on brutality, drug abuse, and the use/misuse of ECT, and developing tactical papers for our development; I also continued as education director, giving lessons and lectures two or three times a day. Ronald was instructed to work with me; as the only other group member on parole, he was to act as my "runner" – and was also told to be as quiet as possible so that we would have someone working in safety if the rest of us were jumped. Other people worked as information gatherers, talking with people in their own Houses and seeking to establish greater links around the prison.

This period was nerve-rackingly exciting for me: although I still had doubts and hesitations about my role as "leader", I was witnessing the growth of a prisoners' organisation which I had been seeking to establish for some time. As the days passed, and more and more information came in, I spent increasingly shorter periods of time on my own; this meant less sleep, for only at night could I continue with my analyses of Broadmoor, the state, and the position of the RAC(B) as a contemporary and future phenomenon. My relationships with my comrades, and with our friends outside, became better and better, and our sessions of criticism/self-criticism increased our individual and mutual strengths and understandings. With hesitations, fumblings, errors, arguments and disagreements, we were building something that Broadmoor had never seen – a true collective, a network of support which the authorities had consistently stated could never be.

I spent at least two hours a day out of Kent House, meeting with brothers in the other Houses and discussing our position on a number of issues; sometimes I took statements from people who wished to complain about the treatment they had received. The screws in these other Houses knew what I was doing, and several times I was called into an office and quizzed about the plans of the group; I used the time to emphasise that it was not our intention to start riots or mass uprisings, pointing out that our complaints were justified and that we were fighting a battle which was being waged in other prisons around the country. If I was asked about relationships with screws, I answered that the organisation we were building had no interest in harming screws, merely isolating the brutes and seeking some sort of working relationship with the rest: Broadmoor was merely one small part of the system, I argued, and it was that system we were committed to attacking – the screws should unite with us, for they shared the class position of the prisoners. At times the arguments became heated, but several screws made interesting and relevant points.

Four to six weeks after we originally distributed the Provisional Manifesto we had consolidated our network of supporters around the prison; we had over thirty people scattered around the Houses who gave firm support to the RAC(B), and the committee itself had been extended to seven people. (Some of our supporters are still in Broadmoor, so I shall refrain from giving more names. These people identified so far have all been known to the authorities since 1972.) We were slowly growing stronger, and it was time to examine our next step. Then, without warning, our options were cut back; we had to make a quick decision about our future.

Phil Hall, a young prisoner in Gloucester House, the semi-parole unit, sent a message that he wanted to see me urgently; I went over to him within an hour of receiving the message. He told me that he had decided to make a roof-top protest about conditions in Broadmoor, and asked for help. We talked for about half an hour, with me pointing out the dangers and consequences of such an action; I also questioned his determination, arguing that half-hearted protest would seriously damage the momentum of the RAC(B) – Phil was adamant that he wanted to make the protest. I told him to wait; it was necessary for the committee to discuss this before I could commit us to assisting him.

Back in Kent House, I convened an emergency meeting of the committee to discuss Phil's action and his request for assistance. For about an hour we talked, examining Phil's motives, discussing the possibilities of mobilising support around the prison, seeking some rapid understanding of the implications and consequences of a direct action protest at this time. Finally, we concurred that (i) the protest was legitimate and should be supported, (ii) the RAC(B) should take the responsibility for organising it, (iii) it should be made as a political rather than a personal statement of anguish, and (iv) as a consequence of the preceding decisions, one of the committee should go onto the roof with Phil.

Once we had agreed that the protest should take place, the rest was fairly straightforward. Phil was not an experienced climber, he was young and impressionable, and our representative had to be completely identified with the committee in order that, no matter what the authorities did to criminalise or medicalise the protest, it would be seen by the cons as an essentially political act. I was asked to volunteer – the profile we had drawn fitted me like a glove: I was an experienced climber, had been used to arguing and "leading" impressionable people, and I was totally identified with the committee.

I left the committee and went back to see Phil Hall. He was waiting nervously for our answer, and when I told him of our decision he was, to put it mildly, very pleased. I told him that we would be making the climb that evening, but that I needed a couple of hours to organise things with the committee and also to distribute my belongings around the group – this latter activity being secondary, for we had been sharing everything we owned and it was simply a matter of taking things out of my cell and putting them into the classroom. Before leaving, I told him how we would meet – he was to walk along the bottom wall of Gloucester House exercise yard and then make his way up to the railings alongside the Terrace, and I would pick him up there.

For an hour and a half I sat with the group and we discussed what was about to happen, making plans for the negotiations I would have with the authorities. I was given clear instructions on the major points to raise, but left with considerable leeway about the procedure I was to adopt. When we were finished discussing things, I moved most of my belongings into the classroom and stored them in the communal cupboard. Into two boxes I placed a copy of our information file, several books by Marx and Mao Zedong, a couple of notebooks, some spare tobacco, and a quantity of chocolate and fruit: all this was coming on the roof with me. Then each member of the group gave me a cuddle, telling me to share it with Phil once we were aloft.

Phil was waiting at the spot I had designated, and it was a matter of moments for him to clamber over the railings and join me on the Terrace. We moved swiftly to the canteen, going to the spot where I had left my two boxes – then we climbed up the struts and onto the glass-covered roof of the waiting area, and from there onto the roof of the administrator's office. From this vantage point we could reach the top of the church and, with some assistance from a lightning conductor, climb onto the roof of Kent House. This was where we planned to make our base.

As we were moving onto the administrator's office roof two screws arrived; someone had seen us from the screws' mess-room in Kent. We couldn't be reached by the screws, so we laughed at their demands that we return: "This is a protest," we said, " and we're not coming down for some time!" One of the screws remained to watch us, and the other one went off to phone 222, the emergency number. Ten minutes later there were about six or seven screws outside the canteen.

For the first couple of hours Phil and I sat on the church roof, talking. Then I went off and climbed onto Kent House roof; Phil joined me ten minutes later. In the middle of the roof there was a five to seven meter channel, shaped as a flat-bottom V; a similar channel was on the outcrop where the searchlights were located. (The building was shaped like an F, with the base joining onto the church via a link made from the administrator's office, and the two arms pointing away from the main gate. The top arm of the F was flat, the roof being that of a new dormitory with wash-rooms on the two lower floors, and the bottom arm had a regular roof with a flat-bottomed V in the middle – there was a dormitory underneath this roof, too, with day-rooms on the two lower floors.)

Leaving Phil in the central V, I climbed down to one of the top-floor cells and, reaching in through the bars, pulled a couple of blankets off the bed; I threw them up onto the roof. Unfortunately, before I could get all the bedding a screw came rushing in through the cell door – I left, quickly. Back together on the roof, Phil and I made our way to the flat roof at the end: this was to be Base One. The comrades I had left in Kent were all crowding at the window of the classroom, shouting encouragement; several other brothers were doing the same from windows on the gallery. Suddenly, we heard the sounds of Bob Dylan's tribute to George Jackson floating up to us; a portable record player had been moved into the classroom, and our comrades were serenading us in our struggle. Within ten minutes there was silence and the windows were deserted – the screws were reacting to the support being given us. Interestingly enough, the cons at the windows of Essex House, the full-parole unit, were not pulled back – but as they were almost unanimous in their hostility to us, this came as no surprise. We settled in for a long protest.

We were on the roof for just under seventy-two hours – three nights and two full days. During that time we harangued the screws, participated in arguments with Udwin and McGrath, scratched slogans on the roof-slates, and spent much time discussing politics. It was Easter, and I horrified several onlookers by stretching my arms over the cross on the church roof and hanging myself into space: McGrath, whose Catholic protestations, allied to his profession, put him firmly in the tradition of Torquemada, was less than amused by my humour.

After our first night Udwin climbed up onto the canteen roof to negotiate; we spent about half an hour discussing our relative positions. At this time, too, we had a flask of hot soup delivered to us – another thing which didn't endear us to the screws. Nothing was resolved during the first bout of negotiations, so the waiting went on. We spent the time sun-bathing, with Phil asking and me answering questions on the place of Broadmoor in relation to the state.

During the negotiations with Udwin I had asked him about his imposition of solitary confinement on the comrades we had left in Kent House; he told me that they would stay locked up until Phil and I left the roof. Although we had expected some such move as this, we were very angry, but we took comfort from two very heartening occurrences during the preceding night. Firstly, we had removed the sky-light from over one of the dormitories and managed to make contact with some sympathisers; they had given us a couple of extra blankets and a pillow. Secondly, just before midnight, when it had been raining heavily for several hours, one of the screws standing watch on the Terrace had decided that he wasn't taking any more – after arguing with his colleagues for several minutes, egged on by us shouting encouragement, he stormed off the Terrace and went home. On balance, we felt that we were winning.

The second round of negotiations brought some progress; we were offered a private enquiry into our allegations, with the publication of its findings. We went away and discussed this offer, but decided to hold out for our original demand for a public enquiry; Udwin told us he would discuss the matter with his colleagues and superiors. He didn't hold out much hope.

Our second night passed quietly, and we slept soundly from about midnight on; we were confident that we couldn't be attacked without warning because of our location – and our threat that we would grab any attacker and leap off the roof with him/them. The next morning was also quiet. Then Udwin arrived to negotiate again.

We were told that we could have a private enquiry, supervised by a senior civil servant, with any prisoner being able to give evidence. In addition, our comrades would be released from solitary and no further action would be taken against them. We two would be taken to the Punishment Block, but would not be locked in cells and would be permitted to hold our papers without intervention. We said that we would consider the offers, but would make no decision until the following day. Udwin argued that we would get no further offer, and that we should give in immediately; we refused. The rest of that day we spent discussing the offer; we recognised, unwillingly, that it was probably the best that we could get.

The next day, after a good night's sleep in the open air, we called for Udwin and told him we were prepared to climb down. He told us that we should come down through the sky-light we had previously opened – which confirmed our suspicion that someone had talked about our communication with the dormitory. We opened the sky-light and found several screws standing with Udwin, so we stated that we wouldn't come down until they were removed; they were sent away. Then I told Phil to go down – and added that I was staying aloft until the enquiry was convened. Phil refused to go. For ten minutes or so we argued, then I walked away from him and went to the edge of the roof: I was considering jumping, thinking that it might prove most beneficial if I died and thus added dramatic emphasis to our struggle. This infantile romanticism was something which still inhibited my political development and analytical competence. Udwin came out onto the roof and, walking over to where I stood, took my arm and invited me to go with him: although by the time he arrived I had decided to join Phil in descending, this act was an example of Udwin's personal courage and medical style.

We went down together, and within minutes we were locked in the Punishment Block. We had a bath and then went to the day-room, our papers intact and un-examined. The protest was over.

During the week or so we waited for the private enquiry to begin, I concentrated on writing a memorandum to my comrades on the RAC(B); I sought to analyse our action, wanting to obtain the greatest possible political benefit from what we had done. I couldn't send the document out, but I knew that they would get it eventually.

This analysis, the first of several, began with a general account of the time spent on the roof. I was severely critical of myself, arguing that I had indulged in romantic posturing and had failed to utilise the time properly by continuing a heavy political indoctrination of young Philip. I examined the negotiations we had had with Udwin, and noted that he had dominated them; I had been too passive, too locked in a relationship of dependence with the man. Then I looked at the tactic itself, and concluded that it was completely legitimate and could give the prison population genuine benefits if we could push through the enquiry and also maintain the consistency of our arguments against the prevalent abuses. In a brief appendix I criticised all of us on the committee for acting hastily; the action was a good one, with firm political legitimacy, but we had rushed into it rather than plan it thoroughly and thus ensure maximum external support and publicity. I gave the document to Phil to read and comment, but all he said was that I was too harsh on myself – a clear example, I thought, of my failure to encourage his political development.

The enquiry, when it came, proved to be a farce: one man conducted it, a Divisional Nursing Officer from some local psychiatric hospital. Our allegations were dismissed as groundless, although at least two people refused to be intimidated and maintained that they had been victims of serious criminal assault.

After discussing what had happened, Phil and I decided that it was necessary to show some anger at the way we had been fooled – we thought it would be appropriate if I went up on the roof again. Accordingly, a couple of days later, while we were out on exercise, I strolled over to the wall of the building and quickly clambered up the bars on a window until I reached the second storey. While I stood there, laughing down at the screws, everyone else was taken inside; McGrath arrived soon afterwards. He attempted to talk me down, but I was having no more of their tricks – then I found, much to my embarrassment, that there was no clear route to the roof! On top of this, the cold was settling in fast and my muscles were beginning to tighten; I was in real trouble, but I couldn't simply go down without giving the screws and McGrath a major victory. I had to make the climb.

While the screws stood around laughing at me, I stood on a ledge three and a half inches wide and surveyed the wall – the only way up was by stretching out my arms, curling my fingers around the edge of the building and into the protective shield around the drainpipe, and then inching slowly upwards. I started off, knowing that this time I stood every chance of failing – and dying, or being seriously injured. I made it to the top floor, but then I was faced with the problem of a two-foot overhang just below the roof; by this time my muscles were shaking and I couldn't feel my hands. Somehow, I managed to keep going, although it took me about five minutes to make this final ascent: I reached the roof and threw a clenched-fist salute into the sky as the screws gaped, open-mouthed, in the exercise yard below. If they had known how weak I was, they would have come through the sky-light to get me – fortunately, they were too surprised that I had completed the climb.

I couldn't stay up for long: about four hours later, sitting in the attic, I sprained my right arm in trying to stand up. It was so cold that I didn't notice that my arm was trapped underneath a pipe, and in pushing myself to my feet I tore the muscles in the arm. When McGrath called to me through the sky-light I conceded defeat; the nails were taken out, and I was helped down. A couple of minutes later I was back in a cell on the Punishment Ward.

Udwin was most upset with me, but he had to agree that I didn't have much choice if I was to have any political credibility – especially, a couple of weeks later, when the result, but not the evidence, of the enquiry was published. I told him that the betrayal was complete, but he argued that he had kept his bargain. An interesting example of how perceptions can differ. The next thing to happen was Phil's move back to a front block; the authorities, secure in their "vindication" at the enquiry, decided to be magnanimous. I stayed – soon to be joined by two of my comrades from Kent House.

One Brian, in return for renouncing the RAC(B), was to be released very quickly; the other two comrades, Phil Batt and Bryan Knight, were sent to join me in Monmouth One – their "crime": wearing red-star armbands in support of our protest, and in defiance of McGrath's orders. We had one senior cadre still operating outside the block – Ron Greedy, my "runner", who continued to act as my liaison with the rest of the prisoners.

When Bryan and Phil joined me in the day-room a few days later we spent several hours discussing recent events, making plans for re-establishing contact with our friends and comrades outside, and deciding on the tactics we would employ during our stay in punishment. We were determined to make the most of the time.

We spent about three months on Monmouth One (the official name for the Punishment Block), during which time we kept ourselves as a political unit: we worked together, ate together, and, after refusing to speak with him under any other arrangements, were interviewed by Udwin together. The screws didn't like our collective approach, but we didn't really give a damn about that.

Our criticism and self-criticism sessions were very heavy, but my comrades agreed with young Philip that I was too harsh on myself: I continued to argue that my position as the "leading" cadre necessitated a refusal to be soft on myself. We had re-established contact with our people outside

Broadmoor, and we exchanged letters with them about our actions and the tactics we should follow for the future; we sought assistance from any genuine political source, and at this time it was readily given. We were still growing, personally and politically – much to the annoyance of our "keepers".

Eventually, over the disagreement of the screws, Udwin moved all three of us onto the open ward of Monmouth Three. We quickly settled in, continuing our political work among the other cons: we also decided to continue a battle with McGrath over compensation for the property which the screws had stolen from us when we had been moved out of Kent House. We were mainly concerned about our books, nearly £100 worth of them. We never were compensated.

Shortly after we moved up to Ward Three Udwin called us all into the office for a meeting. After telling us that he appreciated the "sincerity" of our behaviour, he cautioned us about the length of time we would spend in the prison unless we altered our approach. We had previously discussed among ourselves the possibility that a deal would be offered, so we were not surprised at the next stage of the meeting: we heard that Bryan "could" be released within a year, and Phil within eighteen months. Nothing was said about me, so Bryan asked about my prospects – and we were told that it would "take more time to get Alan released".

The offer from Udwin was conditional upon a lowering of the political climate we had engendered; we had to "pull our horns in" and stop putting pressure on the prison. The screws were of the opinion that Phil and Bryan weren't as committed as I was to the politics of our behaviour, so the initial offer was aimed more at them than at me – but if they were released, then it was thought that I would be isolated. A relaxation of the pressure we exerted, followed by the release of two of the leading figures of the RAC(B), would be a major victory for the establishment as long as I didn't continue to push on my own. All of this was known to us when the offer was made; we said that we would consider it.

For over a week we considered the offer, examining the various problems which could arise from acceptance or rejection. We sought comments from as wide a circle as possible; several people were surprised that we hesitated, but it wasn't only our future we were deciding. Ronald was categorically against the offer, arguing that it would mean an agreement with the authorities such that the other prisoners would suffer; he was also concerned that I would be savagely harassed as well as isolated. Phil and Bryan were unsure, knowing that the personal benefits accruing to them could easily bias their judgement. Young Phil, having already accepted a similar deal – with our agreement – supported acceptance of the offer. I reserved judgement, listening to everyone's opinion and taking my time to analyse as much as possible.

Finally, it became obvious that no decision would be reached until I committed myself, one way or the other. I met Ronald down the field and told him that I was going to recommend acceptance of the deal: I felt that we could make significant political gains, in the long term, by showing that concerted action could be successful, that the other cons would understand our decision when they saw that I continued to maintain a firm political position, and that the direct benefits available to Phil and Bryan could strengthen our internal position by their external actions. Ron was furious, arguing that I was being betrayed by a desire to sacrifice myself for others; he maintained that if the others had any real political understanding they would take the decision out of my hands and reject the offer. I told him that he had to abide by the decision, otherwise we would degenerate into a rabble. His final comment was that he would accept whatever I did, but he still didn't agree with me! I went back to Monmouth to tell the others.

Udwin was unsurprised to hear that Phil and Bryan would agree to his conditions, but he tried to get me to go along with them. I argued that I would not involve them, but nor would I refrain from any actions which could further the politics fought for. He seemed to accept this, saying only that he hoped I would not turn myself into a martyr – after all, my behaviour with my brother had indicated a tendency towards a martyrdom complex! Maybe there was some truth in that when I was younger, I answered, but no more . . . but thanks for the advice, doc.

Two cooperative political acts remained before the RAC(B) split into those original cadres who were to be released, and those who were to remain imprisoned. The first occurred when we received a request to call our supporters into action for a sit-down strike on the sports field – we refused, arguing that there was an implication for violence in the action, especially since the people who wanted to organise it had openly stated that they wanted a fight with the screws. We stated that our position on violence was supportive, but that it had to be a response by the mass of prisoners – not something aimed solely at releasing the frustration of a few people. Interestingly enough, the people who made the request for our support on this occasion didn't retreat from us as a result of our refusal; they continued to work with me over the years which followed.

The second of these final acts wrote finis to our cooperation: Phil and Bryan left me isolated, and I went down onto the Punishment Ward alone. The event occurred in a particularly stupid manner – as a result of one person complaining about the rest of the ward watching a *Doctor Who* programme on television.

It was a Saturday evening just after Christmas, 1972. A vote had been taken as to which TV channel was to dominate the evening's viewing, and a rather cumbersome programme had been worked out; most of the time we would watch ITV, but for a short time BBC would be on so that we could watch *Doctor Who*. A complaint was made to the office that many of the people who had voted for the programme weren't watching it, and the screw in the day-room ordered that the channels be changed. We saw the order as provocative, pointing out that it was the result of one person's desire – and against the wishes of the majority. The screw was adamant; he switched the TV over, and I stood up and switched it back. Then the situation degenerated into pure farce.

For about an hour, several screws wandered in and out of the day-room, muttering dire threats of what was going to happen to us all. We ignored them, sitting in tight little bunches around the room; no one watched television because it had been switched off after the channel-switching contest between the screw and me! Then things seemed to settle down for a few minutes; we were left in the day-room without any screws present. Suddenly three screws walked into the room, rolled their shirt-sleeves up and began to harangue us. They concentrated on the front row of seats facing the TV – where Phil, Bryan, several of our supporters and I sat. We argued fiercely for a while, then, in response to a comment from one of the screws about all prisoners being "animals", I walked (or perhaps "stalked" would be a better description) over to them and said that any further comments along those lines would result in a violent confrontation. (My words were undoubtedly less restrained than this, but I cannot remember the exact terminology. There is no doubt, however, that I was threatening.) After more mumbles two of the screws left the room – but not before I had gone off to collect three prison-made knives for what I thought was the forthcoming riot, only to have them taken by Phil and hidden in a chair-covering. This was the closest I came to initiating a violent response against the screws and, although they didn't know about the knives, they recognised that fact. Ten minutes after we were locked away for the night, several screws came to take me downstairs to the Punishment Ward.

As I was led out of the cell, quietly and without anyone laying hands on me, I called out: "Phil, Bryan, it's all on top. I'm going down to Monmouth!" There was silence from their cells, and one of the screws said – somewhat sadly, I thought: "You're on your own again, Alan." We went downstairs, and I was locked in a cell – once again I was in punishment.

I didn't see Udwin for a couple of days, during which time I maintained a hunger/thirst strike. On the Tuesday morning, when he finally came in to talk with me, Udwin was singularly unsympathetic: he told me that I was a bloody fool for giving the screws a reason to take me. As I sat, pathetically slumped over his desk, he told me to go back to my cell and drink something before I became completely dehydrated; he wasn't prepared to entertain my complaint of victimisation. Deflated as well as dehydrated, I went back to my cell – I knew that I had some serious thinking to do.

For several days I was kept locked up, and then I was allowed out into the day-room. During my confinement, and for a few weeks after it, I concentrated on examining how I had been growing over the past few years. I recognised that, although my political commitment was serious, there was still a large part of my thinking which was romantic, idealistic, and heavily influenced by a naïvely egotistic desire to sacrifice myself. Further, I was still working within a framework which accepted the status quo; I fought the screws, but considered Udwin as a personal "therapist". The contradictions were obvious, and I had to work through them: I had been analysing external events, sometimes looking at internal developments, but had developed no coherent views on the interaction between the two. I hadn't developed quite as much as I had thought.

Looking back, I tried to isolate the factors which had caused this uneven and, in some ways, distorted development. I noted that my initial reaction against the violence of my own direct experience had resulted in a hesitancy toward asserting myself; I was cautious lest I used politics as an excuse to exact vengeance for personal slights. Also I distrusted my own emotions, recognising that I had not really been in contact with them for many years: my involvement with Allison had brought me out of an emotional wilderness, but that relationship had been assaulted by the effects of my past insofar as I had been both possessive and easily unbalanced. Another major factor was the tremendous excitement I experienced as I flexed my intellectual muscles.

Although I had read widely over the years, there had been no real pattern to my work; I had been so indiscriminate that my intellect had been barely involved, with little analysis and even less involvement of my views of the world. Since 1967/68 I had deliberately sought to be more critical, more analytical, and my exposure to so many exciting ideas made me susceptible to the liberal problem of multiple choice – I was trapped in Mao's ninth type of liberalism: "As long as one remains a monk, one goes on tolling the bell." Committed to Marxism, Leninism, Mao Zedong Thought, to class analysis and class struggle, I was nonetheless permitting my lumpen experience, and its consequent vacillation, to interfere too much with my thinking and my work.

Having identified what I considered to be the two principal contradictions in my own experience, I turned outward to identify what factors in my social environment contributed to their debilitating effects. Once again I examined the role of the "patient", analysing the consciousness which grew from it; I also looked at the specific relationships within which that role was embedded. I noted both the psychological and external factors which prompted the bulk of my brothers to accept a position of inferiority and dependence: there was a need to accept being a "patient" in order not to examine too closely the processes whereby they had arrived at being incarcerated, and this acceptance led to a peculiarly narrow view of the world – many cons refused to recognise the endemic brutality, preferring to attribute what they did see to some personal failing on the part of the person being brutalised by physical assault. They would not see the environment itself as being brutal and dehumanising. Because of the allegedly "therapeutic" nature of the imprisonment, the staff were perceived as being essentially concerned with the well-being of the inmates, and this perception couldn't be maintained unless examples of the environment being anything other than "therapeutic" were rejected.

The relationships of subordination followed on from the misperception of the environment as "therapeutic": there is a tendency to accept a position of inferiority vis-à-vis "medical" authority when an "illness" is involved. The psychiatrists, with their totally medical model of the social environment, perceived every sign of disagreement as evidence of some fundamental disorder; refusal to accept the role of "patient" simply represented some symptom of mental disorder. Thus in relationships with psychiatrists it was necessary to demonstrate complete acceptance of the ordained role – which included the environment in which that role occurred – or some response of power would obtain, usually an increase in drug level, or the administration of ECT, or, ultimately, prolonged imprisonment. Paradoxically, a consistent attitude of rejection could lead to some new diagnosis, including that of mental health (!), on the basis of the consistency itself – but this could take years, and involve a long period of very unpleasant reactions from the staff.

On a day-to-day level, most relationships with authority involved the screws – it was quite usual to have only one or two interviews with a psychiatrist in any twelve-month period. As the majority of the screws were time-servers, interested only in working the minimum hours for the maximum pay, there was a tendency to view them in their everyday aspect as just ordinary people doing a job; this led to an acceptance of their very human qualities of humour and tolerance as being paramount. But these qualities were, in fact, the exception rather than the norm: frustration, irritation, and a casual indifference predominated. On each unit one or two screws represented "humanity", and the bulk of their colleagues existed in the reflected glow that these people gave off. Consequently, although the threat or the actuality of direct physical brutality was endemic, its actual occurrence, and thus impact, was not a constant reality, and this resulted in relatively harmonious relationships being routine. Given the majority acceptance of the role of "patient", and routine relationships with the screws being essentially passive, it was difficult to generate/develop any real emotional strength or expressiveness; these qualities depended on a sense of one's personal worth, and an independent attitude toward authority. Equally, the role of "patient" and passive dependence on screws actively discouraged any notion or development of interdependence – and this reinforced the "official" view that cooperation among cons was impossible.

From this analytical resumé I drew certain pragmatic conclusions. Firstly, I had to live my emotional life independently of the stultifying pressures of Broadmoor – and, simultaneously, I had to beware of the destructive claustrophobia which would result if I didn't turn those emotions, and their expressiveness, outward. Secondly, I had to strive to achieve a closer integration of my intellect and emotions; it was pointless, for example, to have an ideological commitment to combat sexism if I didn't combine an emotional expressiveness with my intellectual grasp of the problem. These conclusions were not easy to accept, and they were even harder to implement.

The difficulty of the personal re-evaluation I had experienced in 1967/68, followed by the intensive period of study I had undertaken, had led to liberal errors in my thinking and my work – but that period had been emotionally devastating, causing me a great deal of anguish. Now I was forced to repeat the process or content myself with a half-finished job. Further, I recognised that my development could easily lead me into greater isolation from my fellow cons, and in consequence I would probably face yet more periods of re-evaluation occasioned by subjectivist errors. The paradox was heart-rending: serving the people could, in the concrete circumstances surrounding my work, lead to my alienation from the people! I decided that I had to take the risk; any other course would be a betrayal of everything I believed.

During this period of re-evaluation I had not been completely isolated; several people visited me, and I was involved in a regular correspondence with several others. My parents were still coming in to see me on a regular basis; our relationships were improving dramatically, and I felt closer to them than I had ever done. David had recently married, and he brought his wife, Ingrid, in to visit me. I found her to be really beautiful, a viewpoint I still maintain. Richard and Jenny, too, were frequent visitors: their support and encouragement was a tremendous influence on me, and in this period we consolidated a relationship which has lasted for many years.

My correspondence was both internal and external; I remained in contact with Allison, sharing some of my difficulties with him, and also wrote to my erstwhile comrades. Outside Broadmoor, I was exchanging political analyses and commentaries with several people – this enabled me to try out some of my ideas on an "educated" audience. I needed this encouragement, and without it I would probably have dropped down into completely subjectivist errors; I doubt if I could have recovered from that.

Just over three months after I was moved down into the punishment ward, Udwin moved me back upstairs onto Ward Two. He wanted to capitalise on my separation from Phil and Bryan, so I didn't go back to Ward Three. Moving upstairs was a wrench, because Ron Greedy had recently arrived in Monmouth One; he had been falsely accused of assaulting another con, and the opportunity had been taken to get him out of circulation. (The screws had recognised by this time that he was involved with the RAC(B), but I think this played only a tangential part in his victimisation. It seemed that his publicly asserted homosexuality was the main contributing cause – the screws didn't like Ron's refusal to be meek and apologetic about his preferences.) We discused my move, and finally agreed that it was necessary – but I still approached Udwin and requested that Ron be moved up to join me as soon as possible. He came up three weeks later.

The rest of the year was relatively quiet: with the original RAC(B) now disbanded, I set about reorganising it, making it a more flexible group. With Ronald, I constituted a collator's centre in Monmouth Two; in each House I arranged for at least two people to continue political discussion, and they had the additional responsibility of channelling information through to me whenever it was necessary. I also opened tentative negotiations with several screws whose desire to be thought of as "nurses" made them susceptible to our propaganda; the information I obtained from them over the years enabled me to make defensive arrangements in advance of Prison Officers Association assaults on the cons. There were several sources providing information to us, but quite often we were unable to publish data because we had to protect our informants. For example, I once managed to get time to read a copy of the introductory lecture given to new screws by the Security Officer – and noted with interest the way he characterised all visitors to cons, without exception, as being either criminals or mentally deranged persons. This information would have had a profound impact if I had been able to publish it, but the person who provided the copy was fearful of being identified so I could only add the data to my files.

Political meetings down the sports field continued, often attended by a dozen or more people. In addition, I was continuing my own studies with a view to starting with the Open University in 1974; I had decided to drop my "A" level work, choosing to go straight for a Degree instead. When, after applying for entrance independently of Broadmoor's Education Office, I found that I had been accepted as an undergraduate, I asked Udwin for financial assistance; he agreed to fund me with a 100 per cent subsidy from the Education Fund, designating my studies as "treatment". I was more than satisfied with the arrangement.

On the level of personal relationships, I found two new people entering my life. Don D'Eath, the social worker with responsibility for Monmouth House, started coming in to speak with me – I think Udwin had encouraged it as a way of assisting my studies. We quickly became friendly, and soon afterwards another social worker, Veronica Pearson, joined Don on the visits. These two people had somehow managed to maintain a critical and independent outlook despite their involvement in Broadmoor's machine; we spent many pleasant hours discussing a wide variety of stimulating topics. When, later in the year, my appetite began to collapse in response to the strain I was under, Veronica used to make me the occasional jelly in an effort to stimulate my eating – we would all sit round the table in the dining-room, playing bridge, talking, while I was encouraged to eat! We also went off to my cell on occasion, although this was later in my first year of Open University studies, and continued our discussions in relative privacy.

Don had started to visit me early in 1974, just after the

academic year started, and Veronica came in a month or so later. I was studying a Foundation Course in Social Science (D100), and found that my wide reading in the past had, if anything, over-prepared me; the work I was doing was too basic. Wanting to extend myself, I spent about four times the necessary time studying each week, and read several more texts than were required of me. My social-worker friends were of great help to me during the early part of my studies, but their major contribution to me was personal; I became very fond of them, and by the latter part of 1974 found myself trusting them regardless of their involvement with Broadmoor. This personal relationship was so beneficial to me, and, I believe, to them as well, that it had to be noticeable to the screws – and they didn't like it. Ultimately, we all suffered because of it.

Although, during 1974, I was busy with my studies, I continued to be politically active: my meetings down the sports field continued to attract people, and they often involved lively and critical discussions. People continued to come in and visit me, ranging from Richard and Jenny Turner to Martin Kaufman (a fellow Maoist) and my family. With my parents, I was still getting closer; we were working through the mutual misunderstandings and anguish of our past. David and Ingrid came in a couple of times, as did Francesca, my sister – she was soon to leave England, getting married and moving out to New Zealand.

Phil and Bryan had left Broadmoor by mid-1974, and Ronald and I found ourself meeting ever more harassment as the remaining members of the original RAC(B): we heard increasingly of people being intimidated for attending our meetings, and several cons stopped participating because they were told that such conduct would prolong their stay in the prison. Some of this harassment spilled over into the OU, although that wasn't really necessary because education was a long-standing area of rabid disagreement with the screws.

Four people started with the Open University in 1974, the other three having been late applicants once it was recognised that the university would accept us. None of the others were politically active, and this stood us in good stead when the pressure got heavy; the screws couldn't use political radicalism as an excuse to hit us. We had a hard job keeping both the idea and the practice of university study in Broadmoor alive, but we persevered – and started our own "tradition" that year by having a 100 per cent success rate with the people who sat the exams.

Throughout this year of personal, political and educational harassment I continued to develop: although Allison left the prison, something which simultaneously pleased and pained me, I managed to maintain an emotional growth thanks to the network of encouragement and support available to me both inside and outside Broadmoor. Intellectually, too, I was becoming stronger; the discipline involved with OU study was of great benefit to me. The screws remained very antagonistic, arguing that I was an "extremist", and Udwin warned me that I was taking too much on; he said that I was too involved in the welfare of other cons and should concentrate on "getting on and getting out" – one of his favourite lines. Even Ronald warned me that I was pushing myself too hard, and the comments from Don and Veronica were similarly cautionary. I ignored them, answering that I couldn't slow down or refuse to help the cons who came to me. In October, the axe fell – and I found I couldn't handle events properly.

In late summer or early autumn, a con named Alan Poutney was assaulted, while being visited, by a screw named Griffith. The incident apparently involved a push, but Alan and his visitor were sufficiently incensed by it to seek legal advice – then Alan issued a private summons against Griffith alleging criminal assault. (The Thames Valley police, in whose jurisdiction Broadmoor lies, were at that time following a policy of refusing to accept or investigate complaints from prisoners; the Chief Constable didn't want us "wasting" his time. Accordingly, the only recourse for someone wishing to make use of British "justice" was to take a private action.) When the case got to the Magistrates' Court, Griffith was convicted and fined: he stood to lose his job and his pension, but not his liberty.

The Prison Officers Association were outraged: it seemed that the "divine" right of screws to assault prisoners with impunity was no longer to be sanctioned. They called a "work-to-rule" – meaning that they stopped all visits to prisoners, confined us to our wards, and refused to manhandle us in case we brought criminal charges against them. This latter point pleased us tremendously, but the other two impositions caused a great deal of suffering – which of course was exactly what the screws wanted. It was October when the pressure started building, and by mid-November there was much anguish as cons lost their annual visit. (Many people could only afford to visit someone in Broadmoor once a year, and this tended to be toward Christmas; as November drew to a close, more and more cons moved to the edge.)

Udwin permitted the cons on Monmouth Two and Three to mix, and I was constantly shuttling between the wards as people called me for advice or support. In addition to the "work-to-rule", the screws had initiated an appeal; they argued, quite legitimately, that the 1959 Mental Health Act specifically forbids private prosecutions against screws without the difficult-to-obtain sanction of a judge in chambers. They were asking for their privileged position under British law to be maintained – a perfectly understandable desire. With several other cons I was busy writing some of the arguments Alan was sending as instructions to his barrister; this was an additional pressure on me.

At the end of November, I was called into the office; it was time for Udwin to discuss with me the question of my release. He told me that I was still too heavily involved in other people's welfare; I had to tone down the politics and concentrate on myself. I told him to go to hell – there was no way I could pull back under the present circumstances. Then I listened as he stated that I was pushing too hard, and that I wouldn't be able to maintain this pace much longer. Finally, he told me that I wouldn't be released for several years, regardless of the assurances he had given the previous year. I felt that I had had enough; it was time for me to take action to protect myself.

On the night of December 7th, 1974, with two other cons, Ken Adamson and Pat Carey, I went through the bars of a cell in an attempt to escape from Broadmoor. Ken and I had cut through the bars over a two-day period, timing the act so that we could go on the night of the Christmas film – this year, because of prevailing circumstances, shown in Ward Two day-room. Straight after the film, we went directly to Ken's cell and climbed out into the exercise yard. We didn't get far: a chance meeting with a screw drove us up onto a low roof, turning an escape attempt into a protest demonstration.

The action had been precipitate: Pat had suggested the move about a week before we went, and the hacksaw blade –

obtained from a "friendly" screw – had been in our hands for only three days. Ken had not really wanted to go, making his decision essentially because of an emotional involvement with me; my own bitter angish after Udwin's comments about my staying in Broadmoor made me too selfish to recognise his doubts and hesitations. Pat had recently been refused his release by the Home Secretary on the advice of the Aarvold Committee, a group of people who were concerned with state security rather than mental health, and was understandably bitter about the position he found himself in. My mood was such that anything which seemed to offer some prospect of getting out of Broadmoor looked good – and Pat knew that.

Being convinced that we would get out, we had left a number of red herrings behind: in each of our cells we had hidden pieces of paper with comments about assistance we had received from screws, barely destroyed addresses, and a map with routes to the West Country pencilled in. Pat had obtained – from the same screw as the hacksaws, I believe – a box of .22 ammunition, and we had planned to drop this next to the spot where we would steal a car; the police might be less willing to come after us if they believed us to be armed. I had also fashioned two prison-made knives, intending to use them to pry open a car window – or threaten any policeman foolish enough to get in the way. When we climbed up onto the roof after being surprised by the screw, we left the bundle containing the ammunition in the exercise yard – and then had some fun telling the screws that we had hidden explosives in with the clothing. Our amusement was short-lived; we were trapped.

We spent the night on the low roof, surrounded by screws, unable to move in any direction. In the morning, I attempted to scale the wall of the building; I couldn't do it, being too cold. We had negotiated with Udwin through one of the windows, and the other two wanted to go down – I didn't like the idea, knowing that there was nowhere for me to go any more. As Pat and Ken went down the ladder, I managed to reach the windows on Ward Three; I couldn't manage the overhang. I tied a piece of flex from the tv aerial around my neck, laughingly informing Udwin and the assembled screws that if I didn't make it then I would at least remove the problem of deciding my future – then I climbed up the bars and tried to reach up over the guttering. Ken was on the ground by this time, and being held by two screws; he started screaming at me to give up, tears interrupting his pleas. I almost jumped – but climbed down instead. A couple of minutes later we were all in solitary.

Ken was moved back upstairs to Ward Two just before Christmas, and Pat was as quickly permitted to leave the cell and go into the day-room; I was kept in solitary. When, a week or so after our attempt to escape, the screws won their appeal against the private prosecution, they called off the "work-to-rule" and gloatingly told the cons that they were still on top: a deputation of three came to my cell to laugh at me and ask if I was going to kill myself in protest. It seemed that I was back to the position I had been in during 1967/68.

Early in January, I heard that Veronica Pearson, who had gone off to university (Bristol, I think) to work for her MA, wouldn't be returning to Broadmoor; Don had had his contract terminated. The screw who told me this also said that their relationship with me had been the prime cause; he also said that some of the documents we had left behind incriminated them. Initially, I was furious, thinking that my friends had been "framed" – then I began to wonder if Pat had deliberately or inadvertantly mentioned them in his scraps of paper. I didn't know, and there was no way I could find out. This information was the final straw, and once again I collapsed into myself: it seemed that, despite my good intentions, I was still causing distress to people I cared for.

Sitting in my cell, I withdrew into depression; the problem of subjectivist errors had finally overwhelmed me. This depression was not as savage as the one I had experienced in 1967; bad though I felt, I was no longer committed to a view of myself as totally worthless. But . . . there were additional problems this time: the beatings I had had when I was younger, plus the months in cold and damp solitary-confinement cells, had gradually been exerting an influence on me, and I was in constant pain. In addition, the disease in my jawbone flared up again, and this resulted in raging headaches from which there was no respite. Emotionally drawn and physically distressed, my appetite, tentative at the best of times, collapsed; I started on the intermittent anorexia which was to plague me for several years.

Sometime in January I was allowed out of the cell; I went each day to the day-room, sitting in a corner and reading or thinking. On exercise, I managed to speak with Ken when he came to the window, but he was getting increasingly friendly with a recently arrived youngster named Hywel Davis and was just not inclined to spend much time speaking with me. He was also, I think, justifiably somewhat bitter at my insensitive behaviour at the time of our escape attempt. Ronald couldn't get to the window much, so I was effectively isolated.

I came close to giving up completely, even going so far as to talk with a couple of screws about my prospects if I withdrew from political activity: fortunately, they made it clear that I would be expected to repudiate everything I and the RAC(B) had done, and this was totally unacceptable to me. Although I was depressed, my confidence shaken, and doubtful about my ability to go on, there was no way that I could go that far back. I knew that my actions had involved errors, but my position was essentially correct in political terms. Unsure that I could personally handle the situation I was in, and knowing that the screws would reap considerable benefits if they could break me, I decided that the best way out was suicide; I just had to find the way.

Late in February, Udwin permitted me to spend three hours a day on Ward Two in order to continue my OU studies; it didn't work, and I had to withdraw from my courses that year. I continued going upstairs and sitting in a cell which had been put aside for study; I just kept reading and thinking. Having decided that I was going to kill myself, a lot of the depression had lifted; I found myself enjoying the reading I was doing, and actually managing to expand my analytical skills. It seemed that, having decided to die, much of the pressure on me evaporated! Finally, in May I think, my chance came; I went out one evening to play bowls, and climbed onto Dorset House roof instead.

I had been receiving pain-killers to combat the muscle-wrenching agony in my back, and I had managed to keep twenty or so of them to take up to the roof with me. My intention was to swallow the pills, sit on the edge of the roof, and, when I was unconscious, roll off. Things didn't quite go as I planned.

My memories of this event are almost non-existent: soon after reaching the roof, I swallowed the pills – and they took effect too quickly. I remember having a nightmare inside the attic, being enveloped by snakes/ants/rats and trying to cut them off my arms with broken slates. The screws later told me that I threw slates down at them, but I have no recollection of that. Eventually, late that night, I was somehow persuaded to climb down a ladder which had been provided; I woke up the next morning in a cell on Monmouth One.

When I woke up I was completely disoriented; I had difficulty believing I was still alive! Not knowing what had happened, I assumed that I had given in and surrendered without complaint – I found out very quickly that this wasn't the case. Two screws came and got me from the cell, taking me along to the office; I found myself facing two senior ward screws, a Charge "Nurse" and the House "Nursing" Officer. They asked me what it would take for me to refrain fron confrontation with the authorities – they wanted to make a deal!

The discussions we had that day and the next covered my activities, my commitments, the needs of the staff and the needs of Broadmoor. Eventually a deal was concluded: I was to remain quiet and non-antagonistic, maintaining a low political profile, and in return I was assured of a rapid amelioration of the conditions of my detention. A week or so later Udwin ratified the deal, extending it to include the following bargain: I refrained from direct political activity, confining myself to writing and quiet personal negotiations on issues I felt important, becoming only peripherally involved in the defence of other prisoners, and in return I would be left in peace by the authorities and released by the time I was thirty (1978). From an act of personal despair, the low point of my development since 1967/68, I had reached a position where the authorities were prepared to negotiate with me.

Over the next few weeks I managed to get the opportunity to discuss the deal with Ronald and a few other people; they were unanimous in urging me to accept and implement what had been offered. I also got the chance to speak with Jenny, and she too thought I should go along with the bargain if I thought that political benefits could derive from it. (Soon after this my visits from Richard and Jenny came to an end for a while; a ban was imposed on my receiving visits from anyone other than members of my family. This was the second such ban, the first having been imposed by McGrath in 1972, but at least I could write for a while longer.) So with some reservations, mainly resulting from a feeling that I was receiving benefits denied the other cons, I accepted and honoured the deal: I consoled myself with the thought that I could at least maintain some political activity, even if it had to be low-profile.

For the rest of 1975 I was located on Monmouth One. Within a month I had been given a job in the laundry, a position which enabled me to get time out of the block because I had to go and collect new clothing issues from the main store; I also got the opportunity to visit the open wards above Monmouth One in order to speak with people who needed new clothes. This job was far from being innocuous; too frequently it was used to improve the financial position of the holder, for he could arrange new clothing issues almost at will. An additional benefit for me was that I could sit in the laundry-room alone and unobserved – this left me free to continue my studies. The two screws I worked with most of the time, George Temple and Bill Haslam, were both reasonable: George was a joker with an underlying seriousness, his main bad point from my perspective being total support for the POA; Bill Haslam was one of the gentlest men in Broadmoor, something which often brought him into conflict with his fellow screws. Bob Barber, the senior Charge "Nurse" on the block, left us very much alone in the laundry; he was one of Udwin's principal supporters in attempts to get Monmouth One opened up, and he suffered from a terrible failing – he actively practised nursing!

In my studies, some of them aimed at preparation for my 1976 OU work and some aimed at developing my personal and political competence, I applied myself conscientiously. Following my depression and realisation of subjectivist errors, I let myself be guided by Mao: from his work on "Our Study and the Current Situation" I noted the following passage with care – "Many things may become baggage, may become encumbrances, if we cling to them blindly and uncritically. (. . .) Having made mistakes, you may feel that, come what may, you are saddled with them and so become dispirited; if you have not made mistakes, you may feel that you are free from error and so become conceited. Lack of achievement in work may breed pessimism and depression, while achievement may breed pride and arrogance. (. . .) All such things

146

become encumbrances or baggage if there is no critical awareness." This seemed to apply to me and the way that I had made serious mistakes and been overwhelmed by them; I resolved to analyse the "encumbrances and baggage", seeking to continue my development and the value of my work.

Another passage from Mao inspired me to examine the basis of the errors I had made, simultaneously encouraging me to recognise that I was not alone in failing to note the social basis of mistaken behaviour: "Often, correct knowledge can be arrived at only after many repetitions of the process leading from matter to consciousness and then back to matter, that is, leading from practice to knowledge and then back to practice. Such is the Marxist theory of knowledge, the dialectical materialist theory of knowledge." ("Where Do Correct Ideas Come From?")

Reading the *Selected Works* of Mao, as well as many other volumes of work by leading Marxist thinkers/practitioners, led me to sharpen my analyses of myself and the social environment in which I was located; my work on lumpen consciousness took on a new impetus. I noted the way that declassed people, living on the margin of civil society, were exposed to the blunt reality of state control; there were few superstructural buffers, such as law, "common" morality or religion, to intervene and protect us from abuses. One consequence of this was a tendency to rely overmuch on individual competence, a form of accentuated bourgeois belief in entrepreneurial activity! This individualism bred the extremes of conceit and depression; we fell into delusions of grandeur or total incompetence.

I began to recognise that my selfish concentration on my own well-being – exhibited, paradoxically, through a conceited and self-sacrificial "service" to the other cons – had blinded me to the social consequences of my actions: the RAC(B) had become identified with Alan Reeve, and the responsiveness of the other cons was based on a personal relationship with me rather than any real political consciousness. In spite of these errors of mine, several brothers had begun to develop a genuine political consciousness of their position – but I had failed them by permitting their personal relationships with me to become the dominant expression of their politics. No matter how personally unpleasant the act would be, I had to encourage a whole-hearted criticism of my

147

style of work and leadership. I also had to critically analyse, once again, the development and functioning of the RAC(B).

Following our arguments within the prison, the propaganda activities of Richard, Jenny and other comrades outside, the roof-top protest and subsequent "enquiry", and the action of Phil and Bryan in coming to the Punishment Block, certain concrete benefits had resulted. The incidence of physical brutality had begun to decrease, many cons had had their "medication" re-assessed (i.e. lessened), Udwin had initiated reform in the Punishment Block, opening it up somewhat and bringing cons out of solitary after shorter periods than was previously the case, and several screws had served notice on their colleagues that they intended attempting to practise nursing for a change. There were also structural changes, epitomised by the ending of the practice of making cons strip naked and stand shivering on the gallery for three or four minutes prior to being locked up at night. Although these were essentially cosmetic changes, hardly undermining the structural abuses which made Broadmoor a centre of state terrorism, they did improve the quality of life for most prisoners. But we had managed to obtain these reforms almost by accident. It was not responsiveness to our political analyses and/or demands which had forced the authorities to act; it was the threat, explicit in our existence, of prisoner organisation. We had failed to properly identify the levers of power which we had manipulated, and this resulted in our failing to capitalise on Broadmoor's fearful responsiveness.

In our Provisional Manifesto, we had made serious political errors: we had naïvely concentrated on slogans to the detriment of analyses, and we had also exhibited an adventurism by failing to link the specific instances of oppression in Broadmoor to their counterparts in civil society beyond the walls. These errors were compounded by our hasty and ill-conceived acceptance of Phil Hall's desire to protest on the roof; our action resulted in the leading cadres being removed from regular contact with the bulk of prisoners, and this permitted a reformist consciousness to develop in the prison without our providing serious political leadership. It was at this time that the subjectivist error of rooting political developments in personal relationships began to manifest itself most profoundly, and we had uncritically permitted this to happen. Clearly, as the initiator of political discussion in the prison, as the leading cadre of the RAC(B) and as the person most regularly identified with the process of "rebellion", I was responsible for this state of affairs: concentrating on the purity of my own political development, I had failed to provide the necessary leadership and guidance.

These reflections and analyses did not occur in total isolation: when I went upstairs to speak with people about clothing I took letters with me, and these were passed on to other people. From the feedback I received, I found that my brothers were strong and growing in political consciousness – but they still exhibited a defensiveness about me, seeking to protect me from what they considered harsh self-criticism. This was a tendency which was to remain for the duration of my stay in Broadmoor: while many cons rejected me and my work, fearfully referring to me as "that mad commie bastard", and many others regarded me as something resembling a prisoner-cum-social-worker, those cons who developed a political perspective rooted in Marxism consistently behaved protectively toward me – I remained something apart, always considered an extremist and yet referred to as something resembling a political guru.

By the end of 1975 I was being treated as a visitor on the block; I even had a television set in my cell, permission having been granted so that I could keep abreast of OU programmes. My position was anomalous, to put it mildly. The deal, inspired I think by a lingering humanitarian impulse combined with a pragmatic desire to obtain some respite from my political activism, was supported by the bulk of the screws, and this resulted in fairly amicable relations with most of them. I continued arguing my position, forcibly, and now there were many screws who were prepared to engage in debate; although only one or two of them commented on it at this time, they were treating me as a political prisoner.

My relationship with Udwin continued to be something of a paradox: I felt something close to affection for the man, even though I recognised his form of liberalism as being particularly dangerous – he disarmed opponents by being sympathetically reasonable. It was quite common to hear screws warning cons not to trust him, and on occasion it seemed that there was a POA policy aimed at breaking his power in the prison. The ambivalence of our relationship often caused me some amusement: I detested his liberalism, seeing it as one of the components which prevented many cons from recognising the real nature of Broadmoor; held in contempt his professional hypocrisy in being willing to function as a political jailer for the Establishment; and yet felt affection for him as one of the few people who had tried to get close to me. No matter how contemptible or dangerous I considered him, I couldn't fail to recognise the profound effect he had had in pushing me toward a radical re-evaluation of myself and my position in life. Knowing that I was emotionally drawn to him, I had to take great care that I did not subordinate political ideas and practices to some protective consideration of his welfare.

Overall, during this year I had managed to recover from the mood of personal despair with which I had ended 1974: emotionally, I was stronger, having benefitted from a recognition that last year's low point was just another stage in my growth, and politically, too, I was far stronger after my months of reflection and analyses. Despite my anomalous position, occasioned by an unprecedented bargain initiated by the authorities, I remained politically active; I couldn't make "public" utterances, but I could write and engage in private discussions. Among those brothers who were politically conscious I retained some influence, and I looked forward to the process of mutual growth which I saw ahead of us. I had not risen, like a phoenix, from the ashes of a personal disaster, but I had consolidated my political consciousness and finalised my commitment to Marxism, Leninism, Mao Zedong Thought.

During 1975, Monmouth Two and Three had been re-designated as Somerset One and Two; the stigma of the Punishment Block was causing some screws around the prison to treat everyone from the House as if they were in need of closer than usual observation. In late January, or possibly early February, 1976, I was moved up to Somerset Two.

My OU studies, suspended in 1975 because it was too difficult to continue in Monmouth, had now restarted; I was signed up to take a course in Decision Making. Once again I found the work relatively easy, but I continued my pattern of reading wider and deeper than was called for by the course material. Decision-making processes intrigued me, especially as I brought a Marxist perspective to an essentially liberal course; it was interesting to see the rationales offered for class domination, and the way that the myth of "democracy" was maintained by reference to pluralist models based on voting patterns. Some of the material, such as that dealing with the inequalities of health care resources between different regions in Britain, was new to me, but the analyses provided were common enough – they fell into the usual pattern of bourgeois justification.

In addition to my studies with the OU, I was continuing my private research into a materialist conception of social "deviance"; I began revising/re-writing my notes on Broadmoor and its relation to the state, looking outward at the same time to compare the categorisation, stigmatisation, and general oppressive measures taken against specific social groups. One particular dimension of this research was concerned with the way that tactics were developed in specific institutions and circumstances and then generalised to deal with other, apparently quite different, patterns. I found what I considered to be some interesting correlations.

The medicalisation of crime was by this time fairly generally known about; the "liquid cosh" used to control prisoners in civil prisons was not a humanitarian concern but rather an indication of the way that social dissent of any form was increasingly coming to be regarded as symptomatic of mental disorder. Criminological theories which seemed to recognise the social basis of crime were all the rage in universities, but the models accepted and utilised by the prison service were rooted in the stigmatising concepts of forensic psychiatry. The academic criminologists were offering insights into the social inequalities which motivated much crime, and began to explain the consciousness of the criminal, but forensic psychiatry was reinforcing the bourgeois conceptualisation of deterministically individual responsibility. In the battle of theory the criminologists were winning easily – but the forensic psychiatrists had the big guns because their models were accepted at the Home Office, and as a result they were winning the practice.

Another area in which "deviance" research was being generalised was Northern Ireland: an anti-colonialist war of liberation was being characterised as a criminal clash of interest, with the freedom fighters of the IRA stigmatised as mentally deranged "terrorists" and the reactionary forces of Paisley and company dismissed as mere misguided vigilantes. The British government had already started its argument that prison conditions in Northern Ireland were among the best in

Europe, a tacit recognition of the special status of the fighters in that colony; but they were (and are) still using tactics familiar from prisons on the mainland: brutality, isolation, psychological terrorism predominated in the institutions, and a consistent public campaign of vilification outside them. Interrogation procedures, too, had been perfected from the armoury of forensic psychiatry; they drew (draw) on techniques of coercive modification rooted in behavioural psychology and aversion "therapy".

Some of these analyses found their way into my OU assignments, but I recognised that I was working with inadequate data most of the time and I was still tentative about presenting my own analyses – it took another couple of years before I became confident enough to let my academic work stand or fall on its own logic. For the present, most of my private research remained in my files or was used as the basis of discussion and correspondence.

Throughout 1976 and 1977 I concentrated on my studies, my private research, consolidating my personal development and quietly encouraging several brothers in their political and personal growth. I was still functioning as something of a prisoner–cum–social–worker, but this was done quietly and didn't often bring me into conflict with the authorities. In fact, several brothers were sent to me by the screws; they recognised that people were more prepared to listen to another con on certain issues, and some of them were beginning to accept the notion of mutual self-help as being inherently valuable. With the bulk of the screws, however, I was still involved in a wary truce; they wondered how long I would be able to maintain a non–controversial position in the face of provocation. (Reports of brutality were still occasionally reaching me, and several screws asked me if I would content myself with merely offering advice and information on complaint procedures. I wondered about this myself!)

In the early days of the "deal" I found it very difficult to refrain from public comment, but my comrades, my friends and family, and many brothers kept up a consistent pressure on me to "be cool". Udwin didn't come in to see me very much in this period, but when he did he told me that I was fulfilling our bargain and that he would fulfil his obligations, too.

Bryan Knight and Phil Batt had both been back to visit me after their release, encouraged to do so by Udwin. On one occasion Bryan had been recalled to Broadmoor for an interview with Udwin; he had been having problems maintaining himself in Reading, where he had been sent, and the interview was designed as a cautionary procedure. After seeing Udwin, Bryan was "instructed" to come and talk with me; Udwin obviously thought that I could offer more encouragement to my former comrade. Unfortunately I couldn't do much.

Bryan's difficulties in Reading didn't abate, and he ran back to his home town of Peterborough. Udwin decided to leave him there instead of recalling him, and I thought this would help him to make the transition to outside life again. One day I found out how difficult it was for some people to adjust; I heard that Bryan had been charged with murder. The facts, as they were explained to me by a screw who had access to the official papers, were that Bryan had given shelter to another man in the house he shared with his woman friend. This man had broken into the gas meter and Bryan had demanded that the robbery be reported to the police – he pointed out that he stood to lose his freedom for life if it was thought that he had done the job. The man refused to cooperate, deciding instead to attack Bryan – who fought back, and in the struggle killed the man with a blow to the head. On the basis of these facts it seemed to me that Bryan would probably be sentenced to four years imprisonment for manslaughter – but I reckoned without the bias which a period in Broadmoor inevitably inserted into a Court case. The sentence was life.

This sentence undoubtedly devastated Bryan, and its effect on me was almost as bad; he had been a good comrade, and I felt shattered that this could happen to him without my being able to do anything. I went to Udwin, seeking permission to write to my friend, but was "advised" that the prison authorities would not look favourably on such correspondence; inter-prison political discussion was frowned upon. Another factor which caused me some concern was the effect of the sentence on me – I asked Udwin if the Home Office would be using Bryan's alleged crime as a weapon against people in Broadmoor: he told me that they wouldn't, because that would reflect unfavourably on the institution.

Soon after this a rumour swept Broadmoor that Phil Batt, too, was in prison again; it was said that he had been sentenced to ten years for some unspecified offence. I have never been able to get this rumour rejected or substantiated by the authorities, but I didn't hear from Phil again. When, about a year or so later, I heard that Phil Hall had been sentenced to a short prison term, the bad news was complete: of the comrades who had been released still quietly supporting the RAC(B) and its policies, none remained free or available. I wondered how much of the problems my friends had faced had been attributable to my errors as their political mentor.

Following the successful completion of my studies in 1976, I chose to read for Social Psychology plus Soviet Government and Politics in 1977. I had decided to major in those subjects which would enable me to function as a political psychologist, feeling that my developmental process would increase my skills in this area: my primary concern was relations of power between individuals and groups, and this particular discipline seemed the most useful to me. My private research had led me to concentrate on image development and management, and I began collecting data for a research project once I had completed my Degree: I felt that the concentration of relations of power in a prison would offer insights into the repressive techniques, ideologically based, used in civil society as a whole – and I had hopes of identifying counter-levers useful to revolutionaries. My confidence in my own analytical competence had by this time begun to assert itself, and I was no longer fearful of working independently. Marxism was not just an idea for me, it had become completely integrated as a way of life.

My personal relationships were continuing to improve: with my family I had finally accomplished a warm and companionable relationship based on mutual acceptance and love, and this was the pattern with my other friends around the country. In Broadmoor, I was getting on well with most of the cons I came in contact with, although there was still a trace of trepidation involved with many; my "arrangement" with Udwin and the screws didn't stop either the harassment I experienced (although this did lessen considerably) or that experienced by other people who came into contact with me. Even in "retirement", I was considered a "dangerous communist agitator" by the more hard-line screws – it was rather flattering, in a perverse sort of way!

Allison, who had been recalled to Broadmoor for a couple

of years, and who was soon to leave again, was becoming increasingly interested in spiritualism – this led to some interesting and argumentative discussions, but as neither of us felt able to move from our position we just had to make the best of it. Our relationship was, if anything, closer than ever, though no longer as passionate as was previously the case; both of us drew much encouragement and support from the love we shared. Some of his more reactionary views caused me a great deal of concern, but I recognised that this was an example of what Mao had called "contradictions among the people"; he was a political opponent, but certainly not an enemy – and besides, I was well aware of the social pressures which had shaped his life and thinking. I had been able to accept homosexual love as just another valid expression of human emotional concern, but Allison, five years older than me, had experienced more of the anguish and ostracism accorded to this "unacceptable" sexuality. While for me gay consciousness was just one facet of my existence, an expression of emotional involvement and commitment to a person who happened to be a man, and did not preclude my loving other people, including women, for my lover it was a fundamental apect of his very existence. Too many people forget that sexism has crippled men as well as women, and that we should resolutely oppose – and smash – its every manifestation.

In December 1977, on Christmas Eve, I think, Udwin called me into the office and told me that he was going to submit a recommendation for my conditional discharge; the staff and the psychology department were totally in support of this development. Understandably, I was very pleased to hear this, but I was also wondering just how the Home Office would respond. I was well aware that reformist agreements made by agencies in civil society to politically disarm class-conscious workers are often abrogated by the superior agencies of state control – and, as my analyses of Broadmoor showed it to be a microcosm of relations existing in the state and civil society, I thought it quite possible that the "arrangement" between the Broadmoor authorities and myself might not be acceptable to the Home Secretary with his wider political "responsibilities". The Broadmoor authorities were merely servants of the state, and any "bargains" that they entered into could easily be repudiated by their masters. (During my studies of Decision

Making in Britain, I had analysed negotiations between unions and management in nationalised industries, noting the way that "deals" were suspended, altered, or simply abrogated by the incumbent government – in Marx's succinct phrase the "national management committee of the bourgeoisie" – regardless of the wishes even of their own designated management teams. These analyses had led me to characterise negotiations in Broadmoor in an analogous fashion, and early in 1977 I had written a memorandum to myself in which I had applied this analogy to my own situation: I hoped that I would be released, but my own analyses told me that it was unlikely.)

While I concentrated on informing my family, friends and comrades of Udwin's decision, word spread quickly around Broadmoor about it. Several screws went out of their way to tell me that they would not have signed the staff agreement to my release, but I pointed out that the responsibility lay with people of at least Charge "Nurse" level – and it was highly unlikely that they would ever reach so high. Two conversations with screws have remained vivid in my memory: the first involved a screw asking me how I thought I would deal with the problem of being imprisoned as a thirteen-year-old boy and released as a thirty-year-old man – I told him that I had an excellent support network of friends, family and comrades, and that this would enhance my self-confidence and assist me in getting over any problems. In addition, I pointed out that I had at least the opportunity (perhaps!) of starting my life as an adult, while Barry Richards, the boy I killed, did not have even this; I said that Barry's memory would be a sobering and stabilising factor.

The second conversation was with a screw who had made no secret of his opposition to my coming out of solitary confinement, let alone being released; he had consistently stated that any con who became political was dangerous, and my tendency to commitment made me doubly so. The screw asked me if I would be politically active on the outside, and I told him that I would, to the limits of whatever was possible in my circumstances. He then queried me about my continuing work with prisoners and prison conditions; I told him that this was only one small area of the state's apparatus of coercion and control, and I would be working with my comrades on the whole spectrum of oppression and exploitation. Finally, after telling me that he thought I had become stronger, harder, even more political and revolutionary over the past couple of years, he asked me if I supported armed struggle, violent revolution, and such groups as the IRA and the Red Brigades. I told him that revolutionary violence was a class question, not something dependent on individual whim; the concrete conditions existing at any given historical moment determined the issue of violence. On groups such as those he had mentioned, I answered that I unreservedly supported the right of people engaged in wars of liberation to determine the tactics appropriate to their situation. In a phrase – "Yes, I unequivocally support revolutionary war, the human expression of a human desire to end oppression and exploitation." He was rather surprised that I answered as I did, and as he turned to go told me that, like all communists, I subordinated morality to a political dream. I followed him down the gallery, stopped him outside the office, and quoted the following piece at him: "A revolutionary Marxist cannot begin to approach his historical mission without having broken morally from bourgeois public opinion and its agencies in the proletariat. For this, moral courage of a different calibre is required than that of opening wide one's mouth at meetings and yelling 'Down with Hitler!' 'Down with Franco!' It is precisely this resolute, completely-thought-out, inflexible rupture of the Bolsheviks from conservative moral philosophy not only of the big but of the petty bourgeoisie which morally terrorises democratic phrasemongers, drawing-room prophets and lobbying heroes. From this are derived their complaints about the 'amoralism' of the Bolsheviks." I left him standing, staring after me, as I strolled back to the day-room.

When I told Ronald about this conversation, and mentioned that the quote was from Trotsky's *Their Morals and Ours*, he asked me why I didn't quote Mao. I answered that Trotsky had made some good points, and this was one of them, so I used it. We both found it amusing that the screw, familiar with the way that I worked, had forgotten my habit of quoting long passages from political authors if I thought that they had written something in such a way that I couldn't improve on it. One other thing we noted carefully: if this screw had seen that I was getting stronger and harder, then undoubtedly reports of this had reached the Home Office.

My family and friends were very pleased to hear that I might be released soon, but my comrades shared my doubts about the Home Office. The logic was obvious: if my detention was dependent on psychiatric opinion as to my "psychopathy" – as the law and the letter from Mark Carlisle, one-time Under-Secretary of State at the Home Office, stated – then the psychiatric statements which unanimously declared me mentally competent should inevitably result in my release. Because I was detained under Sections 60/65 of the 1959 Medical Health Act, I could only be conditionally discharged; the Home Secretary would retain the right to recall me during any period up to the end of my life, but this should only be consequential upon some definite evidence of mental disorder on my part. This was the thought-process of my family and friends: my comrades, like me, thought that the law was not really involved in my case – it was a straightforward political question, and this could have the effect of making my existing sentence one of "natural life".

Udwin submitted the formal papers recommending my release early in January, 1978; we were still on target for my release before I was thirty. I continued with my studies, this year reading two courses in economics – Micro-economics, and National Income and Economic Policy. On Somerset Two I was left very much alone, free to pursue my own interests within the confines of the ward. I was getting on reasonably with most of the screws, including "Tiny" Davis and Grantley Thomas, the two Charge "Nurses". Grantley, the first black Charge "Nurse" in Broadmoor's history, was thought by many of the cons to be rather abrupt, but I always found him courteous and helpful; he was one of the few screws who tried very hard to function as "nurses", and I never heard any allegations of abuse levelled at him. He was very encouraging to me during the waiting period.

A couple of months into the year, Udwin came to me and said that I was to be interviewed by a member of the Aarvold Committee before a decision would be taken by the Home Secretary regarding my recommendation for discharge. I was furious, though not overly surprised: Udwin had told me in 1971, when the idea of this Committee was first discussed, that it would not have any effect on me – I didn't believe him then, so I was not particularly shocked.

The Aarvold Committee was established in the wake of Graham Young's trial for murders committed subsequent to his release from Broadmoor. Its brief was to act as an advisory team for the Home Secretary whenever the release of someone with a long criminal record or substantial public notoriety was contemplated. Many people thought that they were a medical team, but they weren't: as the Blue Paper on reforming the 1959 Medical Health Act (1979 or 1980, I think) stated, medical questions were the province of psychiatrists and Mental Health Review Tribunals, while the Aarvold Committee was specifically to deal with questions of public security. This Committee, whose recommendations are very rarely over-turned, operates independently of the judiciary, shrouded in secrecy, and with no right of appeal. Interposing themselves between certain, but not all, prisoners detained under Sections 60/65, their criteria for advising the Home Secretary are com-pletely removed from the medical considerations which the 1959 Act makes paramount: the result of this is that prisoners detained on allegedly psychiatric grounds may continue to be detained in a place legally defined as a psychiatric prison, without recourse to any legal protection, for reasons deter-mined by political considerations. I don't think Udwin was surprised to find that I was furious about their involvement in my release.

I can't remember the exact dates, but I think that I was eventually interviewed by a Committee member in May, 1978. Waiting to see the man was a worrying period; my parents, especially my mother, were understandably anxious, and while I attempted to reassure them I didn't hide my own doubts about the way things were going. They were not yet prepared to accept that I was a political prisoner, but the way that events were following the process I had outlined to them made them begin thinking about what I had been saying on this point.

The interview itself was relatively easy, with most of the questions following the line I had anticipated: I was asked questions about my life, my development, my relations with other people, especially my parents, my studies, the circum-stances surrounding my murder of Barry Richards – and then a few, simple, "not particularly important" I was assured, questions about my politics. "Are you a communist?" "Yes." "Are you a Maoist?" "Yes." "Do you intend to be politically active if you are released?" "Yes." After thanking me for being "so honest and cooperative", the man asked me if I had any message I wanted delivered to the Committee. I answered that I would stand on Dr Udwin's recommendation, especially as it had been unanimously supported by the other departments in Broadmoor. That concluded my first meeting with a representative of the Aarvold Committee.

Thirteen weeks after the interview, Udwin called me into the office and told me that his recommendation had been rejected; no reasons were given. My first thoughts were for my parents – how was I going to tell them, what could I say? Udwin asked me if I wanted him to contact them, but I rejected his offer; this was something I had to do for myself, no matter how unpleasant it was. I sat down and wrote them a letter, telling them how sorry I was that they should have to go through this additional burden after all that had happened; there may well have been a note of self-pity in the letter, although I tried hard to avoid it. My own feelings were fatigue, a sense of bitter satisfaction at having my suspicions confirmed, and a rather weary unhappiness at the prospect of more time in Broadmoor.

Over the next few weeks, as news of the decision spread around the prison, a number of cons came up to me to commiserate and, something more gratifying, to apologise for contemptuously rejecting my arguments in the past. Now that "Udwin's pet", the prison's own Maoist, was suffering the consequences of maintaining a consistent political position, a number of sceptical cons were reconsidering their own position – and myself and my political position were gaining in stature because of the way that this problem had been foretold. I was suddenly in great demand as cons sought information and explanation about the Aarvold Committee and the way that the Home Office worked.

Interestingly enough, it wasn't only cons who commiserated with me; several screws made the trip to Somerset Two to tell me that they thought a mistake had been made. Of course, many screws were either indifferent (like the majority of the cons) or openly gloated at the result: that was as I expected, so it caused me no grief. I made use of every reaction, commiseration or gloating, even indifference, as long as it was expressed, to hammer home the political reality of the situation: it was futile relying on negotiations with, or goodwill from, liberals and reformists, because the fundamental relations of power remained unaltered and therefore detrimental to our interests. Only a comprehensive recognition of these relations of power, located in a consciousness of our class position, could lead to the unity which is our fundamental strength, and only this unity could alter these relations of power by forcing a revolutionary restructuring of the state and civil society. It might seem that this was a large lesson to draw from the Home Office's rejection of one individual's recommendation for release, but I pointed out that I was only the tip of the iceberg: in my case political involvement seemed obvious, but it was the rationale behind that involvement which was important – repressive tolerance does not extend to consistent political opposition in the face of the state's need to control and ideologically dominate the civil population. As an individual I was unimportant, but as a representative of a developmental process which incorporated class consciousness and a resolute opposition to state control by the bourgeoisie, my insignificant person posed a threat.

The analyses, and the arguments which embodied them, were accepted by only a few people, but at least they brought politics back into the centre of my discussions with people; that was enough for the moment. My relations with the bulk of the people I came into contact with were very wary: for some of them there was the apparent fact that my credentials as a "revolutionary" had been endorsed by the action of the Home Secretary, while for others there was a lingering fear that I might "freak out" in anguish and despair. Because I wasn't taking my position "personally", retreating into depression and self-doubt, I confused many people; my quiet, relatively good-humoured behaviour, combined with my even more determined consistency in making political points, was not something familiar as the response of a prisoner faced with the likelihood of a lifetime "inside".

My parents, who had rushed down to comfort me as soon as they received the letter telling them of the rejection by the Home Secretary, were incredibly encouraging and supportive all through this period. Our relationship now was firm and mutually loving; we had worked through the doubts, hesitations and misperceptions of my early years, and had arrived at the point we had sadly missed so long ago. My father was still not particularly demonstrative, something which distressed me on occasion, but I was confident of his love. As a child, with the narrow concentration characteristic of that period, I had concentrated only on my own misery, abstracting from my relationships the factors which that misery made dominant. Later, as an adolescent, I recognised that my father's undemonstrative manner masked a real love for me, but my own continuing misery made me too self-centred to reach out to him. Now, as an adult, secure in my own personality and able to recognise the diversity of expressiveness in human behaviour, I could express the love I felt for him and knew that, in his own way, he reciprocated it. With my mother, too, my relationship was warm and comfortable – but it had not taken so much to re-establish this, because my early estrangement from her had been primarily the result of my rejection of my father. Whatever the future held, I was confident that we would never again be separated in the same manner as when I was a child, and this was a tremendous source of comfort.

Richard and Jenny Turner were also visiting me during this period and being both supportive and encouraging; the ban had been lifted, and the first visit occurred around the time of my interview with the Aarvold Committee member. It is difficult to express the dimensions of the relationships I share with these two people: friends of long-standing, comrades with political differences, and a large element of love. Instrumental in my development, both personal and political, they had been unwavering in their assistance, and the fact that they were again in direct contact gave me a tremendous lift.

When, on November 14th, following Udwin's recommendation and the support of the screws, McGrath again granted me internal Parole, it was confirmed that my quiet handling of the Home Secretary's rejection had been the correct tactic. It was also confirmed that I could once again engage in open political discussion; my position had, ironically, been strengthened at the moment of apparently total weakness.

In 1979, with only one and a half Credits required for me to obtain my BA, I chose to read a Foundation Course in Technology, and a higher-level course in Internal Politics and Foreign Policy. I was rounding out the shape of my Degree, still determined that I should be able to function as a political psychologist. Udwin was continuing to give me a 100 per cent subsidy, so I could use what little money I had to extend my own library.

Just before mid-year, Udwin told me that he was moving

me to Essex House, the full-Parole unit; he told me it was preparatory to re-submitting a recommendation for my release. I was still wary of moving to Essex, but he pointed out that he was estabishing a "study dormitory" there and I was an obvious candidate. I moved.

During our few interviews in the early part of 1979, Udwin emphasised to me that the one major problem I faced with the Aarvold Committee was my political commitment; I told him that I was aware of this, but I had no intention of retreating from my position in the face of threats. When, early in the year, I decided, as an option in International Politics, to write a paper on the anti-colonialist war of liberation going on in occupied Ireland, planning to relate the tactic of guerrilla warfare to problems of foreign policy faced by the British state, it had been made clear to me that this type of work, no matter how academic, would reflect badly on me in the eyes of the Home Office. My OU counsellor, Rosemary Thompson, had grown nervous about my deciding to use this option and had referred the matter to Udwin – he had called me into the office, accompanied by Roy Croucher, the "Nursing" Officer, and cautioned me against following my plans. Croucher told me that I would "have the Special Branch up your ass when you get out if you go in for this". I was determined to press ahead, but unfortunately I was frustrated by lack of access to documents I needed; I wrote an extra essay instead. (I was eventually awarded a distinction for my work on this course, and I was even more annoyed that I hadn't been able to pursue my plans on the optional paper.)

After I moved over to Essex House, my family and friends, all of whom were becoming increasingly frustrated by the lack of any visible moves to continue the struggle to get me out of Broadmoor, started to write to Udwin. He was singularly unhelpful, answering that it was a matter of time. I, too, along with my comrades, was anxious to get involved in the second round of the fight; I had hopes of exacting much political capital from the coming confrontation. The one thing which deeply disturbed me was the effect on my parents: my mother was ill, something brought on largely by worry over me and the situation I was in, while my father, too, was suffering.

Sometime in the third quarter of 1979, a couple of months after I had moved to Essex, Udwin told me that he was re-submitting his recommendation; once again he had the unequivocable support of the Psychology Department, and this time the additional factor of another agreement of support from a new group of screws – those in Essex. Alf Lister, the Charge "Nurse" who signed the recommendation, had known me since I arrived in Broadmoor, and now I had a double reason to be grateful to him – early in my imprisonment he had saved my arm from permanent damage by using his skills as a masseur after I had ripped all the muscles during a game of cricket. In the face of disagreements from some of his colleagues, he backed Udwin on the question of my release.

Once again the contest was under way, and I wondered if the Home Office, faced with yet another unanimous medical recommendation, would chose to acquiesce – or give more credence to my claims to being a political prisoner. My analysis of the situation made it clear that I stood no better a chance this time than last, but I knew that things weren't always as clear-cut as analyses – or analysts – would have them.

Tony Black, the Chief Clinical Psychologist for all the institutions known as "Special Hospitals", had told me that his recommendation this time wasn't as superlative as the last; he had been advocating that I be released since 1972. (I had applied for a Mental Health Review Tribunal a couple of years after I was imprisoned, but this had been in the nature of an enquiry into their proceedings rather than a serious attempt to be released. In 1972 I had made a serious application and Tony had supported me, going so far as to make a personal appearance to present his arguments.) Now, as he pointed out, there was a risk that whatever he said would be rejected simply because he had been supporting me for so long – and anyway there was nothing new he could add: I was fit, showed no signs of any mental abnormality whatsoever, and should not be detained in Broadmoor. I told him of my analyses, as I had done in the past, and he commented that while he didn't agree with everything there didn't seem to be any reason to reject them all.

Udwin informed me that I would be interviewed again by an Aarvold Committee member in October, but for some reason this was postponed. Then I heard that the meeting would be in November – and again it was postponed. I was very tired, emotionally drawn, and these postponements were getting on my nerves. Although I didn't expect to be released,

I couldn't help hoping that this time the Home Office would give in – making political capital appealed to me, but the idea of being a small-time martyr didn't. (I don't think I wanted to be a "big-time" martyr either, but there wasn't any question of this!) The strain on my parents was even worse, because they didn't have any political axes to grind.

Concentration on questions of release aside, I was continuing to develop personally. Early in 1979, on Udwin's advice, a young brother had periodically visited me on Somerset Two; he had simply walked up the stairs from Somerset One, which had recently been re-designated as the Adolescent Ward. He was a trifle nervous of me at the beginning, being more impressed by my reputation and the warnings of the screws about me than by the reality of meeting me. His name was Bob Windell, and we were soon to become very close friends – and, later in the year, to become a public scandal. Another youngster, Alan Holland, had moved to Somerset Two at the end of the previous year, and he too was to become a close friend.

Bob and I initially met infrequently, the main purpose of the meetings being coordination of our work; we were both studying Technology with the OU. I drew heavily on his technical and scientific background, while he gained from my experience at gathering and preparing data for essays. Alan, who had begun his OU studies with a Foundation Course in the Arts, was still rather distant with me. Over the year, after I moved to Essex House, Bob and I drew closer; he would often come and join me for walks on the Terrace – I was barred from the Adolescent Ward, as were the rest of the prisoners on Parole.

During the year, when I heard that Allison had been sentenced to life imprisonment for burning down a church or two, Bob was the person I talked with; he knew of my relationship with Allison, knew of the love I had for him, and was quick to offer comfort when he heard the bad news. Allison's imprisonment hit me even worse than Bryan Knight's had; he had been such a tremendous influence on me, the first person I had loved, and the first one to offer me unconditional support. I grieved for him, and felt a raging bitterness at the way that his life had been so badly distorted by social opprobrium and authoritarian intervention resulting from his homosexuality: he was just one more victim of the all-pervasive sexism of British social life. I wept for his wasted life, and was reconfirmed in my determination to struggle for revolution.

At the end of the year, Bob, who was organising the Adolescent Ward's Christmas party, invited me to attend; I was working as deputy editor of the prison magazine, the *Chronicle*, and this was reason enough for me to attend. During the party we danced together, holding each other with affection – and the screws went quietly wild. When we returned to our respective Houses that night, Bob had his Parole card suspended and was confined to the Ward; no action was taken against me, and I did not know what was happening on the Adolescent Ward until the next morning. It was a storm in a tea-cup, for Bob was reinstated on Parole a week later, but I was enraged that he should be subjected to a punishment while I was left alone. I spoke with Udwin, who told me to consider myself cautioned, and heard that no action was taken against me because this type of behaviour was quite "normal" for me. Bob sent a message via another con, saying that I was not to react to this piece of provocation, but I was hard put to keep quiet.

At the end of the week, when I had the opportunity to talk with Bob, I heard that the punishment was the result of the bigotry of one screw whose hysterical reaction against anything resembling human emotions between prisoners was a by-word.

Apart from these personal relationships, I was attempting to inject some semblance of political thought into the prison magazine – a difficult task, made worse by the need to work indirectly. I had become deputy (or assistant) editor shortly after moving to Essex House, and the editor, Barry Stone, agreed to allow me a column of my own each month. I called it "Commentary", and attempted to make it a voice of the prisoners. In addition, I wrote reports on events around the prison, attending as many functions as I could so that I could report, verbatim, how people felt about them. The screws didn't particularly like my work, feeling that I was biased against them – but I reported how people felt, and I was determined to quote as many as possible.

One spin-off from my work with the magazine was a closer involvement with the Female Wing, something which had not been possible in the past. Our sisters were universally treated worse than the males: with male screws active on the Wards, although allegedly subordinate to the female screws, sexism was rampant, sexually motivated assault an occasional pastime, and psychiatrically approved drug abuse frequent. The abuse of the 1959 Mental Health Act – if such a term can be applied to this process, considering that the Act itself is an abuse – was, if anything, more prevalent on the Female Wing.

In my attempts to discuss sexism with some of the sisters, I found myself facing the same problems as on the Male Wing – taking a close look at the social reality of their position was too uncomfortable for many cons because they couldn't afford to contact their own anger at the treatment they received. Political protest just earned you more time, many people told me, and pointed quietly at me to prove the case. I couldn't blame anyone for their quiescence, their fears were well known to me, but that didn't stop me plugging on and trying to reach through to them. Some sisters did struggle against sexism and attempt to combat the inhumanity of the Female Wing – for example Carol Rigby, who despite a physical illness which left her in intense pain much of the time, quietly did everything in her power to serve her sisters. Carol did not work politically, in the sense that I did, but I was impressed by her courage and perseverance.

Another facet of the environment in which I had been struggling and developing was racism, institutional and individual. Like sexism, racism was part of the cultural norm which, in the name of rehabilitation, many screws attempted to foster and/or maintain. Several screws were long-standing members of the National Front, and their racist attacks are directed as much against black screws as they are against black cons. Men like Grantley Thomas, George Otu and Andy Roberts, all black, are often used as examples of the way England is being taken over – and some screws deliberately provoke racist cons into verbally or physically abusing them. A sexist and racist consciousness is as much part of the cultural heritage of prisoners as it is of the general population, and this makes it extremely difficult to combat: on several occasions I was threatened with physical assault because I criticised anti-black, anti-Irish or anti-Jewish sentiments. The threats came most frequently from cons, although many of them, I think, were inspired by racist screws. I tried to show the manner in which one could be racist without really meaning to be, quoting the way that I used to refer to Udwin as "that South African Jewish bastard", arguing that both sexism and racism were in the structure of consciousness itself, being manifest in language as well as relationships, but I don't think I was very successful. But even if I didn't manage to reach through to many other people on these issues, I would at least continue to work on myself.

Just before Christmas, 1979, I heard that I had successfully completed the year's studies and was therefore graduated as a Bachelor of Arts with the Open University. My mother wasn't available to hear the news directly, having gone to visit my sister in New Zealand – partly because she hadn't seen her for some time, partly as a respite from the pressures she was under consequent upon my situation – but my father sent the message through to her; he came to visit me immediately. The degree meant little to me, except in terms of a stepping stone to the PhD research on image management which I wanted to do, but for my parents it was a happy occasion; they had long wanted to see me obtain academic qualifications at this level. I was pleased that I had been able to give them something, even if it couldn't be myself!

Several weeks after hearing about the BA, on January 30th, 1980, I had another meeting with an Aarvold representative. The interview followed the same pattern as previously, but this time, when asked if I had a message for the Committee, I answered: "I'm tired, very tired, just tell them that." Having been asked about my continuing political commitment, I didn't really think that there was much chance of the Committee's advice to the Home Secretary being any different from the last time. Seven weeks later, on March 20th, after a very wearying wait, I heard that my assessment was correct – the recommendation had again been rejected.

Udwin's demeanour when he told me the news was very sombre; more so than seemed warranted, I thought. After all, the rejection wasn't completely unexpected. Then I heard of an additional problem – McGrath, suspicious of my coolness in the face of such adversity, had decided that I should be withdrawn from circulation for a while. My Parole card was to be suspended, and I was to be moved back to Somerset Two until his, and a section of the screws', fears were allayed; I was permitted no choice in the matter. On one point, however, I dug in my heels – I refused to be escorted, and I demanded that I be allowed to complete the move in my own time, subject only to the time limit of that day's Parole check, six o'clock. Udwin agreed to my conditions, and also specified, on my prompting, that I would be in Somerset House for no longer than one week provided that I took no untoward action.

Leaving the office, I went upstairs to the dormitory, knowing that my friends, especially Bob and Alan, were waiting to hear what had happened. I caught sight of Ron as I went up, and called him to one side to inform him; he was, predictably, enraged, but immediately offered what comfort and encouragement he could. I told him that he had to stay cool, and that I would appreciate assistance in moving some stuff over to Somerset. Then I went into the dormitory to speak with Bob and Alan – a task even harder than explaining to Ron.

My friends were bitterly disappointed, but they too offered what comfort and encouragement they could. They had believed that I would get out on this attempt, not yet being convinced of the soundness of my analyses; this rejection completed my arguments, and they never again questioned the logic of what I was saying. I left them for a while, going off for a walk on the Terrace by myself: partly I wanted to be alone for a while, and partly I wanted to show the screws that I was still determined not to break under the strain. Then I returned to the dormitory and, with the assistance of Bob, Alan, Ron and a young brother named Paul, I moved myself over to Somerset.

Barry Carlton, the Charge "Nurse" on Somerset Two at the time I arrived, had known me for several years; we got on reasonably well, with him always cracking jokes about fixing me up with a "normal" love-life. I kept telling him that he was sexist, but it did no good – and, in fact, he was actually more sensitive than his manner usually indicated. He let me arrange my belongings in the cell, then he called me into the office and told me that he had arranged a game of bridge for the evening; I was to be his partner. There was nothing else for me to do after Parole ended, so I agreed to the game – and I was rather pleased that he had shown some understanding of the position I was in, going out of his way to keep me occupied during that first evening. (I didn't actually need this type of protective attitude, but I wasn't going to reject it; anything which encouraged screws to express human feelings was good as far

169

as I was concerned. And this went double in the case of those with a "macho" reputation such as Barry.)

At half past eight we finished the game of bridge, and I went off to my cell; at nine o'clock we were locked away for the night. I had made arrangements to have my light left on as long as I wanted it – there were some difficult letters I had to write. For several hours I thought about what I could write, and to whom; I decided that I would content myself with three letters for the moment. To my parents, I wrote a brief note outlining what I had heard and explaining that I had been moved to Somerset Two as a result of the institutional paranoia manifested by McGrath and some of the screws; I asked them not to worry too much about me – a rather stupid request, actually, as their concern would not disappear simply because I asked it to – and assured them that I would not be giving up. The second letter, to Richard and Jenny, was even briefer; I gave the facts, and commented that the struggle would continue. The final letter, to Jane Grundy, a sister I had met only a couple of months before, gave information about my rejection by the Home Secretary and added that I would not now be able to visit her in New York as I had hoped. After completing these few notes, I lay down and tried to sleep; I made it early in the morning.

As it turned out, the letter to my parents wasn't needed; they arrived, coincidentally, to visit me two days later. When I was informed that they were at the Main Gate, I requested that they be brought over to Somerset House, where I was to have the visit, without comment; I didn't want them hearing the news from anyone else. One of the screws who brought them over disregarded his instructions and, I have no doubt, took great pleasure in imparting the information about my latest response from the Home Secretary. The visit was fraught, with all of us trying to give comfort to everyone else – but we survived it, and I said goodbye at four o'clock confident that our unity would continue.

Sometime during the visit my father telephoned Dr Udwin in order to get more information about my prospects. Prompted by my comments concerning the political dimensions of the Home Secretary's decision, my father asked for clarification on the question – and was told that my political commitment "certainly hadn't helped" my recommendation, though Udwin would not elaborate (22nd March, 1980). I think that this was the last straw for my parents; they still did not totally accept the idea that I was a political prisoner, but their confidence in "justice" prevailing was shattered, and they no longer questioned my political analyses.

On Tuesday, 25th March, Udwin came over to Somerset Two to speak with me; he made it clear that he could do no more for me, my prospects for release were out of his hands. I reminded him of his promise to provide me with a signed statement as to his impotence, given after I had received the first rejection – but he reneged, saying that it wasn't possible. We talked for half an hour or so, with him telling me that he would do everything he could for me inside Broadmoor, and me reiterating that my interest was in getting out. During the course of our discussion, he mooted the idea of appealing to a Mental Health Review Tribunal; neither of us was foolish enough to believe in their impartiality, but such an appeal would enable me to bring in additional medical comments to support my release. I would also be able to seek the assistance of legal advisers – and this could strengthen my hand in any future negotiations. We ended the discussions with Udwin assuring me that I would be returning to Essex House the next day, six days after I had been moved to Somerset; I would be back on Parole again.

Returning to Essex House, I quickly re-established the rhythm of my studies – Cognitive Psychology, and Research Methods in Social Science and Educational Policy, both needed to translate my BA into an Honours Degree. Within a week I had also sent out more letters describing the recent development and assuring people that the struggle would continue: regardless of what happened to me, the oppor-tunities for disseminating information on the political control of psychiatry and imprisonment made it imperative that a drive toward confrontation continue.

The support network I had forged within Broadmoor was still operative, with Bob, Alan and Ron continuing to offer me both comfort and support: this mutual support group was probably one of the most successful endeavours of the gener-ative work of the original RAC(B), although in its present form it went further than we had initially envisaged. Apart from the people I've mentioned there were others involved, with several groups overlapping; everyone gained, both

171

personally and politically. During the period of maximum tension for me, I doubt that I could have survived if these friends hadn't given so much of their time and energy in an effort to ensure that I was not totally isolated – and my continued involvement in the personal problems of other people enabled me to resist the temptation to become completely self-centred and self-sufficient.

My relations with Bob were sometimes strained during this period, as I sought to prevent myself taking out on him the anguish I was experiencing over the pressures my position imposed on other people; his ability to express emotion, and yet not be enveloped by it, was a source of constant pleasure to me. Along with Alan Holland, he demonstrated a maturity in personal relationships which should have gained more recognition from the Broadmoor authorities – but such relationships were (and are) frowned on by the authorities, so no credit was forthcoming. Although these two young brothers continued to defer to me on many personal and political issues, I knew that my position as "tutor" would soon be redundant; they were fast becoming my equals in competence.

With Ronald Greedy, the oldest and closest of my friends in Broadmoor, notwithstanding the ambivalence of some of his political remarks, Bob and Alan constituted the team of advisors I called upon when I examined the question of an application to the Mental Health Review Tribunal. We discussed the strategy of such an application in terms of its ability to generate political benefits, considering it as the last legal route to forcing the Home Secretary's hand. I also consulted Nigel Price, a fellow OU student (and recent graduate) and dormitory member, whose views I respected – regardless of our widely divergent political opinions! There was unanimous agreement that the application should go ahead, although differences of tactics emerged; only Ronald completely agreed with my desire to force a political confrontation by making my main argument rest on the Home Secretary's political involvement in allegedly medical questions. I submitted the application, telling my friends that I had noted all their arguments and would bear them in mind as the proceedings developed.

Richard and Jenny Turner, supportive as ever, wholeheartedly agreed with my plans to go to the Tribunal. They volunteered to come as witnesses, offering their experience of our long-standing relationship as evidence of their interest. In addition, they discussed the case with some friends, John and Lesley Punter, who volunteered to offer me a home in Reading if this would assist my release. Jenny also took on the position of coordinator and arranged to get me a lawyer – and then helped me to enlist Liz Goldthorpe, a London solicitor, when the first lawyer proved unacceptable. Judith Grundy, Jane's sister and another of Jenny's friends, brought her own experience in the London newspaper industry into the struggle; she mentioned the case to a journalist on the *Times*, and I gave an interview based on the autobiographical "Review" I had prepared for anyone interested. This support network outside Broadmoor, which had other members as well as those I've mentioned, was in addition to the ones operating within the prison; along with my parents, all these people went to great lengths to ensure my survival as a human being rather than just another preoccupied prisoner fighting for release.

In June, I think, Jane Grundy came over from America for a holiday in England. Although spending a couple of days with her parents, her base was in Reading – from where she came, frequently, to visit me. Jane is a professional photographer, concentrating on social issues, with extensive academic administrative experience and a deep interest in community politics; I learned to engage a sense of micro-politics with my more macro approach as a direct result of our relationship, and gained tremendously thereby. There was a strong emotional rapport between us, and we grew closer over the week or so of the visits: at the end of the period we decided to become engaged, an expression of the love which had developed between us. Although the formal engagement was relatively soon disavowed, its sundering was accompanied by as much love and humour as its avowal; the closeness of our relationship continued unabated, and our correspondence remained as full of the mutually growthful interchanges as previously.

By the beginning of August, although my fatigue had reached the stage where I was never free from a bone-deep sense of weariness, I was spending almost all of my waking hours either studying, corresponding on the politics of imprisonment, or preparing for the forthcoming Tribunal. Liz Goldthorpe, although preparing for Law Society examinations, was working hard on my case, and Sarah Forster, the barrister brought in to assist with the actual Tribunal appearance, was also heavily engaged. Our legal discussions had reached the point where Sarah was maintaining that I must refrain from political infighting with Tribunal members, and reluctantly I had agreed – providing the Tribunal didn't initiate the question. Liz had arranged for an independent psychiatrist, whose name I have forgotten, to come and interview me; we knew his report was going to be important, for it was on the psychiatric evidence that my arguments rested. I was not overly concerned, secure in a personal confidence that any independent psychiatric opinion must find me mentally competent.

The interview with the doctor Liz had fixed up lasted about an hour and a half, I think; it was very interesting, with the usual questions about my life and current attitudes. At the end, I was asked if there was anything I wanted to know, and I stated that my key concern was whether or not Udwin's view was going to be supported. The doctor told me that he was convinced that Udwin was correct – there was nothing the matter with me, and I should be released without delay. Once again I had been declared mentally competent, this time by an independent examiner at least equal to Udwin's stature in the profession; we were ready to face the Tribunal. Our last concern was whether or not the doctor's report would be ready in time for the hearing – it was, just.

The Tribunal was convened early in September, and we quickly heard that it would require two sessions because of the number of witnesses I had called. Udwin had suggested that I rely on medical evidence plus the assistance of my lawyers, but everyone I was working with had thought that it would be better to show the strength of my support by bringing in witnesses. My parents were present, as were Richard and Jenny, Gilbert Adair and Pat Farrell, Judith and Simon Grundy, my two lawyers, and me. In addition, we had letters of continuing support from John and Lesley Punter, and Jane; we also had the report of the independent psychiatrist. Liz and Sarah had spent several hours the previous night ensuring that all the evidence was in order, and some of it had been photocopied in its raw state so that it would be available.

After Sarah had made an opening statement, I was called into the room and the questioning began. Things began inauspiciously, with a question as to why I was proceeding after two rejections from the Home Secretary. I answered that there were two possible approaches to my release: either people who had committed murder should be hanged or put to death in some other manner, or the possibility of rehabilitation should be kept open – if the former view prevailed with the Tribunal, then we should end the farce immediately; if the latter view was dominant, then all the evidence pointed to my fitness for release, and the Tribunal should decide accordingly. I went on to argue that for three years my Responsible Medical Officer, Dr Udwin, two sets of staff, and the Psychology Department, had consistently maintained that I should be released: these people were employed by the DHSS and supported by the Home Office; they did not share my political views or commitment, although they were very much aware of them, and they did not receive any favour or payment from me, my family, or my friends. In addition, they were all aware of my personal history, and they had extensive experience of interacting with me in an adversorial manner. Concluding my argument, I pointed out that for many years, in accordance with legal requirements, the people who now so consistently and unanimously supported me had submitted unquestioned reports which advocated my continued detention – if their opinions had been acceptable over the years, then surely they should be acceptable now.

Although the logic of my argument should have sufficed, I had to endure many more questions. The Tribunal concentrated on my political development and continuing commitment – Sarah had guessed wrong when she thought that they wouldn't touch on this subject! I stated my position quite calmly, refusing to be drawn into arguments: the lay member of the Tribunal asked if I was aware of the fact that the Home Secretary had the legal right to impose restrictions on my activities after release, and did I think that I could abide by them if they conflicted with my political commitment? I answered that I was aware of the Home Secretary's powers, and that I had already agreed to abide by the restrictions Udwin would impose – further than that I wasn't going, but he seemed satisfied.

The last batch of questions came from the Tribunal's psychiatrist who wanted to know more about Billy Doyle's death. I told him that I maintained my innocence of the actual killing, but accepted some moral responsibility because I had acted as lookout – although unaware of, or disbelieving, what was going on. He seemed to be unimpressed by my comments.

After I left the room my parents were called in. The questioning they endured surprised Liz and Sarah, and enraged my father. In addition to being quizzed about my politics, my father found himself being asked by the chairperson about his feelings concerning my intellect! The chairperson asked if my "obviously high intelligence" didn't make my father fearful of me; he answered that it made him proud, not fearful, and that he found nothing surprising in my knowing more than him in subjects which I had conscientiously studied for many years. The chairperson said that he found my intelligence frightening, even if my father didn't. When asked about their views concerning any possible political activity I might engage in once I was released, both my parents answered that this was a question only I could answer – but it was no one else's business as England was still supposed to be a "free" country.

Richard and Jenny were next, and they too had a couple of questions asked about my politics. Most of their questions, though, were about the relationship we had had over the years. After a very short time they came out. Judith and Simon went in, and Simon answered the first question about politics by saying that this had nothing to do with the point at issue – they were only in the room for a couple of minutes. Finally Sarah came out, accompanied by the Tribunal's secretary, and said that Gilbert and Pat wouldn't be required; the Tribunal felt that they had nothing more to offer. (This decision had the effect of denying Gilbert and Pat any compensation for coming to the meeting – a rather petty way of hitting out at the number of witnesses I had called – but I managed to pay their expenses out of the emergency fund I had built from my pay over the year.)

While the questions concerning expenses were being dealt with, Sarah told me that the Tribunal would convene again on October 16th, at which time the "professional" evidence would be dealt with. It was a six-week wait, and after I had said goodbye to everyone and returned to Essex I wondered how everyone would take it. I was still worried about the way that my mother's health was suffering.

The wait was full of tension for me; I wanted to get the process out of the way. I knew that there would be little pressure on me once the decision was taken: if I was rejected again, I had nowhere to go, and that meant that I could concentrate on other alternatives. Once again my friends in Broadmoor surrounded me with their love and support; Bob, Alan and Ron even started buying me tobacco so that I could build up my emergency reserve again.

In October, when the Tribunal met for the second time, Udwin, Tony Black and Alf Lister were called to give evidence. All three of them maintained the consistency of their recommendations; the evidence was still overwhelmingly in my favour. Liz and Sarah told me that they could do no more for the moment, it was now a question of waiting. As a final comment, Sarah told me that in her long experience of dealing with Tribunals, she had never handled a case in which the defendant had so much positive support. I wondered to what extent that would matter – the Home Secretary hadn't let the evidence influence him in the past, so why should he do so now? The evidence of the Aarvold Committee, that non-statutory body which gave personal advice, could still influence the Tribunal, and even if it didn't the Home Secretary could still favour it above all else.

After the Tribunal I concentrated on my studies for a few weeks; the exams were particularly difficult this year, pre-occupied as I was with other matters. Just before Christmas I heard that I had successfully completed the work and would be receiving confirmation of an Upper-Second Class Honours Degree as a result. The way was now clear for me to apply myself to the research on image management which I intended to offer as the basis of a PhD. My parents were, once again, pleased to hear of my academic success; I was just happy to have completed the work while handling the stress of the Tribunal.

Once again I spent Christmas and New Year in Broadmoor; the third such "holiday" since what was supposed to be my last one. In 1979 I had, just before Christmas, broken my nose during a football match, and in consequence had spent the entire period of the "holiday" at the card table in Essex. I decided to repeat the process this year, spending the days going around the other Houses to spend time with friends, and the evenings playing cards. Between December 24th and January 1st I spent several hours, with Alan and Bob, talking with a youngster who had just moved onto Somerset Three from the Adolescent Ward; a brother named Alan Wilbourne. This new addition to our support network was known to the other two because of their mutual experience of the Adolescent Ward, but I knew of him only by reputation. Ronald, too, occasionally joined us for the meetings on Somerset Two but, as with most other times of the year, his main interest was going to Gloucester House to spend time with Chris Reid – the young brother who with Ron and me had formed the prototype of the support network now in operation. The special relationship between Ron and Chris was something we all respected, and most of the time only Alan Holland joined them in Gloucester.

On New Year's Eve, Bob, Alan, Ron and myself congregated on the Terrace to discuss the forthcoming year; once again I was in a minority of one with my suspicion that I wouldn't be released. Of the others, Ron, who had returned to Broadmoor ten years or so before with a new conviction for murder, had little immediate prospect of release and was primarily concerned with the possibility of Chris Reid's being moved to a relatively new "Special Hospital" called Park Lane – located just outside Liverpool. Bob's main interest for the moment was getting moved to Essex – anything to get off the claustrophobic Adolescent Ward – while Alan was seeking to negotiate some sort of "deal" with Udwin. Although each of them had problems "doing time", they were still intimately involved in my struggle – thus, once more, giving the lie to the notion that prisoners are unable to empathise with other people. Although I sometimes had bitter arguments over a variety of topics with them, I loved these brothers; they were a constant source of comfort, support, and sheer bloody-minded encouragement in the face of what seemed a ceaseless flow of establishment-imposed anguish. I knew that, whatever happened to me, there were other people in Broadmoor to continue the struggle I had been waging for so long – and they would probably do things better than I had because they had grown together rather than in isolation. Regardless of the environment, I was proud to be seeing the New Year in with this group.

The early part of 1981, with what I considered the final card – the Tribunal – having been played, was relatively tension-free for me; I was still constantly tired, but I felt able to concentrate on building up my data files and preparing an abstract to submit for PhD funding. My preoccupation was still relations of power, and I had chosen to examine problems of image formation and management in a penal environment as the research vehicle of that preoccupation.

I started from the position that "deviance", of whatever variety, was defined according to a set of social norms, and from this derived two distinct sets of power relations – that between the person doing the labelling and the person being labelled, and that between the class originating the social norms and that class upon whom they were imposed. My research was intended to concentrate on the specific consequences of these two sets of relations for a group of people labelled as "deviant", with the focus being on the self-manipulation of personal and interpersonal image in terms of a coherent sense of identity. Among other things, I had hopes of developing the Marxist concept of "false consciousness" and using it as a means of elaborating a comprehensive grasp of the dynamics of bourgeois ideological hegemony. It was a large undertaking, and I knew that under my existing circumstances I had little hope of doing anything other than sketching out the line of enquiry I would take with post-doctoral work.

Only three people in Broadmoor – Bob, Alan and Ron – knew the full extent of my interests, but several people knew the outline of the work I intended for my doctorate. Unfortunately, no one could help me with in-depth discussion; the specialised nature of the work made my academic isolation even more profound. Alan Holland did provide me with some very interesting material which could be used in my doctorate, and that deserves mention, if only as a further indication of the environment in which I had developed.

Alan was involved in a psychological assessment programme which was allegedly aimed at modifying the link between male sexuality and violence. The initial programme consisted to exposure to several films, some of them explicitly sexual and/or violent in nature; the concern was states of arousal, measured by self-report and electronically monitored penile response. I was interested in the way that subsequent behavioural modication techniques, utilised when a high positive correlation was found between sexuality and violence, were based on cultural norms which emphasised the prevailing sexist biases. Alan and I had several interesting discussions about this contradiction, and I especially noted the way that he understood that sexism was merely covert violence – and also noted, with pleasure as well as academic interest, his conclusion that these programmes emphasised mechanical sexuality at the expense of human emotional expressiveness. It was fascinating to see that Alan's image framework was sufficiently dynamic to envisage a relational format far superior to that which currently exists.

Institutionalised sexism wasn't only manifest in the psychological assessment techniques being imposed on the prisoners, or in the running of the Female Wing; its most profound existence and effect was in the consciousness which people brought to their relationships. In March, I was asked to go to another House to speak with someone who hadn't been long in Broadmoor – he had heard quite a lot about me, and felt that I might be interested in a story he had to tell. For about an hour I sat and listened as, haltingly, he told me of how he had been raped by several men, and how he had been unable to obtain help, comfort, or protection. He was a homosexual, but he had not solicited the men or behaved in any manner which could have provoked the assault – except in that he was young, small, and beautiful. I had heard several tales of homosexual rape, and the most interesting thing about all of them was the fact that the perpetrators were "normal" men; the viciousness of the initial assault was usually compounded by a savage beating as a farewell gesture. On this occasion the unusual detail was the social awareness of the victim – and the insights he gave me into some of the difficulties men face in relation to sexism. There was a rape crisis centre in the town where the rape occurred, but the man felt unable to telephone for help or advice; he told me that once, fearful of walking about in the dark because of the way that other men called out to him, he had gone to the centre to seek advice – and been told, quite politely, that men were not welcome. The homosexual "hot line" informed him that he should arrange to be accompanied at night. These two responses, he felt, showed a lot about the way that sexism was demonstrated even by groups and individuals who claimed to be fighting it. Just before I left him, he told me about an incident on the Admission Ward when he had complained to a "doctor" about some remarks passed by several screws – he was called into the office about half an hour later and, after being cautioned about making any more complaints, he faced a screw who exposed himself and said: "You're going to get this up your ass if you don't watch out." I thanked him for telling me about his experiences, and assured him that, although I'd use the information in my work, I would not identify him.

Several months had passed since the Tribunal sat, and the waiting was becoming increasingly oppressive. My friends were having great difficulty in maintaining their optimism, and my frequent bouts of irritability were obviously wearing on their nerves. I spent more and more time discussing politics with them, often using it as something of a shield against the emotional stretching which the waiting was imposing on me: I consistently maintained that I didn't expect the Home Secretary to shift from his position of rejection, emphasising that it was a political question and not a personal one, but I could never completely escape from the emotional involvement, the hope, which was based on the fact that I needed to be free if my personal and political development were to be integrated into the activism of which I spoke and dreamed.

My development had been in the manner of "two steps forward, one step back", with plateaus marked by painful and self-critical consolidation. Although the political value of my actions had made an impact on the lives of all the cons, I had never managed to directly contact more than five per cent or so of Broadmoor's total population of about eight hundred – and too often the results of my work had been laid at the door of Alan Reeve, prisoner, rather than being seen as the result of political forces. As I looked back over the previous twelve years I saw many errors and few accomplishments, but I knew that I had helped to change the face of Broadmoor and participated in the political growth of several people.

I spoke with many people, seeking to gain a broader perspective on my work over the years, and, while appalled to learn that a few thought of me as a cross between George Jackson and Antonio Gramsci, was satisfied to hear that many more simply considered me a prison rebel with a political theory. I knew that the extremely small number of prisoners who did think in political terms would be able to build on this beginning: I had become a relatively big frog in a very small pond rather than a red fish in "the sea of the people", but there were highly effective tadpoles behind me who would work more successfully because I had stood out.

On May 4th, a Bank Holiday Monday, Jenny came to visit me. On her last visit she had mentioned the possibility of bringing someone else in with her, a young woman named

Patricia Ford, but I wasn't sure if this would happen because Pat always seemed to have something else to do on the relevant day: this time she didn't, and we finally met. About eight years previously, when I was writing to a woman named Kate, Pat had read my letters and had wanted to visit me, but something always intervened; we had heard of each other, but had never spoken.

The visit is memorable primarily because although Jenny had told me that I was finally going to meet someone who could talk as rapidly as I did, Pat remained silent for most of the time. When, at twelve o'clock, the visit ended and I walked back to Essex, I remember thinking to myself that once again I had made someone nervous with my tendency to hammer political points. The next day I found out that I was wrong; Pat arrived at ten o'clock to visit me again. This was the beginning of a personal and political relationship which, despite errors, anguish and anger, has survived and matured, forming a partnership which strengthens both of us.

During May, Pat visited me almost every day – much to the annoyance of several screws. On one occasion, which gave Pat the opportunity to note some of the more sexist manifestations of the people who claimed to be society's "guardians", an unidentifiable screw called out from one of the windows in Dorset House: "Hey, Reeve! Get your hands off her, you dirty bastard!" I jumped off the bench on which we were sitting and started to run across the Terrace toward the House – and Pat caught hold of my arm and told me to sit down again. Fuming, I complied, and for several minutes we talked about the way that the screws could so easily get under a prisoner's skin. After the visit, I spoke with Alf Lister, telling him of what had occurred; I don't know what he did, but the incident wasn't repeated. However, I eventually received a note telling me that my allowance of weekday visits was finished – I could only be visited on the weekend for the rest of the month. A petty revenge, I felt. I complained to Udwin, pointing out that as I was simply marking time, waiting for what was obviously going to be a favourable answer from the Home Office (!), I should be allowed as many visits as my friends were prepared to make – he gave me an extra four for the month.

In June, concerned that Pat's concentration on me was causing problems for her relationships with Jenny and other friends, I wrote to Jenny and said that I hoped it wasn't the case; Jenny wrote back and assured me that I was misperceiving. Quite possibly, my worry was a generalisation of a problem I saw developing between Bob and me – he was getting the brunt of my nervousness, while Pat and other visitors were seeing me at my "best". It wasn't just Bob, either, for several cons approached me and said that they had noticed my preoccupation and irritability. The waiting was really beginning to have an effect on me; I didn't expect to be released, but the waiting, the not knowing, these were difficult to take. I wanted this three years of indecision over with – I needed to know just where I stood, just what the options were for my future.

Through friends, I had managed to get a "pipeline" into the Home Office, and I heard that the decision had been taken on my release; the continued delay was because "certain technical matters (had) been referred to the DHSS". After consulting several people, I resolved to send telegrams to Margaret Thatcher, Elizabeth Windsor and William Whitelaw; none of us expected dramatic results, but the possibility of gaining some political benefits from the move seemed to make it worthwhile. The telegrams were sent in Jenny's name, and we received two responses: from Buckingham Palace came a note addressed to Mr Turner – an interesting insight into the expectations and thoroughness of royal secretaries – which said that the "telex" had been passed on to the Home Office, and from Whitelaw's Department came a polite note of acknowledgement. Thatcher was obviously too busy contemplating human rights in the Soviet Union and Afghanistan to worry about such things in Britain; her telegram disappeared into oblivion.

Sometime toward the end of June, on a Saturday morning, Jenny and Pat came in to see me – and I found out that, once again, my release had been blocked by the Home Secretary. Jenny had received a letter that morning from the Home Office, and it told her that Alan Reeve was not to be conditionally discharged but, instead, offered a transfer to a relatively new, more secure "Special Hospital" – Park Lane. Although we were all upset, I felt a tremendous sense of relief; there were no hiding places left, no excuses, no doubts, for now I knew with certainty that I could expect nothing other than death or permanent incarceration from the British state. The Home Secretary had removed any possibility of my weakening and seeking to effect a compromise with my class enemies.

Discussing the matter with Pat and Jenny, I decided to keep the news to myself; I would wait and see how long it would take Udwin to tell me, and if there was any attempt to place me in solitary because of the result I would be able to answer that I had known for X amount of time and had handled the problem without cracking up. I told a number of my friends in the prison, but not my parents; I wanted to wait until they visited me, not feeling able to break the news by letter. Udwin informed me about ten days later, telling me that he had only just that day received the details himself.

At the same time as I heard the news from Udwin, I received a letter from an Under-Secretary of State at the Home Office; he was almost apologetic, and strongly advised me to accept the new deal that my Responsible Medical Officer would be offering. The details were quite simple: without any guarantees, I was to accept voluntary transfer to Park Lane, and my case would be re-examined in a couple of years. I pointed out that such a move would isolate me from my family, my friends, the entire support network which had grown up over the years – and was answered with the statement that perhaps the existence of this group was part of the problem. When I pushed him, Udwin told me that the senior civil servants supported my release; they had overturned the Aarvold Committee's recommendation and substituted their own which said that I should go – but they would not give me any guarantee regardless of this "support". I said that I wouldn't move, but that I would be prepared to talk further about the matter.

Early in June I heard that Dr McCulloch, Physician Superintendent of Park Lane, was coming to Broadmoor and would personally discuss with me the opportunities available in that prison; I looked forward to the interview. In the meantime, I faced the prospect of explaining what had happened to my parents. I found that they already knew, having received a letter informing them of the decision at the same time as Jenny. It was a very difficult visit, especially when I explained what Udwin had told me about the civil servants; my parents, understandably, thought that with this additional support there should have been no question about releasing me. I told them that I had rejected the offered move to Park Lane but that

I would be discussing the matter with McCulloch in a few days.

The interview was fascinating; McCulloch is a very smooth operator. We talked about my life for a short while, and then concentrated on recent developments. I heard that my politics would not be used against me in Park Lane, and that I would be encouraged to continue my research interests – even getting access to McCulloch's computer so that I could run auxiliary statistical checks! In addition I would be given the opportunity to forge links with the other prisoners, and no disciplinary action would be taken against me if I formed political discussion groups or even set up a union! There was one drawback – McCulloch couldn't guarantee that, even if he found after a two-year check period that he agreed with the people who had been so consistently recommending my release, the Home Secretary would concur. The reality of the deal being offered was that I should move to Park Lane and just continue serving a life sentence. I told him that I would move, that I had been impressed by the details of what was on offer to me in this new prison, but that I had one more thing to do in Broadmoor first.

On August 9th, 1981, I did the "one more thing that I had to do in Broadmoor" – I escaped.

The period of my life covered by Part Three began with a sense of almost total isolation and despair – it ended with an act that screamed defiance at the entire structure of the state. My escape was a personal act, but it carried a political statement with it; I was re-entering the world as a fugitive not from "justice" but rather from political persecution. In 1967, in a cell, in darkness, alone and fearful, I began a process of personal and political growth which, although it caused me much grief and often estranged me from my brothers and sisters in the prison, enabled me to affirm my own humanity and to touch the humanity of others. In 1981, with a sister, a lover, a comrade, I chose to insert myself into the world; together, we repudiated the structures which separated us as people and as comrades, making a final and unequivocable commitment to the revolutionary struggle of our class.

As I have recalled this period of my life and recounted it here, I have increasingly noted the way that this life is only comprehensible in terms of the relationships and environments in which it has been embedded. As this is an autobiography, I have been the nexus of the relationships, thus assuming a disproportionate importance, and this has undoubtedly been complicated further by errors over chronology and personalities – but this is the life that I have remembered, the one that I have lived. It would be easy to write much more, telling in more detail, for example, of the way that my relationship with David altered over the years, or paying more attention to the way that my parents and I drew closer, but I experienced these things in the manner in which I have written of them: I was living an embattled life, and most of my energies were committed to simply surviving the environmental tensions which were both the cause and the consequence of those battles. Equally, the compression of time, the truncated memories, these are products of the time and manner in which I lived: I was no self-sacrificing or self-effacing martyr, totally unconcerned with egocentric desires, but I did try to subordinate personal interests to wider political consciousness.

The periods of radical reassessment and consolidation, initiated in conditions which give the lie to Britain's claim to enlightenment, civilisation, or humanity, have been the salient points in my life since 1967. I have deliberately chosen not to make these pages a catalogue of inhumanity, naming names and locating places, describing with the vivid urgency of my continuing pain the acts of brutality, degradation, and psychological terrorism which are the mundane facts of life in British penal institutions, psychiatric or otherwise – and this was primarily because I felt that the subjective recounting of one life, in such a way that it was seen to be the story of many lives, would be of more benefit than such a catalogue.

When I chose, with my comrade Patricia Ford, to free myself from Broadmoor, I knew that being a fugitive was no pleasant activity, no state of comfort or perpetual happiness. But the decision was not completely personal, for I made it as a revolutionary, knowing and being committed to the truth that the duty of the revolutionary is to make the revolution. As a slogan issued by the Irish anti-colonialist freedom fighters so aptly states: "Until all are free, we are all imprisoned." My freedom, like this book, has value only in its ability to emphasise the human reality of this slogan.

The struggle continues.

Afterword: the end of the beginning – escape, problems, political testament

> "The struggle by the oppressed for freedom threatens not only the oppressor, but also their own oppressed comrades who are fearful of still greater repression."
>
> Paulo Freire, *Pedagogy of the Oppressed*
> (Quoted by D'Arcy,
> *Tell Them Everything*, 1981)

> "We must not become complacent over any success. We should check our complacency and constantly criticise our shortcomings, just as we should wash our faces or sweep the floor every day and remove the dirt and keep them clean."
>
> Mao Zedong, "Get Organised!"

When, on August 9th, 1981, I escaped from Broadmoor, I did so in a manner, and under conditions, which added significantly to the consequent problems of being a fugitive. Contrary to the fanciful constructions of the newspaper industry, the route I took involved free-climbing over two walls and a fence; the hook and flex I had started out with was not particularly useful, mainly because I hadn't realised how difficult it was to climb up such thin material. One other disturbing factor was the fact that I fell over twenty feet before I managed to successfully complete the escape; I went over the walls with a broken bone in my back and another in one of my feet. To complete the catalogue of problems, I have to mention the barbed wire on which I ripped my hands to shreds – it didn't stop me, but it certainly slowed me down! When I met Pat, I collapsed, exhausted and almost fainting with pain.

Apart from these details, the circumstances of my escape must remain unexplained; I cannot give details which could be used by state agencies of repression to justify attacks on other people. In the first three days I almost died twice, and I was paralysed from the waist down for several hours; the strain on my heart was almost too much, and it took prompt action from Pat to start me breathing again. It was several months before I began to mend – an as yet uncompleted process.

I remember few details of the opening days of my freedom, being preoccupied with a simple desire to survive the pain and an all too frequent tendency to collapse. When I did begin to notice my surroundings and take an interest in the world, I had great difficulty in managing my emotions – the sight of children playing, their voices raised in pleasure, the animals walking about so freely, the streets, hills, trees, the gentle courtesy of those old people whom I engaged in conversation, all these things brought tears crowding into my eyes and, on occasion, overflowing down my cheeks. I had no problems handling money, choosing and buying things, but I was some-times overwhelmed with the colours, the textures, and sheer diversity of items available. These things weren't of short duration; it was an emotional experience which occurred over several weeks and, to a lesser extent, continues to occur.

My preoccupation with pain, allied eventually to the emotional experiences I have outlined, added greatly to the burden Pat was carrying: I had forgotten that all this was new to her, too, because she had never before been a fugitive. Initially, the arguments/disagreements we had were those experienced by any two people who suddenly begin to live together, but gradually the niggling problems of our par-ticular situation began to intervene and damage both of us. We found that the specifics of maintaining a "front" insidiously pushed us into adopting the sexist separation of roles which neither of us accepted as legitimate; the pressures of seeming "normal", of refraining from the overt display of our political commitments, of not causing controversy or hostility, all these forced us inward into a claustrophobic relationship rooted in an enforced monogamy. Our position as fugitives isolated us both socially and politically; we nearly split up as a result, driven apart by factors which we had not anticipated.

In November, prompted by a discussion about the writing of this book, when we noted the preoccupation and concentration which would be required of me, we began to examine the distortions imposed on our relationship. For two months we discussed the problems, intermittently and with much anguish; nothing was resolved, and we faced the possibility that we would be forced apart by circumstances. Entering 1982, we faced a new problem, but one which was intimately related to the discussions and arguments we had been having – I became emotionally withdrawn and occasionally impotent as a result of re-living the life of which I was writing.

Our problems were crippling both of us: Pat, still wrestling with the difficulties of a transition to underground life, also had to grapple with a less than satisfactory amount of emotional support from me, while I had to struggle with my tendency to retreat from emotional involvement and still continue writing a book which was ripping me apart. Superficially, it seemed that the major contradiction resided in the distortions of consciousness which our circumstances imposed on us – but this was far too simplistic a position to adopt. We found it necessary to examine the structures of personal oppression which still remained in our consciousnesses, seeking the influences which made our current lifestyle so damaging to us.

Sexism is an all-pervasive factor in contemporary life, inserting its influence into every facet of our relationships and consciousness; even the language we use reflects its structure of oppression, with the idioms of power being "masculine" and those of powerlessness being "feminine". Although a communist and a feminist, Pat's consciousness of personal relationships, derived from her experiences of being female, includes the notions of self-sacrificial supportiveness, domestic organisation almost to the point of obsession, and a passivity characterised by self-doubt concerning her own intellectual competence coupled with a tendency to use emotion as a means of getting her own way. My "masculine" parallel to Pat's consciousness includes protectiveness bordering on the patronising, virtual disinterest in domestic organisation, and assertiveness characterised by intellectual self-confidence, a coldly aggressive argumentativenes, and a tendency to hold my more sensitive emotions in check rather than display them. Neither of these portraits is completely accurate, for both Pat and I consciously rejected them as representative of ourselves – but they are the bases of the distortions which were interfering in the way that we organised our lives and developed our relationships. Like everyone else attempting to prefigure in our lives the future our political commitments aimed to build, we have faced the difficulty of overcoming the "dead hand of the past" which weighs so heavily on our consciousness of the present.

Our problems continue to interfere with our relationships, but we are both confident that, regardless of whether we stay together or not, our mutual love and friendship will remain intact. Personally and politically, we will continue to grow, critically developing ourselves and constantly reaffirming our individual and mutual commitment to the revolutionary struggle of our class.

My escape was effectively the end of the beginning for me; I had travelled far since the despair of a solitary confinement cell in 1967. It has not been a primrose path, with excitement and pleasure marking the route of my progression since August 9th, but I would choose no other. I left many brothers and sisters in Broadmoor, and I cannot forget the inhuman conditions in which they live, or the identical conditions imposed upon many thousands of others. But . . . prison conditions are only one small fragment of my concern, for those conditions mirror the social and political realities of a class, the working class, my class, and only action which liberates that class from its subordinate position in the state can create a truly human country – and world.

I am a child who became a rebel without a cause, who became a prisoner, who re-found a class and thus a cause, who became a communist, who became a political prisoner, who became a fugitive. My future is unknown, but without reservation it is committed to struggle, to class war, to the international revolution . . . having found my humanity, I shall not fail it now.

Alan Reeve,
1981/1982.

Appendix (Amsterdam, August–September 1982)

August 6th, 1982; a Friday. Comrade Patricia and I had been in Amsterdam for almost a year, living together for almost a year, free together for almost a year. My escape from Broadmoor had brought me the first year of freedom I had known since I was a child; August 9th, three days away, was to be the anniversary. We had planned a party, Patricia and I, and we had invited several of the *krakers* [= squatters] we knew; our guests wouldn't know why the event would be so important and exciting for us, but their kindness and support made them welcome additions [. . .]

Earlier in the day I had breakfasted with Patricia and several other people; we had all gathered in her house, across the road from mine, in order to provide a protective shield in the event of her supposedly cancelled eviction actually taking place. Although, a couple of months previously, we had decided to have separate houses, we still effectively lived together; during the days we each concentrated on the work which we found important, and at night we dined together and chose which of our respective houses we would sleep in. At about eleven o'clock, when the other people had left once it became clear that the eviction would not take place, Patricia and I discussed our shopping plans for the weekend and the projected party. We had just under 100 florins each, and we had to plan carefully for this money was intended to last us for a week or possibly two. Among the decisions we took was the one which was to lead me back to a prison cell: it was my responsibility to buy some cheap wine for the party, as much as was possible on my meagre budget. I decided to visit the Dirk van de Broek off-licence on Lijnbaansgracht, a place I had passed several times but had never entered.

Having some writing to do, following through some ideas for the second volume of *Notes From a Waiting-Room*, I returned to my house and spent a couple of hours or so typing. I had decided that I would go shopping in the afternoon, and shortly before one o'clock I changed my clothes preparatory to leaving the apartment. At this point my earlier innocent decision to go and buy some wine took on the element of disaster – when I changed my trousers I picked up my gun, usually left lying in the bedroom, and put it in my pocket, still wrapped in a headscarf.

I had bought the gun about a month previously, having gone looking for one several weeks before that. Buying the gun was a reflection of my increased nervousness as the anniversary of my escape drew nearer. My one overriding fear was being taken by the police and returned to England, for I knew that the authorities would use every inhumane and degrading skill they possessed in the effort to break me and demonstrate their absolute power to the other prisoners. Determined to prevent any use of my broken-minded body, the consequence of the tortures employed in psychiatric prisons in England, for the purposes of increased control over my brothers and sisters in the prisons, I had resolved to kill myself if the threat of being taken became a reality. My reasoning was simple – a gun would guarantee my having the opportunity to destroy myself before the police could take me into custody. Comrade Patricia and I had discussed my fear, both of us aware of the background of experience which underlay it, and she had agreed, after the event, that the expenditure had been worthwhile. Both of us knew that I was in no physical condition to escape a police raid, and equally both of us knew the techniques of mind-destruction and distortion available to the prison authorities: the techniques had been developed in the psychiatric prisons and perfected in the internationally condemned interrogation/torture centres used against the freedom-fighters in occupied Ireland's war of national liberation against colonialist Britain.

So – I left the apartment, picked up my bicycle from comrade Patricia's house, and cycled off to Lijnbaansgracht to buy some wine. As I left Boetzelaerstraat, I had nothing on my mind except buying the wine and getting back home so I could continue writing up my ideas: I didn't get the opportunity to return home, and both the notes and ideas I was working on have disappeared – destroyed by police actions following the events which were shortly to unfold.

The journey to Lijnbaansgracht, though short, took me several minutes: the previous weekend I had collapsed when muscular spasms made the pain in my back too severe for me to handle, and although I felt somewhat better after spending two days laying on the floor, the experience had reasserted my need for physical caution in movement. When I arrived at Dirk van de Broek's I placed my bicycle against a lamp-post, locked it, and, carrying my rucksack, walked the few metres to the shop.

As I entered the shop my intention was quite honest; I intended to look through the drinks available, choose the finest wine within my budget, pay at the cash desk and leave. I had not anticipated that I would see an opportunity to shop-lift more potent drink than wine. Looking around, it seemed to me that the security in the shop was inadequate; the workers were congregated at one end, talking, and the whisky section was unobserved. Quickly, I took two bottles of whisky and slipped them into my rucksack: I decided to walk around to the cash desk, choose and pay for a bottle of Cola or 7-Up and leave with the windfall of two bottles of whisky. Pushing one of the shop's baskets, I walked deeper among the shelves of drink, casually looking over the selection. Then I saw some Cointreau, a drink I knew to be a favourite of Patricia's – and one she had not had the opportunity of tasting much over the previous year because of its cost. I think we'd bought one bottle soon after we had arrived in Amsterdam when we still had a few English pounds in our wallets.

The whisky I had taken was a luxury I thought would be appreciated by everyone at the party on Monday, but the Cointreau – that was a luxury which would have special meaning for Patricia, one she would criticise me for because of the risk, but also one which would afford her a great deal of pleasure. Unfortunately, looking through the lattice-work shelves, one of the storepersons saw me take the Cointreau; I did not see him, and, unsuspecting, walked on toward the cash desk where, showing a bottle of 7-Up I had chosen, I paid for my purchase.

Leaving the shop, I began to walk back toward my bicycle; I was stopped after I had walked about five metres down the road. Two men intercepted me, the taller of whom, with a moustache, told me that I was 'controlled'. He spoke Dutch, a language I have only a minimal vocabulary in, but I understood his intention. It was obvious that my detainers wanted to look inside my rucksack, so, with a shrug, I opened it and the speaker reached inside and withdrew the bottle of Cointreau: I understood the next comment to mean that I should accompany the men back into the shop. Turning around, I began to retrace my steps – and suddenly remembered, two or three metres later, that I had a gun in my pocket!

When I was 'controlled', I reasoned quickly to myself that the situation wasn't terminal: I might be able to talk my way out of it by being the 'stupid English tourist' and handing over all my money. If the police *were* called and I was taken into custody, then I would simply face a charge of shop-lifting which, because it was so trivial, would hardly involve a full-scale check on me with England. Unless the police were in a state of high alert for me, with my dossier from England fresh in their memories, it seemed to me that I could still emerge from the situation with no more than a bad scare. But my possession of the gun changed all this, making me a suspect for full checking by the police. I panicked, threw my rucksack up into the air in the hope that the two men would try and catch it and thus be slowed down, turned on my heels, and ran toward the bridge.

Although I was moving fast, I knew before I had gone fifteen metres that I could not escape this way. Each step I took was shooting waves of raw agony through my back, and my left leg was operating out of rhythm as the partial paralysis I had been experiencing made itself felt. About ten metres or so from the bridge there was a yellow sand-box and I swerved towards it, slammed my right foot into it, twisting my ankle, and, turning, ran at a slower pace the way I had come; my pursuers ran past me, stopped, then renewed the chase. Now, the transition in my feelings was complete: from nervous anticipation, through panic, to an overwhelming terror – I knew that if I was taken into custody now I would end up back in England, back in the psychiatric prison with the Home Secretary continuing my detention on the grounds of my political commitment, back in the hands of authorities whose full range of mind-breaking drugs, solitary-confinement cells and physical brutality would be brought into play to ensure my numbed and uncritical obedience to their manipulations. Still running, I reached into my pocket, pulled out the gun, unwrapped it, turned – and pointed it at my pursuers, aiming just above their heads.

Seeing the gun, the two men stopped, their bodies twisting and their hands thrown wildly into the air – the classic movie version of shock. For several seconds I stood still, breathing hard: the training I had imposed on myself over the years had taken over, and without any concious decision I was operating in such a way as to minimise any possible damage to other people while still trying to protect myself. Backing away from the men I made my way to the corner of the road and into another street; several metres further on I turned right, moving in an unknown area but seeking to put distance between myself and the shop. Halfway down this new street I looked back over my shoulder – the man with the moustache was following me, maintaining a watch which could bring the police directly to me. Knowing that I had to prevent pursuit, I walked several metres back toward the man, operated the breech on the gun and put a bullet into the chamber – it had been inoperable until this moment – and, aiming to my left, away from the man crouching behind a car, placed one shot into the car window, shattering it. Confident that this would persuade the man not to follow me, I turned and jogged on, turning left into another street.

Halfway down the street I went into a blind alley, a quadrangle between the houses; there was no alternative exit that I could see, so I returned to the street. I turned left again, then right: my physical condition was deteriorating rapidly, with the pain so severe that most of my energy was being used up in simply continuing to move. I knew that I could not survive this pressure for much longer; then, glancing over my shoulder just before I reached the end of the street, I saw a police car turning toward me. I threw myself around the corner, stumbled on for several metres, then stopped: I couldn't go any further without a break, and could hear a racing motor coming toward me.

The next minute or so was a nightmare of concentration as I blanked out the pain, controlled the trembling in my limbs, and tried desperately to concentrate on the dangers represented by the police car, the police shooting at me, and my overriding need to stay free. Facing the corner, I waited for the car to come into sight; then, when it did so, I raised my gun and, taking careful aim at the centre of the windshield between the two policemen, I fired once; my intention was to make them crash into the canal. The car slowed dramatically, but didn't crash and nor did it stop. I aimed at the right shoulder of the driver and fired again, seeking to wound him and thus remove him from the combat. As I fired the second shot the passenger policeman threw himself out of the car, lay down on the side away from me, and brought his gun into my sight. I turned toward the immediate threat, brought my gun up, saw a movement out of the corner of my eye, turned back to the car and snapped off one last bullet at the driver as the passenger policeman started shooting at me, then began to return the fire.

After exchanging a couple of shots with the policeman on the ground, I ducked behind a nearby car for a few seconds. Knowing that I couldn't stay in a fire-fight for too long, and aware that my rapid movements were bringing closer my eventual and inevitable collapse, I moved out of cover and exposed myself, standing, to the policeman's shooting. Twice he had a clear view of me, each time snapping shots in my direction but not hitting me, then, on the third occasion, I returned his shots, aiming at his gun arm and shoulder. I hit him, and he crawled back along the side of the car protectively.

During the last exchange of shots a car had driven up behind me, and as I moved into the road preparatory to staggering off on my continued flight, looking all the time toward the wounded policeman on the ground, I realised that I desperately needed transport. Holding the gun in clear sight of the driver, I reached into the back of the car which had just arrived and tried to open the back door; I couldn't. Still holding the gun in front of me, pointed in the general direction of the driver, I risked exposing my back to the policeman on the ground and the one in the police car, and moved around the bonnet toward the passenger's side: the woman passenger, with no urging from me, had wisely decided to get out of the car, leaving her seat to me. I got in, closed the door, pointed the gun at the driver and told him to drive on.

For about a minute the driver fumbled with the keys, either deliberately or through nervousness slowing everything down. I told him, forcefully, that he should drive on. We moved off, skirted the police car while I leaned forward in case the driver managed to get a clear shot at me, and made our way along the street. As the driver told me he had been in the marines, I noticed that my gun was empty; the breech was locked back, and even a casual glance would show that it was useless as a weapon. Knowing that even a casual back-hand slap would have finished me off because I was so weak, I decided that I had better get out of the car as swiftly as possible. I told the driver to slow down at a corner, opened the door, stepped out, and gave instructions that the car should keep moving straight ahead. It did so.

Staggering down the street, I turned left and recognised where I was; it seemed that I still had a chance to escape. When I had put the gun in my pocket that morning I had also picked up a small plastic bag which contained two spare bullets, so I removed them and loaded them into the gun. I operated the breech and put one round into the chamber. I could not survive another fire-fight, I knew, so I wanted to ensure that the opportunity would be available to shoot myself.

A bus came along the road and, being near a bus stop, I waved to slow it down; the driver ignored me, possibly seeing the gun I was still holding. Crossing the road, I moved through the bushes and up toward the fence which prevented access to the railway track. I tried to climb over the fence but didn't have the strength. I sat down, thinking that it was time to put a bullet through my brain – but I couldn't give up without another try. Somehow, I pulled myself up to the top of the fence and fell over onto the other side. To my right was the station, full of people who could get caught in police bullets if I was seen; I turned left. About a hundred metres along the track I decided to try and get down on the other side: there was a metal buttress supporting the wall alongside the railway line and I tried climbing down – I fell about two and a half metres, jarring my back and almost knocking myself unconscious.

Now on the Prinseneiland side of the tracks, I moved in the direction of Haarlemmerplein; I knew where I had to go in order to get home. Within seconds I was seen by a police car and, turning down a side street, I stepped behind a truck which blocked any view of me from behind. Moving as rapidly as I could, I made my way toward the bridge I knew I would have to cross if I was to reach Haarlemmerplein – and saw another police car. I turned down an alley, staggered behind some huts and, looking around, realised that I was trapped. Behind me in the street was a police car, on two sides were fences which, in my condition, I couldn't hope to climb, and the final side was the canal. Thinking that I had at least made a good try at escaping, I sat down on the side of the canal and raised the gun to my mouth – and as I did so, I noticed that a rowing boat directly in front of me was merely tied to the bank: I wasn't finished yet!

Untying the rope, I got into the boat and pushed myself away from the bank. The oars were there and I tried to use them, but I had no strength in my shoulders: I paddled frantically with my hands as the boat slowly moved in circles in the middle of the canal. Finally, I drifted within reach of a houseboat; jumping at it, I caught hold of the deck and, half in the water, pulled myself around to the walkway. Getting out of the canal was both difficult and painful, but I finally managed it. I sat on the walkway hoping that no one would come, for I knew that a kitten would have more strength than me.

After sitting for a minute or so I pulled myself up to a kneeling position, took the magazine out of the gun, pulled the breech back to release the loaded bullet, thus locking it in position, checked that both bullets were still alright, and reloaded them into the magazine. I replaced the magazine and released the breech. I didn't realise it but my exhaustion had just led me to a major error – the gun was loaded, but it couldn't fire because I hadn't put a bullet into the chamber.

Even if there had been a route available, I couldn't have climbed back up to the railway track; I had to go from the walkway onto the road if I wanted to get to Haarlemmerplein. A police car was stationed on the bridge, but they hadn't seen me as I crossed the canal: I had to hope that my luck would hold. It didn't. As I walked onto the road the police car started its engine and came after me. Staggering across the road, I headed for the tunnel a few metres away. A woman was just entering it and, as I drew level with her, I grasped her left shoulder and twisted round, meaning to cause her to fall across the road behind me as I moved on. It didn't work – as I twisted round, my back gave way and both the woman and I slid down the wall and ended up sitting side by side against the brickwork, my arm around her shoulder. Almost unconscious with the pain I didn't at first notice that I was being shot at from my right, the direction in which I had been moving. I felt bullets going into my foot and back, hard blows like being punched, and I could feel the woman's body shaking as she screamed: the police were so intent on shooting me that they were indifferent to her life. When I looked to my right I saw a policeman, kneeling, with his gun pointed straight at me; I couldn't see anyone else. I raised my own gun and, putting the barrel into my mouth, pulled the trigger – no result, my error on the walkway had caught up with me. I considered pulling my left hand over and chambering a round, but I knew that I didn't have the strength to pull the breech open. Calling out "Stop shooting; I'll surrender", I moved my arm away from the woman and, drawing on the last of my strength, pushed myself to my feet and staggered into the middle of the tunnel. Facing the policeman who was kneeling and pointing his gun at me, I tried to force my right arm to lift the gun in a threatening gesture – I knew that such a move would result in my being hit by even more bullets and, hopefully, being killed. My arm wouldn't move. Seconds later I was jumped from behind by two or three policeman, thrown to the ground and, after they had slammed their guns alongside my head, handcuffed with my hands behind me. I was back in custody.

The minute or so between being thrown to the ground and then moved out of the tunnel and forced over the bonnet of a car remains a blur in my memory. Exhausted, in considerable pain, and on the point of collapse, I didn't take much notice of what was going on. The exploding flashbulbs of the media photographers kept me conscious, and the threat from one of the policemen – "You're as good as dead; we'll finish you!" – kept me determined. Manhandled into a police wagon, I was driven off at high speed, siren screaming – I don't know where we went because a policeman's foot kept my head pinned to the seat. After a short period, the wagon stopped and I was taken out and thrown back into the back of an ambulance; I assume I was lying on a stretcher.

I don't know which hospital we drove to; for most of the journey I was unconscious. Just after the door had been closed I was kicked several times in the legs and ankles by the policemen (I think there were two of them) sitting next to the door, and at the same time the policeman sitting next to my head kicked me in the face and neck, pressing my face down into the pillow and suffocating me into unconsciousness. Quite possibly I was kicked some more – my testicles were swollen and sore for several days – but I have no recollection of it. I regained consciousness as I was wheeled into the hospital.

As my clothes were being cut off me and the initial examination made, a policeman asked for my name and address; I gave false answers to both questions. Afterwards, as the X-rays were being taken, another policeman, a detective, told me that I was dying and should give as much information as possible to ease my conscience; I told a few more lies. I didn't know how badly hurt I was, but I did know that I had to give my comrade wife, Patricia, a chance to get out of the area before a full police search was launched: also, I wanted to give as much time as possible for our brothers and sisters in the *kraak* movement to arrange some defensive measures before the inevitable police raids. Giving a false name was simple, for it was one I had been using, but I chose an address near to some *kraker* friends so that they would be alerted by police activity.

About half an hour, I think, after the X-rays were taken, the detective told me that I wasn't dying after all. I was rather disappointed about that because, as he had told me both policemen I had shot were alive and liable to recover, I had nightmare visions of being returned to England after all. Within a few minutes, however, I had something else to worry about. The surgeon started operating on my left foot to remove a bullet, and, although he might have given me a local anaesthetic without my knowing about it, I could feel every cut of the scalpel and every twist of the bone as he delved into my foot. I had to keep the leg still, but the rest of my body was shaking uncontrollably as I locked the muscles in an effort to combat the new pain level: I was determined not to scream.

After being cautioned that I must not put my weight on the foot for at least a couple of weeks, and that I must also make sure that it didn't receive any knocks, I was led out, hopping on my right foot, to a waiting police wagon – gauze and plaster were put on my back before I left, covering the bullet wounds there. A few minutes later we arrived at Waarmoestraat police station, and, still handcuffed, I was forced to hop up a flight of steps and into a cell. Dressed only in briefs, handcuffed, with my foot wrapped in bandages and sweating profusely, I must have looked very bad – but the large policeman who stood in the doorway slamming a wooden stick into his hand to emphasise his points as he looked at me, seemed more interested in worsening my condition than bettering it. By now I knew that one of the policemen had died; it had been mentioned to me, in passing, sometime during my exit from hospital.

Rather to my surprise, after a few minutes in the cell I was led out, hopping, and back to the police wagon. On the way to police HQ I was informed that the Waarmoestraat colleagues of the dead policeman had stated that it was their intention to kick me to death – but the higher echelons of the police service felt this might damage their public image so they had ordered me moved elsewhere. Bearing in mind the continuing Ministry of Justice suspicions about Patricia and me being linked to some vast international terrorist conspiracy, I think an additional reason for interfering in the enjoyment of the Waarmoestraat policemen was a desire to sweat information out of me.

My four and a bit days at police HQ were an interesting education in the similarity of police methods between Holland and England: I wasn't savagely assaulted in Holland, but the general inhumanity was identical. Under the careful supervision of the Hulpofficer Justicie I was forced to hop up a couple of flights of steps, handcuffed all the time, with particular care being taken to ensure that my left foot came into frequent and heavy contact with the steps; my fingers were numbed for over two weeks as a result of the tightness of the handcuffs. Also during this period I was pushed and punched in the back, the blows landing on the bullet wounds, and, on one occasion, I was invited to scream when a policeman pushed my left foot into the ground – I declined the offer, thinking to myself that having been tortured by experts in England I should really consider myself quite fortunate to be in the hands of such humane people as these. For the first 24 hours, when not hopping around in handcuffs, I was kept, still naked except for my briefs, in a bare cell. I lay on the floor, cold, shivering, and in pain; but as I kept slipping in and out of faints, it didn't really matter. It did irritate me that I had no water for 36 hours, but I wasn't overly disturbed; the lack of food for three days didn't worry me at all. I spent the time comparing Holland and Britain, to neither of their advantage. The treatment I was receiving, including the white noise and the sexist and racist abuse coming through the intercom, was identical, though less severe, to that imposed on the guerrilla cadres in the colonialist interrogation centres in occupied Ireland. I was in good company, I felt, for the Irish comrades, too, had routinely ignored the tortures used by their British oppressors and had spent the time concentrating on the political struggle.

On those occasions when I was actually interrogated by detectives I was not physically abused; they gave me coffee and cigarettes, and on one occasion carried me to the toilet when I couldn't walk. As I was cooperating, however, even though delivering a calm string of lies, their behaviour isn't really surprising. Their more usual methods of straightforward beatings would have been counter-productive – brutality tends to make me very stubborn, and in my extremely weak physical condition it wouldn't have taken much to make me unconscious or dead. (In addition, statements about an alleged terrorist involvement were already being made to the media – and it would have been embarrassing if I ended up in a hospital or morgue. My arrest was too public for me to quietly disappear or conveniently fall out of a window.)

So – the interrogations were quite calm. I continued my defensive lying because I knew that my comrade wife was still free, and I also wanted to distance myself from the *krakers* in order to minimise any damage to them. Knowing that the real opinions of comrade Patricia and myself would be used to justify attacks on the *krakers*, I explained that they didn't really have any hard political position and tended to be rather childish. It would have been disastrous, I felt, if I pointed out that we considered them, in general, to have a relatively low level of political consciousness, an over-emphasis on spontaneous street actions together with an undervaluation of theory, but that simultaneously the movement as a whole is an excellent nursery for political activists, has good embryonic contacts with and support from a wide general population, operates progressively in a socially and politically sensitive area, and has a small but growing number of activists with highly developed political consciousness, a willingness to learn, a keen interest in theory, and a commitment to revolutionary struggle. With sexism and racism so dominant among the police, I didn't think they would be interested in an analysis of the sexism prevalent amongst *krakers*, or in comments on how it was being recognised and, sometimes, combatted. Equally, I felt this was the wrong time to argue the anti-sectarianism of comrade Patricia and myself. So I didn't elaborate on the need for unity among the people in struggle, or comment on the way that anarchists and Marxists could co-operate in their mutual commitment within the context of the *kraak* movement as a whole [. . .]

When my appointed lawyer arrived to see me on Saturday night, I was quite pleased – his first intervention got me a mattress for the night. No blankets, of course, but it was a beginning.

On Tuesday I moved to the Bijlmer Bajas, had a brief interview with the Rechter Commissaris, and then hopped along what seemed miles of corridors and was located in Demersluis. While I was attempting to recover my breath and ease the agony in my back by sitting on the bed, the Director came in and explained to me, very courteously, that on the advice of the Ministry of Justice I was being held on conditions of special restriction – solitary confinement, supervised visits from lawyers, exercise on the roof, only one visitor permitted from an approved list at any one time, and no physical contact with visitors or anyone else. I admired the furnishing of the cell and its decor – and commented that I would expect nothing else but politically motivated restrictions from the Ministry of Justice. Then, to my great pleasure, I was given a pack of Van Nelle, some cigarette papers, and a box of matches.

After a couple of days, I was given a television set in my cell to ease the isolation; some English books from the library were also arranged about a week later. The Director and the *bewakers* [= warders] were uniformly courteous, and the doctor who dressed my wounds was very considerate – a pleasant change from the police doctor who contemptuously refused to examine me and was indifferent to the blood I was leaving everywhere from my hopping foot. (I, too, was indifferent to it, but for a different reason – I hoped it might lead to some embarrassment for the police if journalists saw a trail of bloody footprints. Of course, it was a pointless hope.)

201

The material conditions of my detention were far superior to anything I had experienced in my many years in English prisons, but the sensual and sensory deprivation imposed by the Ministry of Justice was no less savage and inhumane than that imposed by their British counterparts. The lessons of torture and oppression learned by the British in their savagery against the freedom fighters in occupied Ireland must, I felt, be made available to other reactionary European regimes – either that, or liberal, democratic, tolerant and humane Holland has been experimenting on its own.

My comrade wife, after losing through a miscarriage the baby we had been hoping for, turned herself in to the police on Friday 13th August: I quickly heard about the racist and sexist abuse she had been subjected to, and the threats which accompanied that abuse. That she was detained, contrary to any reasonable standards of human and legal rights, came as no surprise to me: as a communist committed to the revolutionary struggle against injustice, oppression and exploitation, she was (and is) quite obviously a danger to any business estate – and, in addition, as my wife she had to experience the vengeance being directed against me [. . .]

For a couple of days I was returned to police HQ for more interrogation – conditions were the same as previously, only this time I had blankets during the night. I was rather disappointed with the lack of subtlety used in references to my wife; I prefer sophisticated threats, they provide more intellectual stimulation, and sexism is gross no matter how deviously it is expressed. Apart from this, the interrogators were relatively courteous. On my return to the Bijlmer, I wrote a letter of complaint to the Rechter Commissaris, pointing out that I objected to the atmosphere of threat and discomfort I experienced at the police station. The only surprise in his reply, received a couple of weeks later, was his honesty – he stated that he considered it "practically inevitable" that I would experience threat and discomfort. Whatever happened to legal protection, I wondered!

On September 1st, a Wednesday, I appeared with my lawyer in front of the Commissie van Boezicht in the Bijlmer Bajas in order to appeal against the politically motivated restrictions imposed on my detention. It was an interesting experience, one I felt I should get used to as it is likely I will have to go through it many more times during the next few years. I was satisfied with my argument, but delighted with the lawyer's – he did an excellent job, the result of which was shown when I heard several weeks later that we had won the case. The next day I moved to the Pieter Baans Centrum in Utrecht.

Having been taken to the prison hospital in Schevingen for X-rays, a journey complete with motorcycle escort and screaming sirens, I knew what to expect. Sure enough, Starsky and Hutch would have envied the 160 kph trip – especially as the screaming sirens suitably aroused motorists to curiosity. The Pieter Baans Centrum itself is much like the Bijlmer in material conditions, but at least the solitary confinement restriction was removed. (The other restrictions remained until we won a special appeal – the result delivered the day after comrade Patricia was formally recognised as my comrade wife.)

In the PBC I was treated throughout with courtesy and recognition of a common humanity: the conditions surrounding my wedding with comrade Patricia were made less than totally inhumane by virtue of the staff demanding that we be allowed some time together – 54 minutes before the ceremony, 15 minutes afterwards; both occasions supervised – and by their volunteering as witnesses after it was made clear that our own people couldn't attend. (Incidentally, our wedding – on Monday 27th September at 15.35 – was the first time comrade Patricia and I had been allowed to meet with each other.)

Two weeks later I returned to the Bijlmer, to a renewed set of restrictions, including solitary confinement, which I think will follow me throughout my imprisonment in Holland. I don't feel too disturbed by the prospect: the conditions of imprisonment which all detainees experience involve sensual and sensory deprivation, humiliation, degradation, inadequate health facilities, sexism, racism, personality distortion through an imposed child-like obedience and lack of responsibility, occasional physical brutality and constant psychological terrorism, all these as a matter of routine – so the additional restrictions imposed on me by the Ministry of Justice are actually a declaration of the fear which political consciousness arouses in the guardians of "democracy".

At my trial in Holland I presented evidence of crimes I charge against the British government, with reference to political control of periods of detention in psychiatric prisons along with the horror programme of isolation and torture which is not unusual. I had no hesitation in using the court as a platform to expose the British thugs, to affirm the political commitment of my comrade wife and myself as a continuing reality, and hurl my contempt for Dutch injustice into the teeth of the judges. Secure in the love my comrade wife and I share, for each other and the people, resolute and determined in my commitment to the revolutionary struggle, I shall treat my savage sentence as just another step in the long march toward a bright communist future.

Dare to struggle – Dare to win!

Alan Reeve, 29 September 1982

Rudolf Bahro
Socialism and Survival

a vital contribution to the red/green debate

Pat Arrowsmith
Jericho

the novel of a peace camp in the early years of CND

Alan Reeve
Notes From a Waiting-Room: anatomy of a political prisoner

a devastating indictment of the 'special hospital' system

Erik Dammann
Revolution in the Affluent Society

anti-imperialist eco-politics from the Norwegian *Future in Our Hands*
movement

Louis Mackay and David Fernbach (eds)
Nuclear-Free Defence

a symposium for the peace movement with 23 contributors

Jan Myrdal and Gun Kessle
India Waits

a panoramic guide to India's culture and politics

John Collier
The Dynamic of Socialism

a study of the law of motion of post-capitalist society